THE
TORONTO
BOOK OF
THE DEAD

THE
TORONTO
BOOK OF
THE DEAD

ADAM BUNCH

DUNDURN
TORONTO

Cover image: Skull: shutterstock.com/mamita Skyline: iStock.com/blamb
Printer: Marquis Book Printing Inc.

Library and Archives Canada Cataloguing in Publication

Bunch, Adam, author
	The Toronto book of the dead / Adam Bunch.

Includes bibliographical references.
Issued in print and electronic formats.
ISBN 978-1-4597-3806-5 (softcover).--ISBN 978-1-4597-3807-2 (PDF).--
ISBN 978-1-4597-3808-9 (EPUB)

		1. Death--Ontario--Toronto--History. 2. Toronto (Ont.)--History--Anecdotes.
I. Title.

HQ1073.5.C362T67 2017	306.909713'54		C2017-903407-3
						C2017-903408-1

Conseil des Arts du Canada	Canada Council for the Arts	Canadä	ONTARIO ARTS COUNCIL CONSEIL DES ARTS DE L'ONTARIO an Ontario government agency un organisme du gouvernement de l'Ontario

We acknowledge the support of the Canada Council for the Arts, which last year invested $153 million to bring the arts to Canadians throughout the country, and the Ontario Arts Council for our publishing program. We also acknowledge the financial support of the Government of Ontario, through the Ontario Book Publishing Tax Credit and the Ontario Media Development Corporation, and the Government of Canada.

Nous remercions le Conseil des arts du Canada de son soutien. L'an dernier, le Conseil a investi 153 millions de dollars pour mettre de l'art dans la vie des Canadiennes et des Canadiens de tout le pays.

Care has been taken to trace the ownership of copyright material used in this book. The author and the publisher welcome any information enabling them to rectify any references or credits in subsequent editions.

— J. Kirk Howard, President

The publisher is not responsible for websites or their content unless they are owned by the publisher.

Printed and bound in Canada.

VISIT US AT

 dundurn.com | @dundurnpress | dundurnpress |  dundurnpress

Dundurn
3 Church Street, Suite 500
Toronto, Ontario, Canada
M5E 1M2

For Irene and Old Tom

CONTENTS

THE BOOMING METROPOLIS

THE GREAT WARS

THE MODERN CITY

FOREWORD

TORONTO'S DEAD HISTORY IS QUITE ALIVE

Despite being a city of writers and storytellers, Toronto has a pervasive reputation among its citizens that the city isn't as interesting as other places, that it just doesn't have the same kind of stories as other, well, more storied cities. Though the shelves in the Toronto sections of each library branch are filled with Toronto tales, both fictional and true, the city doesn't viscerally own and know its own multifaceted story as well as it should. History-making, then, remains an important endeavour in Toronto, one that requires constant effort to tell and remind the people who live here why this place is the way it is.

Perhaps it's a condition of being a younger city, one that has become the cosmopolitan metropolis it is today over just a few short decades. Or maybe it's the city's deeply rooted colonial condition, where you can't walk a block without seeing or reading a reference to Britain, the mother country. These take people out of their local environs and suggest, not so subtly, that it is there that the really important things happened. Toronto has gone along with all this with partial complicity: this most loyal provincial outpost wasn't called the Queen City by accident. All of this has resulted in a civic mythology that is lagging behind the city Toronto has become.

Yet a rich cache of stories has always been here, waiting to be brought to life. The foundation of storytelling laid down by authors in the past and present is being built on and expanded in innovative ways. It doesn't hurt that Drake, in his pop superstar way, has said it's okay to like, maybe even be proud of, Toronto. Today there's lots of space for other storytellers because there's an audience demand for it, and those stories will take on a variety of formats, like Adam Bunch's most unique approach to Toronto, a public historian who drifts back and forth between fiction and non-fiction versions of Toronto past and present.

Bunch has been mining — and creating — Toronto's mythology for some time. As the creator of the Toronto Dreams Project, he's written a kind of fan fiction for Toronto's history by imagining the dreams of the city's historic figures and attaching those dreams to its very geography. By using postcards as his medium, and physically placing the dream stories he has created in the very places they take place or are connected to, Bunch is actively connecting stories to the city, a trick that ensures they remain rooted here and with a better chance of being remembered.

Mythologies, whether civic, national, or otherwise, aren't built on the absolute truth alone. Imagination plays a role in bringing history to life and helps lodge it in the living memory of those who live in and visit the city. The Toronto Dreams Project *projects* the idea of the city beyond what we already know and suggests there's untold potential and possibility here: it's an exciting place to dream of our own future.

Yet Bunch is also committed to the city's factual history with his Toronto Dreams Project Historical Ephemera Blog, where he compiles the vast amount of research he's uncovered and turns it into compelling social histories of Toronto, work he's shared to wider audiences as the history columnist at *Spacing* magazine. As with his Dreams project, Bunch uses geographic points throughout the city — places we can walk by today and look at and stand in — to connect those histories and stories to the city. Stories connected to geography tend to be remembered because the physical presence of that place is a constant reminder of those stories.

However, Toronto is a city that is always changing, building and rebuilding itself, so even the geography here can be untrustworthy. Whether standing atop a buried creek, in a parking lot that was once a grand or even drab building, or on the waterfront created by dumping fill into the lake, never assume the landscape here hasn't been manipulated or wholly invented. The dead, though, are eternal and remain a direct connection to history. With *The Toronto Book of the Dead*, Bunch combines both geography and the stories of those who've left a mark on this place into an absorbing look into Toronto's thousands of years of human history. Death provides a new lens through which to see Toronto, replete with opportunities for story tangents and historical threads that Bunch follows as if they're tributaries in Toronto's ravine system.

Compared to other global cities, Toronto (it was established as the Town of York in only 1793) is relatively young, but in *The Toronto Book of the Dead* you'll find a city that goes back much further, well before the colonial era that has received the most official attention. And though the city has changed and expanded, there is still geography to attach the stories to. For instance, those who ignore the plaque attached to a boulder there may think that Tabor Hill is just a park in Scarborough with a rather nice hill, but readers will discover through Bunch's account of it that the place is an important one, closely connected to the pre-European contact era. That plaque on the rock by the hill, surrounded by post-war bungalows, tells passersby this is a First Nations ossuary, but doesn't elaborate on how actively the early European settlers tried to assimilate the local population and erase their culture four hundred years ago. In this book, Bunch provides the rest of the story, and while he embraces the colonial history we have, he continually sets it in the context of a much longer and more robust history.

The lens of death provides a particularly acute way of revealing the struggle and violence often associated with creating the city we have today. New York and Paris have violent histories that are part of their lore — think of *Gangs of New York* or *Les Misérables*. Toronto is no different, but so often the history of this place has been sanitized to conform with notions of "Toronto the Good."

The Toronto Book of the Dead comes at a time when the city is running out of cemetery space, when the not-yet-dead who wish to be buried must find plots farther and farther away from where they live. What will that do to future stories? Will the disconnection between geography and humans force stories to exist in an even more ephemeral space? That's a thought to keep in mind while making your way through this fine work of narrative non-fiction, a book that will convince even skeptics that important things happened here, and that we walk among and on top of the literal layers of many thousands of years of history every day.

— Shawn Micallef, co-founder of *Spacing* magazine
and *Toronto Star* columnist

INTRODUCTION

The dead keep silent watch over the Don Valley. There are tens of thousands of them there, their bones buried in the soil not far south of Bloor Street. Their gravestones are hidden beneath the grand old trees that loom above the western slope. Even if you know they're there, it's easy to forget them as you rumble across the Bloor Viaduct on a subway or zip by in a car. But many of them have been resting in the earth on the edge of the valley since long before the Viaduct existed or a highway roared below. Some have been there for more than 150 years, since the Necropolis cemetery first opened its gates.

The Necropolis was a new kind of graveyard. Garden cemeteries were all the rage in the middle of the 1800s. As Victorian cities became more and more crowded, the question of where to bury the dead was a growing concern. There were more people dying than there was space left to bury them — churchyards were filled to overflowing, and shallow burials meant bodies could easily be uncovered by a heavy rain or a curious dog. The living and the dead were being forced into ever closer quarters.

In response, cities began to open large green spaces on the outskirts of town, where the living could visit the dead in the quiet of a pastoral setting, far from the rush and roar of urban life. The new burial grounds of the "cemetery beautiful" movement were as much parks as they were boneyards.

The Toronto Necropolis fit that new mould. The old Potter's Field cemetery at Yonge and Bloor was quickly reaching capacity and would soon be closed: a petition from Yorkville residents demanded the dead be evicted from their neighbourhood. Thousands of bodies — including some of the city's early settlers — were dug up out of the ground and moved to a new home.

The Necropolis was opened for them on a more peaceful spot: perched atop the verdant slopes of the Don Valley; a scenic place filled with trees. A small chapel was designed by one of the city's leading architects, complete with a beautiful white archway that serves as an entrance to the cemetery — a portal through the black iron fence into the graveyard beyond. It feels like a gateway into another world.

That's not by accident. *Necropolis* is an ancient Greek term: "city of the dead." And Toronto's Necropolis does feel something like its own city. (In fact, with a population of 62,000 residents, there are more dead people buried inside the Necropolis than there are people living in all of Fredericton, New Brunswick.) Even today, the Necropolis gives the impression of being a place separate from the modern world. On one side of that graceful white arch: the city of the living. On the other: the city of the dead.

At first, people flocked to the new garden cemeteries in droves. Those elegant graveyards became centres of social life. They were founded in a time before large city parks were common and in the days before many public art galleries and museums had opened their doors. Garden cemeteries became a way for large numbers of people to enjoy green space, appreciate fine sculpture, and explore local history.

In time, as urban populations continued to boom, those pastoral cemeteries on the edge of town were swallowed up by the cities they served. Over the last century and a half, Toronto has grown from a provincial outpost of thirty thousand to a cosmopolitan metropolis of millions. As the city has expanded, many of the graveyards that used to stand well outside its borders now find themselves surrounded by the loud chaos of modern life.

St. Michael's Cemetery, one of the area's first Catholic graveyards, used to stand at the edge of a deer park in the rural reaches north of the city; now it has disappeared behind the office towers of Yonge and St. Clair. Richview Memorial Cemetery was once a quiet resting place for Etobicoke's early settlers; now it stands in the middle of a deafening highway interchange. St. James Cemetery, the city's oldest graveyard still in operation, sits in the shadows of the St. James Town apartment blocks — one of the most densely populated neighbourhoods on the continent.

The Necropolis, originally outside the official boundaries of the city, now finds itself right in the heart of Toronto. The quiet of the graveyard is broken by the hum of traffic in the valley below. As dusk descends, the silver lights of skyscrapers wink on in the distance.

Paradoxically, even as garden cemeteries found themselves surrounded by ever growing numbers of people, their popularity declined. For the Victorians who built them, death was still very much a part of daily life. But in the 1900s, as mortality rates dropped, religion became less popular, and parks and art galleries became more common, the number of visitors to garden cemeteries dwindled. Today, graveyards like the Necropolis still attract joggers, cyclists and *flâneurs* — as well as some mourners — but they aren't the social hubs they once were.

In time, left increasingly alone in their walled gardens, the dead became easier to forget. Their graves were no longer a constant of everyday life; they weren't outside the church every Sunday as townspeople went to pray. The dead were now locked away in their own parallel cities, kept safe behind wrought iron fences, mortality contained.

And so, it became easier than ever to imagine the city of the dead and the city of the living as two distinct realms.

I've been spending a lot of time in graveyards recently — since the summer of 2010, to be exact. That's when I launched the Toronto Dreams Project. The project explores the history of the city in many different ways — including a blog where several of the stories in this book originally appeared — but it's centred around a series of fictional dreams about people from the city's past. I print copies of each dream on custom-designed postcards and leave them in public places related to the true story of that person's life.

And there are few places with a more powerful connection to a person's life than the place where they lie buried. The Dreams Project has sent me venturing into the land of the dead on a regular basis, passing through the gates we keep between ourselves and our ancestors, wandering among their bones in search of gravestones bearing familiar names.

There are many of those in the Necropolis. It's home to some of the most fascinating figures from the history of Toronto: William Lyon Mackenzie, the mayor who became a rebel; George Brown, Father of Confederation and founder of the *Globe* newspaper, fatally shot by a disgruntled employee; the Abbotts and the Blackburns, who escaped racial persecution in the United States and helped make Toronto a vital stop at the end of the Underground Railroad; Joseph Tyrrell, the geologist who uncovered dinosaur bones in Alberta; Kay Christie, the nurse who survived a POW camp in Hong Kong; Jack Layton, the leader of the New Democratic Party felled by cancer before his time. Some of their stories even appear in this book.

There are very few experiences that bring the history of the city more vividly to life than spending time among the dead: standing at their gravesides above bones that were once part of a living, breathing, feeling body, contemplating the lives they led. The more time you spend with them, the clearer it becomes: the boundary between the city of the dead and the city of the living is an illusion. The dead are not so easily contained. Cemeteries cannot hold them.

Toronto — like every city — is a city of the dead. It's the collective creation of all those who have come before us. Their homes are our homes, their roads are our roads, their traditions are our traditions, their stories are our stories. The dead are all around us. They haunt our every waking moment whether we realize it or not.

And so, by understanding the dead — how they lived, how they died, how they mourned — we can better understand ourselves and our city. To know the Toronto of today, it helps to know those stories: of recently deceased loved ones with fresh flowers on their graves, of Victorians interred within the confines of their garden cemeteries, of early settlers laid to rest in small church- yards, of the First Nations and their ancestors who have been buried in the land beneath our feet for thousands upon thousands of years.

You can tell the history of Toronto, from a time long before the first Europeans arrived all the way to the mod- ern metropolis of today, through tales of its dead. After all, every story ends the same way.

FOUNDING

1
THE FEAST OF THE DEAD

The land was torn apart. A big, rumbling steam shovel ripped through the earth, eating away at the hill. Great scoops of dirt were carved out of the ground. This was 1956. A new subdivision was being built in Scarborough; rows of bungalows were set to appear on the land near Highland Creek. But on a spot not far from the corner of Lawrence Avenue and Bellamy Road, a large mound of earth stood in the way. Tabor Hill was nearly twenty metres high, so the steam shovel was brought in to flatten it; the extra dirt would be used in the construction of the nearby Highway 401.

But as the digger tore away at the hill, the work suddenly came to a halt. The machine had uncovered something in the dirt.

Tabor Hill isn't a natural formation. It's a seven-hundred-year-old mass grave. The steam shovel had uncovered an ancient ossuary. Inside were the bones of more than five hundred people laid to rest in the early 1300s.

Centuries before subdivisions, skyscrapers, and highways covered the land where Toronto now stands, it was home to Wendat villages. (Europeans would later call them the Huron.) Hundreds of people lived together in each community. Their longhouses were surrounded by sprawling fields of maize. They hunted in towering forests of oak and pine, carefully managed by controlled fires. Those woods were filled with deer, wolves, cougars, and bears. Every fall, the rivers flowed thick with salmon. Bald eagles soared overhead. Enormous flocks of passenger pigeons filled the sky.

Once every ten to thirty years, when the natural resources surrounding a village had been depleted and needed time to recover, the Wendats would move to a new location. But first, they would mark the occasion with a huge festival — ten days of feasting and gift-giving capped by a burial ceremony: all of those who had died of natural causes since the village last moved were laid to rest in one communal grave. When the first French missionaries showed up, they gave it the name most people use today: the Feast of the Dead.

As the time of the great feast approached, the villagers paid a visit to the cemetery. Over the years, as the daily life of the village carried on, the graveyard had slowly filled with bodies. Every time someone died of natural causes, they were placed on a litter and carried to the cemetery, the villagers following in silence. The corpse was placed in a temporary coffin made of bark, to be kept on a wooden platform two or three metres above the ground. There they rested for years on end, until it was time for the Feast of the Dead.

Then, they were brought back out.

The French missionary Jean de Brébeuf was invited to attend the Feast of the Dead in 1636. His account is deeply coloured by his own prejudice, but it provides a detailed record of the event and the preparations that went into it, including the moment when the bodies were taken out of their bark coffins.

"After having opened the graves," Brébeuf explained in *The Jesuit Relations*, "they display before you all these corpses, on the spot, and they leave them thus exposed long enough for the spectators to learn at their leisure, and once for all, what they will be some day. The flesh of some is quite gone, and there is only parchment on their bones; in other cases, the bodies look as if they had been dried and smoked, and show scarcely any signs of putrefaction; and in still other cases they are still swarming with worms."

The missionary was amazed by the power of that sight — by the raw truth of death. He thought Christians could stand to learn from it. "I do not think one could see in the world a more vivid picture or more perfect representation of what man is," he wrote. "It is true that in France our cemeteries preach powerfully ... but it seems to me that what our Savages do on this occasion touches us still more, and makes us see more closely and apprehend more sensibly our wretched state."

The bodies were then prepared for reburial. The freshest corpses — those still writhing with maggots — were simply wrapped in beaver-fur robes and placed on litters to be carried to the site of the new grave. But the others had their bones cleaned. The remaining flesh was stripped from their skeletons and burned in a fire. Then, the body was taken apart and the bones were bundled in beaver fur.

For days, the villagers would feast, sing, and cry out in honour of the dead. Gifts were exchanged among the living. They held sporting contests and gave prizes to the winners. And then, finally, it was time to bring the dead to the place where they would be buried again.

The Feast of the Dead Brébeuf attended came more than three hundred years after the burial of the bones in Tabor Hill. By then, villages were bigger and were moving more frequently, the territory of the Wendats had shifted north toward Georgian Bay, and the ceremony included communities from outside the village itself. When a Feast of the Dead was being planned, invitations were sent to other Wendat villages, and even to some close allies. They were all invited to come and bury their dead in one communal grave. The bones of many different communities would rest together in the earth for eternity, never to be separated: a powerful symbol of their intimate connection and commitment to one another.

In the days before the reburial, hundreds of people left their villages and began their journey to the site. They carried their dead with them: bundles of bones slung over their shoulders, full bodies stretched out on litters.

As they passed other villages along the way, they would pause to visit and give gifts. Their numbers grew with every stop, an ever larger procession making its slow way toward the site of the grave. Two thousand people attended the Feast of the Dead in 1636. They came from miles around, gathering to bury the dead from eight or nine villages, according to Brébeuf's account.

When they had all arrived, the dead were made ready. Families unfolded the beaver fur to reveal the bones of their loved ones and said goodbye one last time. "The tears," Brébeuf remembered, "flowed afresh."

He described one woman in particular: the daughter of a dead chief. "She combed his hair and handled his bones, one after the other, with as much affection as if she would have desired to restore life to him." The old man wasn't the only relative she had lost in the time since the last great burial. "As for her little children," the missionary remembered, "she put on their arms bracelets of porcelain and glass beads, and bathed their bones with her tears; they could scarcely tear her away."

The dead would be buried in a deep pit. The ossuary at Tabor Hill was fifty feet long; Brébeuf compared the one he saw to the size of a grand square in Paris. Along the edges of the grave, the Wendats built wooden scaffolding from which they hung the bundles of bones. The full bodies were stretched out on bark or on mats. All afternoon and into the evening, they made the final preparations, and gave gifts in the names of the dead.

It was seven o'clock by the time the burial was ready to begin. First, the pit was lined with beaver fur. Then, the bodies of the most recently deceased were lowered into the bottom of the hole. "On all sides," Brébeuf wrote, "you could have seen them letting down half-decayed bodies ... ten or twelve [people] were in the pit and were arranging the bodies all around it, one after another."

Gifts were also buried: kettles, furs, bracelets, and other prized possessions. "You might say that all [the Wendats'] exertions, their labours and their trading," Brébeuf wrote, "concern almost entirely the amassing of something with which to honour the dead ... they lavish robes, axes, and porcelain in such quantities that, to see them on such occasions, you would judge that they place no value upon them; and yet these are the whole riches of the Country."

"One man," another missionary wrote after witnessing a Feast of the Dead years earlier, "will give almost all he possesses for the bones of the man or woman he loved and cherished in this life and still loves after their death."

At dawn the following morning, the bones were added to the bodies in the grave. They were lowered into the pit until it was nearly full. Once they had all been set in place, they were covered with another layer of beaver fur. Then, finally, the rest of the hole was filled in.

The Wendats believed every person had two souls. The Feast of the Dead allowed one of them to leave the body and begin the journey into the afterlife. The other would remain in the bones, resting beneath the earth with the souls of all of those who had been buried along with them.

By bringing so many together in one communal grave, the Feast of the Dead forged strong bonds between the living. "Essentially," Wendat historian Georges E. Sioui explains, "the Feast of the Dead was a gigantic ten-day ritual celebrating the people's unity and their desire to live in peace and to extend the bonds of symbolic kinship to the greatest possible number." It was, he says, "certainly one of the most remarkable and most pivotal features of this civilization."

The 1636 Feast of the Dead came at a dark time for the Wendat nation. The threat of war with their Indigenous neighbours loomed, and smallpox had reached their territory: the first epidemic would kill half the population in just six years. This was an especially important time to cement alliances.

Two Frenchmen had recently been buried in Wendat villages, including the young explorer Étienne Brûlé — who some believe was the very first European ever to set foot on the land where Toronto now stands. The Wendats invited Brébeuf to rebury those French bones in the same communal grave as their own people. It would be a powerful and intimate sign of friendship between the two civilizations.

Brébeuf refused. "We respected their bones too much," he explained, "to permit them being mingled with the bones of those who had not been baptized."

When a Wendat chief offered the missionary a gift of beaver fur, he refused that, too. While he admired some aspects of the Feast of the Dead, he wrote of his hopes that it would die out quickly. The missionaries had not come to take part in Wendat culture. They had come to destroy it. The Jesuits had a clear mission: to wipe out the ancient traditions of the Indigenous nations they encountered and convert them all to Christianity.

"*The only acceptable gift*," as Sioui writes (with his own emphasis), "*was the abandonment of their culture by all of the savages.*" The Wendat historian has no doubt about what Brébeuf's account represents: "This description of the Feast of the Dead is really of the end of a world ... as seen by those who would bring about its destruction. Apocalypse is always dreadful to contemplate. Three and a half centuries later, the shock and horror of it is still palpable."

Today, the dead of Tabor Hill are still resting in the place they were buried seven hundred years ago. The mound was never flattened for the subdivision; instead, the bones were reburied and the mound was preserved as a cemetery: a sacred green space in the middle of a residential neighbourhood. The hill towers over the bungalows that surround it — it's the highest point for miles in every direction. At the top sits a stone inscribed with a memorial to the dead below. From that spot on a clear day, you can see all the way across the eastern half of the city: from the cliffs of the Rouge Valley that mark the eastern border of Toronto all the way to the gleaming skyscrapers of Yonge Street in the west. Millions of people go about their lives in the shadow of those dead souls.

Tabor Hill is far from the only ancient grave in the city. At least twenty ossuaries have been found within the borders of the Greater Toronto Area (the GTA). And preserved in the earth are countless other signs of the people who lived here in centuries gone by — many of them from long before the modern city was founded. Eighty percent of all the archaeological sites in Ontario are Indigenous sites. The remains of entire villages have been discovered beneath Toronto. There are longhouses, hunting camps and portage routes, shards of pottery and ornate bracelets, arrowheads and spear points, and many other remains from the daily life of those who lived in this place hundreds and thousands of years ago.

Tabor Hill reminds us that Toronto is not a blank slate. The land beneath our feet is not empty. It has stories to tell, if we'll listen.

2
THE BEAVER WARS

The year 1687 was a year of war and famine on the shores of Lake Ontario. That summer, on a night in early July, an army camped near the mouth of the Rouge River, at the very eastern edge of what's now the city of Toronto. A few thousand men — professional soldiers from France, militia from Quebec, and their First Nations allies — feasted on venison before bed. They were tired, finally heading home at the end of a long and bloody campaign against the Seneca.

Their war was driven by a fashion trend. Far on the other side of the Atlantic, in the cobblestone capitals of Europe, hats made of beaver felt were all the rage. The demand had already driven European beavers to the brink of extinction. Now, the furriers turned to the Americas to feed their ravenous sartorial appetite. The competition over the slaughter of the large, aquatic rodents plunged the Great Lakes region into more than a century of bloodshed and violence. By the end of the 1600s, there had been decades of conflict. Thousands of warriors had fought bloody battles over control of the fur trade. They called them the Beaver Wars.

This was still long before the city of Toronto was founded, long before the British conquered Quebec, all the way back in the days when the French still claimed the Great Lakes for themselves. As far as they were concerned, the land where Toronto now stands was part of New France. But barely any Europeans had ever set foot on the land: only a few early explorers, fur traders, and missionaries.

There *were* plenty of people, just not French ones. In the late 1600s, the Seneca had two bustling villages within the borders of today's Toronto, with dozens of longhouses surrounded by fields of maize. In the west, Teiaiagon watched over the Humber River at the spot where Baby Point is now (just a bit north of Bloor Street and Old Mill Station). In the east, Ganatsekwyagon had a commanding view over the Rouge.

Both were very important places. The Humber and the Rouge were at the southern end of a vital fur trade route: the Toronto Carrying Place trail, which gave the city its name. The rivers stretched north from Lake Ontario toward Lake Simcoe. From there, fur traders could reach the Upper Great Lakes, where the beaver population was still doing relatively well. Now that the Seneca controlled the Toronto Carrying Place, they could ship beaver pelts south into the American colonies and sell them to their British allies.

That profoundly annoyed the French. They wanted those beaver pelts flowing east down the Ottawa River instead, toward their own relatively new towns of Montreal and Quebec.

By then, the French had already spent decades fighting over the fur trade. They were on one side of the Beaver Wars, generally allied with the Wendats and a variety of Algonquin-speaking nations, like the Odawa. On the other side, the British supported the Haudenosaunee (whom they called the Iroquois): a confederacy of five nations, including the Seneca.

Things weren't going well for the French. By 1687, they still had only a few thousand settlers living in all of New France, most of them centred around Montreal and Quebec. They had tried to expand their control west into the Great Lakes, establishing a trading post — Fort Frontenac — where Kingston is today. But their efforts ended in humiliating failure. They'd been forced to make peace with the Haudenosaunee and their British allies.

The French now worried they would lose the Beaver Wars — and with them, all of New France. They were scared the Haudenosaunee might overrun their settlements, and that their own First Nations allies would soon abandon them to trade with their enemies instead.

Thousands of kilometres and an entire ocean away, in his new royal palace of Versailles, King Louis XIV — the famous Sun King, who reigned over France longer than any monarch has *ever* reigned over a major European nation — decided it was time for a change. The governor of New France was fired. In his place, a new governor was sent across the Atlantic to run things.

His remarkably long name was Jacques-René de Brisay de Denonville. He was a career soldier; a respected officer from an old, rich family with deep ties to the throne. Upon his arrival in Canada, he would write a bloody new chapter in the history of the Great Lakes.

The new governor's first move was to ignore the peace treaty the former governor had negotiated with the Seneca. Denonville sent a hundred men north to Hudson Bay with orders to launch a surprise attack against British trading posts there. It was a rout. The French seized three posts run by the Hudson's Bay Company and just like that, they controlled the northern trade.

Next, Denonville turned to treachery. In the summer of 1687, he proposed a peace council: a great feast with the leaders of the Haudenosaunee Confederacy. Fifty chiefs came to Fort Frontenac that June to meet under a flag of truce. But it was a French trap. When the chiefs and their families arrived, Denonville's men captured them all, taking about two hundred prisoners. Some were tied to posts, bound so tight they couldn't move; some were tortured. Many would be shipped across the Atlantic in chains to serve King Louis as galley slaves.

And Denonville still wasn't done. He'd brought an army with him to Fort Frontenac: three thousand men, including professional French soldiers, militiamen from Quebec, a few coureurs de bois, and hundreds of First Nations allies. He led them across Lake Ontario, a fleet of hundreds of canoes and bateaux, sailing toward the southern shore, where New York State is today: the heartland of the Seneca.

The governor's plan was simple: an invasion to capture and kill as many people as possible. His ultimate goal was laid out clearly in letters sent back and forth across the Atlantic between Denonville, his boss at Versailles, and King Louis himself.

The French wanted, they said, "the establishment of the religion, of commerce and the King's power over all North America." They wanted New France to stretch from the mouth of the St. Lawrence to the mouth of the Mississippi. To do it, they wrote, they would have to destroy the Haudenosaunee. They feared the ruin of New France if they failed.

Denonville's boss — a government minister at Versailles — laid out the plan: "all their plantations of Indian corn will be destroyed, their villages burnt, their women, children and old men captured and their warriors driven into the woods where they will be pursued and annihilated by other Indians who will have served under us during this war."

"[His Majesty]," the minister wrote in a letter to Denonville, "expects to learn at the close of this year, the entire destruction of the greatest part of the Savages."

The army landed near where Rochester is today, at Irondequoit Bay. Then, they headed south toward Ganondagan, the largest of the Seneca villages. Three columns of French soldiers marched through the forest with their First Nations allies. They carried swords and torches and muskets.

But Denonville had trouble finding anyone to capture or to kill. Only a single battle would be fought during the entire campaign. One afternoon, as the French army was approaching Ganondagan through a narrow pass, hundreds of Seneca warriors opened fire on them from behind. There were dozens of casualties on both sides, but the Seneca attack failed. Outnumbered, the Senecas were forced to retreat.

After that, they disappeared. Denonville didn't see another enemy warrior during the rest of his invasion. Every time his army arrived at a Seneca village, they found it already abandoned.

So the governor adjusted his plan. If he couldn't kill the Seneca with swords and guns, he would starve them to death instead.

"I deemed it our best policy," he explained to Versailles, "to employ ourselves laying waste the Indian corn which was in vast abundance in the fields, rather than follow a flying enemy."

For the next ten days, the French army was hard at work burning fields of maize. Acre after acre went up in smoke. Vast stores were destroyed, too: everything saved for the winter. According to the governor's own estimates, his men burned more than a million bushels of maize, plus beans and other vegetables. A "vast quantity" of pigs was slaughtered. Entire villages were burned to the ground.

With winter coming in just a few short months, Denonville's scorched-earth campaign was enough to cause a famine. It wasn't just Seneca warriors who would die thanks to the French: Denonville's war was waged against civilians. Against the entire Seneca people.

"We have, assuredly," the governor boasted, "humbled the Senecas to a considerable degree, and seriously lowered their pride and raised the courage of their Indian enemies."

By the end of those ten days, Denonville's army was tired. It had been weeks since they left Montreal, making the long and dangerous journey up the rapids and waterfalls of the St. Lawrence River toward Lake Ontario. They'd marched through the woods for days, weighed down by their supplies, plagued by mosquitoes. Now they were getting sick, too. "It is full thirty years that I have had the honour to serve," the governor wrote to Versailles, "but I assure you, my lord, that I have seen nothing that comes near this in labour and fatigue."

Meanwhile, some of his First Nations allies were already leaving. There were tensions. Denonville had been badmouthing them in his reports for their "barbarities" and "cruelties" (without even the slightest hint of irony). Some of them were from Haudenosaunee nations themselves — having allied with the French after converting to Christianity — and many seemed to have reservations about the scorched-earth campaign. When Denonville asked them to burn the Seneca maize, they simply refused.

The governor decided it was time to head home.

He took the long way around. First, the army stopped at Niagara. There, they built a new French fort on the spot where Niagara-on-the-Lake is today. Fort Denonville would give the French and their First Nations allies a base of operations to launch future attacks against the Seneca.

Then, they followed the shoreline as it wrapped all the way around the lake — passing the future sites of cities like St. Catharines, Hamilton, and Oakville — which brought them, eventually, to the place where Toronto now stands.

It's hard to tell from Denonville's reports exactly where they stopped each night, but most historians seem to think the army spent two nights within the borders of today's Toronto: the first near the mouth of the Humber River; the second near the mouth of the Rouge.

In his dispatches, the governor doesn't mention anything about the inhabitants of Teiaiagon or Ganatsekwyagon, the Seneca villages on those rivers. Some historians have suggested that Denonville's army must have destroyed them, too. But it's also entirely possible that the Seneca had voluntarily abandoned them years earlier.

Pretty much all the information we have comes from the entry Denonville made in his diary that day — the day we think he woke up at the Humber and travelled to the Rouge. It's not much, but it's one of the very earliest written accounts of the place where Toronto now stands:

"The storm of wind and rain prevented us from leaving in the morning but at noon, the weather clearing up, we advanced seven or eight leagues and encamped at a place to which I had sent forward our Christian Indians from below. We found them with two hundred deer they had killed, a good share of which they gave to our army, that thus profited by this fortunate chase."

The next morning, the army continued east toward Montreal.

Denonville's campaign had succeeded in bringing death to the shores of Lake Ontario, but his greater goals would fail. While the Seneca suffered terribly that winter, the nation was far from broken. The Haudenosaunee would fight back. The Five Nations of the Confederacy launched their own campaigns deep into the heart of New France. They raided French settlements and destroyed farms. Two years after Denonville's army slept on the banks of the Rouge, Mohawk warriors travelled all the way to the island of Montreal and attacked the French settlers at Lachine, burning the town to the ground.

That same year, Denonville was replaced as governor and returned home to France. He got a new job at Versailles: tutor to the king's children.

Back in Canada, the wars raged on for another decade. But some leaders on both sides were working toward peace. By the end of the 1600s, the French had tracked down all of the surviving chiefs forced into slavery by Denonville's treachery. Thirteen of the fifty were still alive. They were finally allowed to return home. Meanwhile, the Haudenosaunee were beginning to worry about the growing power of their British allies. In 1701, a giant peace council was held at Montreal, where extensive negotiations led to a treaty between New France and forty First Nations, including the Haudenosaunee. The Great Peace of Montreal became one of the defining moments in Canadian history.

As for Toronto, in the decades that followed the Great Peace the French established their own trading posts at the southern end of the Carrying Place trail. Fort

Douville was built near Teiaiagon. Fort Toronto was at the mouth of the Humber. Fort Rouillé stood on what's now the Canadian National Exhibition grounds. By then, their allies, the Mississauga, had moved south into the area; they had villages at Ganatsekwyagon and near Teiaiagon, too.

But the days of peace wouldn't last: there would be even bigger wars in the 1700s. The British eventually invaded New France, winning the famous Battle of the Plains of Abraham and conquering all of French Canada. The last of the French forts at Toronto — Fort Rouillé — was burned as their troops retreated.

Then came the American Revolution. The British were overthrown in the United States and those who were still loyal to the Crown were driven from their homes. A flood of Loyalist refugees fled north. Many of them ended up on the northern shore of Lake Ontario, where the British created a new province for them. They called it Upper Canada.

The new province would need a new capital. It would be built on a sheltered harbour between the Humber and the Rouge: at the end of the ancient fur trade route where the First Nations and their ancestors had been living — and hunting beavers — for thousands upon thousands of years. A place called Toronto.

3
ELIZABETH SIMCOE'S NIGHTMARE

As the July sun rose above Lake Ontario early one morning in 1793, a British warship sailed into Toronto Bay. It was HMS *Mississauga*. The ship had sailed overnight from Niagara, arriving while it was still dark, waiting for dawn and a local fur trader to show the way through the treacherous shoals at the mouth of the harbour. On board was the first lieutenant governor of Upper Canada: John Graves Simcoe. He had come to establish a new capital for the new province. The tiny, muddy town he founded would eventually grow into a booming metropolis of concrete and glass, filled with millions of people.

The governor wasn't alone. His family came with him: his wife Elizabeth, their three youngest children, a grey cat with white spots, and a big Newfoundland dog named Jack Sharp.

Although she was embracing a new chapter in her life, Elizabeth Simcoe was no stranger to death. It had stalked her throughout her life, right from the beginning.

Both her parents were dead before she was a single day old. It was death that gave her her middle name: Posthuma. And now, nearly six thousand kilometres and an entire ocean away from home, death would follow her still. Even here, on the distant Canadian frontier, it would haunt her dreams. And with good reason.

Toronto was founded at a dangerous time. The bloody chaos of the American Revolution had ended just a decade earlier. Governor Simcoe spent most of his twenties fighting the American rebels, risking life and limb in the name of the British Empire. He seems lucky to have survived at all: he was wounded three times — once very seriously — and spent six long months in an American prison.

But he also made a name for himself as one of the rising stars of the British military. The unit he commanded, the Queen's Rangers, whose green coats and guerilla tactics helped them blend into the forest, never lost a battle. So when the British created a brand new province in what's now southern Ontario — a home for Loyalist refugees driven out of the United States by the victorious rebels — they chose Simcoe to run it.

Simcoe's military experience was key: another war with the Americans seemed not just inevitable, but imminent. Even with the revolution over, there was still plenty of anger on both sides. As governor, one of Simcoe's most urgent priorities was to prepare his new province for war. An American invasion could come at any time.

That's why he needed a new capital. The seat of government was at Niagara-on-the-Lake, but the Americans would soon be taking over the eastern side of the Niagara River; it was one of the peace terms negotiated in the wake of the revolution. The big guns of Fort Niagara were over there. The old capital would be almost impossible to defend if the Americans decided to invade.

Simcoe's new capital would be much safer. He would build it on the other side of the lake, on a spot where a natural harbour was formed by a long sandbar (the peninsula that would eventually become the Toronto Islands). Since there was only one way into the bay, it would be relatively easy to defend.

In the middle of July, the governor sent a hundred soldiers northward across the lake to begin the work. They were the Queen's Rangers, a new version of his old unit; some of them were the very same men Simcoe had commanded during the Revolutionary War. They made camp at a spot near the entrance to the harbour, at the mouth of what would eventually become known as Garrison Creek. There, they got to work felling trees, hacking away at the ancient forest that towered over the shoreline. Great pines and oaks came crashing to the ground. In their place, a military base began to take shape: Fort York.

About a week after those first soldiers arrived, Simcoe joined them in person, sailing into the bay on the *Mississauga* with his family.

Back home in England, the Simcoes had enjoyed life on a sprawling country estate with a legion of servants to take care of them. At Toronto, life was much more rustic.

The first family of Upper Canada lived in an elaborate set of tents pitched on the banks of the garrison (just across the creek from the construction at Fort York): the same "canvas house" used by the legendary explorer Captain James Cook on his famous travels through the Pacific. The family still had plenty of help and lots of nice things, but life in Canada was certainly much more difficult than it had been back home.

Some of their fellow settlers were shocked by the Simcoes' living conditions. One of them, Peter Russell, expressed his astonishment in a letter to his sister. "You have no conception of the Misery in which they live," he warned her. Some prominent families dragged their feet, staying at Niagara as long as they could before following the Simcoes across the lake.

Still, even in their tents the Simcoes did all they could to bring their British way of life to Upper Canada — in fact, it was an important part of their mission. Simcoe hoped Toronto would someday grow into a shining example of British superiority: a city so amazing the Americans would beg to be let back into the Empire. Arts, culture, and science would all play vital roles.

Democracy, however, was another story. As someone who had spent much of his life fighting against demo-cratic revolutionaries, Simcoe was a firm believer in the value of the English aristocracy; he was determined to import a strict class system. His dream of an official, hereditary, Canadian nobility never did come true, but he and Elizabeth did their best to establish the same kind of genteel, upper-class culture they'd known back home.

So, while the governor busied himself ruling his new province, Elizabeth was charged with the task of bringing a touch of aristocratic society to this remote outpost tucked between the dark Canadian forest and the deep waters of Lake Ontario. She did spend much of her time defying the traditional conventions of an English gentlewoman: exploring the wilderness by canoe, eating a raccoon for dinner in the woods, setting fires in the grass because she liked to watch them burn. But as plans for the fledgling town took shape and the families of other government officials reluctantly arrived, Elizabeth was at the centre of social life in the new settlement. Her calendar began to fill with dinners, teas, dances, balls, parties, and card games with the most powerful Upper Canadian families. She also painted watercolours and kept a detailed diary, providing an invaluable historical record of the city's founding days.

All the while, the threat of war loomed ever larger. And with it, the danger to the Simcoes grew, too. They were among "Mad" King George's highest-ranking representatives on the continent — and they were vulnerable: living in tents on the very edge of the Empire just across the lake from a powerful new nation that loathed the monarchy and might declare war at any moment. The sails of American warships could appear above the horizon without warning, come to seize the new capital and the Simcoes with it.

And the Americans weren't the only threat.

* * *

The revolution in the United States had inspired an even bloodier uprising in France. The French Revolution was in full swing during the summer Toronto was founded. The Reign of Terror began that same fall. While the Simcoes were trying to bring aristocratic culture to their tents on the beach at Toronto, aristocrats in Paris were losing their heads to the guillotine.

Just a few months earlier, the new French republic had officially declared war on the British Empire. And the Simcoes worried the conflict might reach Toronto.

For one thing, it made an American invasion even more likely. In fact, it was when Simcoe heard about the declaration of war that he decided to move his capital out of Niagara immediately — before the French had time to convince the Americans to invade. Reports suggested that French revolutionaries were in Lower Canada (what we now call the province of Quebec) in the hopes of inspiring a revolution there. And French troops stationed in the United States might cross the border to attack the Canadian colonies, too. Anticipating trouble, the Simcoes planned their escape: in case of an invasion, Elizabeth and the children would head to Quebec City, where the strong stone walls were better equipped to resist a siege.

During their first summer at Toronto, the Simcoes received a slow trickle of news from France. In August, they got word of an important British victory over the French rebels; the hero of the hour was King George's own son, the Duke of York. To commemorate the occasion, Simcoe ordered a royal salute: all the cannons on the shore, all the guns on all the ships in the harbour, all the muskets of Simcoe's soldiers were fired in honour of a man waging war against French democrats half a world away. To top it all off, the governor announced that he was naming his new town in honour of the prince. The old Indigenous name of Toronto was dropped. It would now be known as York.

That same month, the Simcoes played host to a pair of French visitors — representatives from a group of aristocrats who had escaped the horrors of the revolution and hoped to settle in Upper Canada. They told a morbid tale of King Louis XVI's botched attempt to escape his republican captors. By the time the Frenchmen told the story, their king had already lost his head. Just a few weeks after their visit, Marie Antoinette would follow her husband to the guillotine.

News of the queen's execution took months to travel across the Atlantic and up the St. Lawrence to York. It was on the first day of March in 1794 that the first lady of Upper Canada learned of the fate of the first lady of France.

Despite being at war with the French, the rulers of Upper Canada marked the occasion with solemn respect. That evening, the settlers of Toronto dressed all in black, postponing the dance they had planned. They might hate France, but they were still staunch monarchists and firm believers in a strict class system. They were exactly the kind of rulers the revolutionaries were hell-bent on overthrowing.

All of this helps to explain the nightmare Elizabeth Simcoe recorded in her diary the following week.

It was, of course, far from the first dream in the history of Toronto. People have been having nightmares on the shores of Lake Ontario for thousands of years. But this brief entry in Elizabeth Simcoe's diary is, at the very least, among the first recorded dreams in the history of the city: "I dreamt some time since that the Gov., Mr. Talbot [Simcoe's personal secretary] & I were passing a wood, possessed by an Enemy who fired ball at us as fast as possible. I was so frightened, that I have never since liked to hear a musquet fired & I am quite nervous when I hear of the probability of this Country being attacked."

It's just a couple of sentences, but those few lines provide a remarkable insight into the emotional life of the town's early settlers. It's a reminder that the city was born at a time of war and upheaval on a dangerous frontier thousands of kilometres away from the heart of the British Empire. It was a beautiful and serene place, but for those first few inexperienced settlers, it was also remote and frightening. The fear was so strong it haunted even the dreams of the most powerful woman in the province.

And Elizabeth was right to be afraid. Death was coming for the Simcoes.

Young Katherine was the first to go.

By the time they reached Toronto, the Simcoes had been married for more than ten years. They first fell in love far on the other side of the Atlantic, in the rolling green hills of Devon. John was a gallant young soldier freshly returned from the American war, still recovering from his wounds; Elizabeth was a petite nineteen-year-old, the niece of John's godfather, smart and curious. They took long walks and horseback rides together along Devon's ancient sunken roads, passing Iron Age hill forts and the hollows where fairies are said to live. Elizabeth would have to run every few steps to keep up with her tall companion. Together, they would sketch the countryside, turning their drawings into paintings when they returned home. They were engaged after just a few months, and soon they took the short trip down the hill to the old church where they got married. With Elizabeth's inheritance, they were able to buy a big country estate nearby.

Elizabeth had been an orphan her entire life. Her father was a military man who fought in Canada during the Seven Years' War; he was aide-de-camp to the legendary General James Wolfe. He was there at the Battle of the Plains of Abraham, one of the most famous moments in all of Canadian history. Unlike Wolfe, he survived. But there were other battles to be fought. The Seven Years' War was raging all over the world: it was the first truly global war, one of the bloodiest conflicts in human history. So, after Canada, Elizabeth's father was sent to Germany. And it was there, for a reason lost to history, that Thomas Gwillim died.

He never knew his wife was pregnant. It was a surprise to everyone: she was thirty-eight years old; they'd never had any other children. She would survive only a few months longer than her husband did; the strain of giving birth was too much. She lived just long enough to see her brand new baby daughter before she passed away.

That's how Elizabeth got her middle name: they called her Elizabeth Posthuma Gwillim because both her parents were dead right from her very first day. She was a posthumous child.

So now, as a young wife, the prospect of pregnancy must have been worrying. It would have been for anyone. Giving birth was a life-threatening ordeal. Some estimates suggest that as many as 20 percent of all English women died in childbirth. But when the time came, it was her husband who was most concerned. Elizabeth put off telling him as long as she could, until she began to have trouble fitting into her dresses and couldn't hide it anymore. When she gave him the news, John was visibly concerned. He was all too aware of what had happened to Elizabeth's mother.

But that first birth turned out to be relatively easy. Elizabeth brought her eldest daughter into the world without much trouble. Four more girls, and then a boy, quickly followed. By the time they left for Canada, the Simcoes had a happy family of six children.

As they set off across the ocean, they left the older kids behind to continue their education — they wouldn't see them again for five long years. But they took their two youngest with them on the journey: they were along for the ride as their parents spent two months sailing across the Atlantic, an entire winter stuck in Quebec City, and another two months struggling up the St. Lawrence River and across Lake Ontario to Niagara. Sophia was three years old by the time they arrived at Toronto; Francis was in his terrible twos. Even with a pair of nurses to help, Elizabeth found the toddlers were more than a handful.

Katherine was the most recent addition to the family: a Canadian-born Simcoe. She was conceived at the end of that first long winter the family spent in Quebec City, as spring arrived, the ice was melting and the days were finally growing longer. Elizabeth was pregnant on their harrowing trip up the St. Lawrence that summer. Her mother had died giving birth in the comfort of her childhood home with her own mother at her side; now Elizabeth would have to do it on a distant frontier.

The time came during the middle of the following winter: on a January day in cold Niagara. Elizabeth suffered through her labour in the canvas house, which was boarded up against the snow. When it was all over, she had given birth to yet another baby girl. They named her Katherine, after the governor's mother, who had died years earlier while Simcoe was away at war fighting the American rebels.

Baby Katherine was still just six months old when the Simcoes moved to Toronto. As spring came to the new town the following year, she was just beginning to walk and to talk. "She was," according to Elizabeth, "the sweetest tempered pretty child imaginable ... one of the strongest healthiest children you ever saw."

But at Easter, just a few weeks after her mother recorded the nightmare in her diary, everything suddenly changed.

When Katherine woke up on the morning of Good Friday, she seemed perfectly fine, playing happily in her mother's room. She'd been a bit feverish, but she was teething so Elizabeth didn't think it was unusual.

That afternoon, Katherine was struck by a series of fits. Her small body convulsed uncontrollably.

Elizabeth must have been terrified. There was no doctor she could call for help; the surgeon still spent much of his time at Niagara. Governor Simcoe was away, too, on a trip to build a strategic new fort near Detroit. She did everything she could for her daughter, staying up all night as Katherine was seized by one spasm after another. But she was fighting a losing battle: given the symptoms, it seems likely Katherine had meningitis, which can still be a life-threatening illness today.

The child's suffering finally came to end after the sun rose the next morning. The youngest Simcoe was dead.

They buried her on Easter Monday, in a small cemetery not far from Fort York — the very first graveyard the settlers made for the new town. Today, it's Victoria Memorial Square Park, at the corner of Wellington and Portland. Some of Toronto's oldest gravestones are still there, keeping silent watch as condo dwellers play with their dogs. A plaque remembers Katherine even now, more than two hundred years after her small bones were laid to rest.

"The loss of so promising a Child," Elizabeth wrote in a letter to a friend back home in England, "must long be a painful thing."

Elizabeth's husband was the next to die. John Graves Simcoe's lungs conspired with Napoleon to kill him.

The governor's health had long been a problem. Elizabeth's diary is full of references to his illnesses: gout, headaches, coughs, and terrible respiratory problems. His biographer, Mary Beacock Fryer, suggests that allergies made him vulnerable to bronchial infection. At Niagara, fumes from fresh paint once drove him into bed for two weeks, forcing him to miss a royal visit from Prince Edward (son of King George; father of Queen Victoria). Life on the frontier was taking a toll.

The stress couldn't have been helping, either. The situation with the Americans was deteriorating. Simcoe was convinced war was about to break out; he was already hard at work trying to secure the support of First Nations allies. He wrote desperate letters to his superiors, begging for the money and permission he needed in order to build adequate defences. They refused one request after another.

That winter, the Simcoes decided it was too dangerous for the family to remain at York. Elizabeth took the children to Quebec, safe behind the city's stone walls.

A peace treaty did finally avert immediate war with the Americans, but by then Simcoe was getting worn down. He requested a leave of absence: he hoped the familiar air of England would soothe his lungs — and that his arguments about the defence of Upper Canada would carry more weight if he made them in person.

And so in the summer of 1796, five years after the Simcoes first arrived in Canada, they sailed back down the St. Lawrence toward the ocean and home. They would never return.

But the dangers that haunted Elizabeth's dreams were far from over. Britain was still at war with France. When the Simcoes reached the mouth of the St. Lawrence, French warships were waiting for them. They were chased out into the Atlantic as some of the other vessels in their convoy were seized. Guns roared in the distance as they dodged icebergs off the coast of Labrador.

Day after day, Elizabeth and the children hid themselves in the cramped quarters below deck. She wrote in her diary that she was "in perfect misery every moment expecting to hear the Guns fire, as I had no Idea what it was to be so frightened.... I could not eat.... It will be a great while before I recover my fight." It took them weeks to sail across the open ocean before they finally reached the safety of home.

Even then, it wasn't over. Britain would be at war with France for most of the next twenty years — and soon the French would have a new leader: Napoleon Bonaparte. Governor Simcoe would spend the rest of his life fighting the Corsican dictator.

When it seemed as if Napoleon was about to invade England, Simcoe was put in charge of defending the West Country — a chance to put his Canadian experience to use at home. A year later, when Napoleon decided to invade Portugal, Simcoe was rushed to Lisbon to help assess the situation.

It was on that trip that his lungs betrayed him a final time. As his ship sailed south, Simcoe was plagued by his old nemesis: fresh paint. By the time he reached Lisbon, he was desperately ill, seized by "asthmatic paroxysms."

He tried every possible cure, but nothing worked. In the end, his doctor sent him home — sailing back to England on the very same poisonous ship he sailed in on.

It was Simcoe's final journey. By the time his ship reached port in Devon, he had less than a week left to live.

He would spend his last few days in his hometown of Exeter, not far from his country estate. His family had moved there when he was a boy, after his father died. Captain John Simcoe had been stricken down by pneumonia while commanding a ship in Canada during the Seven Years' War. Now, half a century later, his son had followed in his footsteps — falling fatally ill on his way to fight his own war against the French.

Growing up, it was mostly just Simcoe and his mother — his brothers all died young. She made sure he got the best possible education and a promising military career. She died while he was away fighting the Americans, taking her last painful breaths in a row of little houses at the foot of Exeter's grand cathedral. Now, thirty years later, her son lay on his own deathbed in that same row of houses.

When the founder of Toronto died, cannons were fired every minute for a full hour. A solemn procession of carriages carried his body east along the straight old Roman road between Exeter and the Simcoe estate. On an autumn day in 1806, John Graves Simcoe was buried in the same rolling green hills where he and Elizabeth had fallen in love all those years ago.

* * *

The dying wasn't done. The war and upheaval of Elizabeth's nightmare had one more Simcoe life to claim.

Torontonians know the name of Francis Simcoe — although they may not know they know it. He was only two years old when his family came to Toronto, but as the governor was handing out parcels of land to settlers, he made sure to reserve a prime lot for his young son. Francis was given a grant of two hundred acres along the western slopes of the Don Valley, from Bloor Street down into what we now know as Cabbagetown.

Soon, the Simcoes built a summer home on Francis's land. They picked a spot in the great pine forest near where the Bloor Viaduct stands today. There, they built a big log cabin, with majestic columns made of towering white pine. It looked out over the green treetops of the valley, where bald eagles made their nests and flocks of passenger pigeons soared by on their migrations.

When it came time to choose a name for the cottage, the Simcoes had fun with it, giving their son's rustic cabin an illustrious title: Castle Frank. Today, the name lives on in a subway station, as well as some nearby roads and a brook.

Even back then, it was clear Francis was headed for a future in the military. As he played on the beach at Toronto, he was fascinated by ships and guns. When Simcoe's cannons thundered their tribute to the Duke of York, Francis was unfazed. The mighty roar delighted the young boy. For his next birthday, he was given a tiny working cannon of his own. He was barely walking and already he seemed destined to follow in the footsteps of his father and his grandfathers: to spend his life fighting for the British Empire.

And he, like them, would die doing it.

He was still just twenty years old when he found himself storming a breach in the walls of Badajoz. The ancient fortress city stood on the border between Portugal and Spain. For five long years — ever since John Graves Simcoe's ill-fated mission to Lisbon — the British and the Portuguese had been fighting the French on the Iberian Peninsula. Led by the famous Duke of Wellington, they'd driven Napoleon out of Portugal and now they wanted to drive him out of Spain. To do that, they would need to hold Badajoz.

And so on a spring night in 1812, after a week of bombardment, the invaders stormed the walls. What followed were two of the most notorious and blood-soaked hours in the entire history of the British army. As Francis and the rest of the men scrambled toward the holes in the crumbling walls, they were slaughtered by the hundreds: cut to pieces by musket balls, trampled to death, blown apart by mines, burned alive by flaming barrels of gunpowder. Thousands were killed or wounded within just a few dozen metres.

Not a single soldier got through the breach. It was, instead, two other attacks on distant sections of the walls — originally planned as distractions — that finally won Badajoz.

The next morning, the Duke of Wellington surveyed the scene. Bodies covered the ground, some in pieces, some blackened, charred, and smoking. Other men were still alive, struggling to drag themselves out from under the pile of fresh corpses. At the sight of the carnage, the battle-hardened duke broke down and cried.

The body of Francis Simcoe was in there somewhere. He met his end during one of the night's many charges. We'll never know exactly how. That morning, a friend of his, a priest, searched through the grisly remains and found him lying among the dead. The reverend performed the last offices over the young soldier's body and made sure he was buried with as much dignity as possible.

Then the priest sat down to write a painful letter, giving Elizabeth the terrible news.

Elizabeth Simcoe had another forty years left to live after her son's death. She had given birth to eleven children and would live long enough to see five of them die — including Francis and Katherine. She spent her entire life as an orphan and more than half of it as a widow. Death is a companion to everyone, but to Elizabeth Posthuma Gwillim more than most.

From England, she kept a close eye on events in Canada. She watched her tiny, muddy town grow into a thriving city of thirty thousand people before she died. She read reports of rebellion and plague in its streets. And she saw her nightmare come true.

Just a few weeks after Francis died at Badajoz, the Americans finally invaded Upper Canada. During the War of 1812, York was attacked and occupied by American soldiers — just as the Simcoes had always feared. Muskets *were* fired from the cover of the Toronto forest, echoing

Elizabeth's dream. The fear of democracy and of democrats that had once troubled her sleep would loom over the city's rulers for decades to come.

Elizabeth grew old on the Simcoe estate, living the rest of her life in the same green hills where she'd fallen in love as a teenager. She died at the ripe old age of eighty-seven. She was buried in those same magical hills, right next to her husband, beneath a little church they had built on their land.

Wolford Chapel is still there today. And now, it's officially part of Canada. More than a hundred years after Elizabeth was laid to rest, that little church in the middle of the English countryside was given to the province of Ontario. The red maple leaf flies over those rolling green hills, an Ontario Heritage plaque stands outside the chapel, and inside you'll find a guestbook signed by many Canadians who have made the pilgrimage to the place where the founders of Toronto lay buried.

The Simcoes never returned to Canada. But at Wolford Chapel, Canada came to them. They rest in the soil of the country they once helped to build.

4
THE MURDER OF
CHIEF WABAKININE

It was dark. Nearly midnight. York was asleep. The tiny new town was still only three years old — the Simcoes had made their final goodbyes just a few weeks earlier. In the time since they'd first sailed into the bay, more and more space had been cleared out of the forest. Trees came crashing down; their stumps were burned out of the way. Now, the first ten blocks of the future capital had been laid out: from Front Street up to Adelaide; from George over to Berkeley. On the eastern edge of town, the modest Palace of Parliament was being built of brick and wood. To the west, Yonge Street had been carved out of the forest as a rugged dirt road — a route to the Upper Great Lakes to replace the old Toronto Carrying Place trail. There was a tavern and a market, but York still had no church, no courthouse, no jail. Many landowners still hadn't moved onto their property. Only a few wooden houses were nestled between the trees and the lake, and only a couple of hundred settlers called the town home. Most of them must have already been in bed on that August night in the summer of 1796.

Not all of them, though. A few men were moving through the darkness near the lake: Charles McEwan and his friends. He was one of the Queen's Rangers, meant to protect the people of Upper Canada and to help build a prosperous new province. Instead, he was about to commit a crime so heinous it would nearly tear the province apart.

In the century since the Beaver Wars, the Seneca had been pushed out of the area around Toronto, moving back south across the lake. By the time the Simcoes arrived, it was the Mississaugas — one of the Anishinabek nations — who controlled the northern shore of Lake Ontario. In the early days of the fur trade, they'd lived in the lands north of Lake Huron (near where Sault Ste. Marie is today), but in the late 1600s, some headed south. Not all sources agree on the details, but Anishinabek oral tradition remembers a series of battles between the Haudenosaunee Confederacy and their own Three Fires Confederacy. A peace treaty finally ended the conflict and established an alliance between the two groups. It was known as the Dish with One Spoon.

By the late 1700s, the Mississaugas could be found throughout much of what is now southern Ontario. Their council fire was at the mouth of the Credit River (where the city of Mississauga is today). In fact, the river got its name thanks to their reputation as trustworthy trading partners. The Mississaugas of the Credit spent their winters hunting in the northern reaches of the watershed and their summers fishing and growing maize at the mouth of the river.

One of their leaders was Chief Wabakinine. He was, they said, big and tall, greatly beloved by his people: a peacemaker who led through consensus. He'd been an important ally to the British for decades. He'd fought with them during the American Revolution, raiding the rebels and helping to convince other First Nations to join the fight.

In the years since, he'd continued to have a productive relationship with the settlers, playing a vital role in the treaty process.

As the Loyalist refugees began to pour into Upper Canada, the British government was looking to secure ever more land for the colonists. The legal framework had been laid out a few decades earlier, just after the British conquered New France. The Royal Proclamation of 1763 — one of the most important documents in Canadian history, reaffirmed by the country's modern constitution — declared the lands to the west legally belonged to the Indigenous people who lived on them. It established a nation-to-nation relationship between the British Crown and those First Nations. Only the government could buy land from Indigenous communities, which they did through formal treaties. The British would eventually negotiate twenty separate land deals with the Mississaugas — and Wabakinine's signature was on several of them.

It was a treaty called the Toronto Purchase that cleared the way for Simcoe's new city — at least as far as the British were concerned. A few years before the governor arrived in the province, the head of the Indian Department met with the Mississaugas to secure the land where the city of Toronto now stands. Wabakinine was there when the treaty was negotiated; he was one of three Mississauga chiefs whose signatures appeared on it.

As the town of York began to take shape, the Mississaugas traded with the tiny new settlement, supplying it with cheap food, including salmon from their fishing grounds in the Credit River.

That's what brought Chief Wabakinine to York on that fateful summer night in 1796. He and some other Mississaugas had come east from the Credit to sell salmon at the market (which stood on the very same spot where the St. Lawrence Market stands today). When they were done, they celebrated with a few drinks and then settled down for the night. While some of the Mississaugas set up camp on the peninsula, Wabakinine and his family went to sleep on the lakeshore, just across the road from Berry's Tavern, curling up beneath the shelter of their canoes.

They wouldn't sleep for long. Earlier that evening, the soldier McEwan had propositioned Wabakinine's sister. He offered her a shilling and some rum in return for sexual favours. And now, he was coming to collect — by force.

Chief Wabakinine was startled awake just before midnight. His wife had seen McEwan drag the chief's sister out from under her canoe. Wabakinine, still groggy, stumbled to her defence, trying to intervene. McEwan lashed out, grabbing a rock and hitting the chief hard over the head. As Wabakinine crumpled to the ground, the soldier kicked him in the chest, scuffled with the chief's wife, and then made his escape.

Hearing screams, the other Mississaugas rushed to the scene along with a couple of settlers. They found Wabakinine and his wife on the beach, both seriously injured. The couple was taken back to the mouth of the Credit River by canoe, where they both died of their wounds.

After decades of friendship with the British, Chief Wabakinine had met his end at the hands of a British soldier.

As news of the killings spread, the Mississaugas demanded justice. Many travelled to Niagara-on-the-Lake, which was still functioning as the capital while York was being built. There, they confronted Simcoe's deputy, Peter Russell, who'd been put in charge of the province now that the governor was gone.

Russell tried to reassure them. Even out here on the frontier, he insisted, English law still applied. The soldier had been arrested, bound in irons, and loaded onto a ship. It was on its way to Niagara, where McEwan would stand trial for murder. If he were found guilty, he would be hanged.

"A man who is capable of murdering one of you," Russell told the Mississaugas, "is also capable of murdering one of us … you need not be afraid that we will not do our utmost to find out the murderer and punish him as he deserves."

The trial was held that December. It was a farce. Four witnesses came forward; all of them had seen McEwan beat Wabakinine with the rock. But in the end, the jury still found the soldier not guilty. There was insufficient evidence, they claimed, that the chief was actually dead. McEwan was set free.

The Mississaugas had little interest in subscribing to the colonial system of justice; they didn't attend the trial, and they didn't give their consent to have the body exhumed as evidence.

"The Great Spirit above has placed him in the ground," a chief explained to Russell, "he might be displeased were he removed."

But many were outraged by the murder and the way it had been handled by the colonial authorities. This wasn't the first time one of their chiefs had been murdered by settlers who then escaped any kind of justice — the same thing had happened in Kingston just a few years earlier. After a century of trade and co-operation, it was now becoming clear to the Mississaugas that the British weren't the trustworthy allies they claimed to be.

The list of betrayals was growing long. Despite their endless promises, the settlers were overfishing and overhunting, razing the forests and polluting the water, destroying the Mississaugas' economy in the process. Settlers were even robbing Mississauga graves. Colonial authorities promised doctors who never came and blacksmiths who never showed up. They promised to support their First Nations allies in a war against the Americans in the Ohio Valley, and then refused to leave the safety of their fort. They were cutting back on the gifts they'd always given as a sign of their ongoing respect and commitment — a conscious ploy to weaken the Mississaugas, to force them into poverty and drive down the price of their land. Even the promises they made during treaty negotiations were quickly proving to be worthless.

The Toronto Purchase was a perfect example. The two sides came away from the negotiations with very different ideas about what the treaty meant. They didn't even agree on which land had been discussed — when the surveyor showed up to chart everything from Etobicoke Creek to Ashbridge's Bay, Wabakinine insisted the treaty only covered the land between the Humber and the Don rivers.

For the British, oral promises meant little — the signed, legal document was all that mattered. For the Mississaugas, the oral agreement was vital — none of them could read the English document, but they had brought hundreds of their people to witness the negotiations.

And as the British soon realized, in the case of the Toronto Purchase the legal document was utterly useless anyway. Just a year after York was founded, Simcoe and his bosses discovered the supposed treaty was nothing but a blank deed. It didn't even describe the land the British thought they had bought. The names of Wabakinine and the other chiefs had been signed on separate pieces of paper and then attached to the blank document after the fact. Even by the sketchy standards of colonialism, it was clear the British had no legal right to the land where they were building their new capital.

They decided not to tell the Mississaugas. The British waited more than ten years and then got the nation to sign another version of the Toronto Purchase — still failing to fully explain what the document meant and that it applied to even more land than the first one. The agreement was so poorly executed that the issues around the Toronto Purchase would remain unresolved for more than two hundred years. It wasn't until 2010 that the dispute was finally settled, with the Canadian government agreeing to pay the Mississaugas of the New Credit First Nation $145 million for the land (the estimated value at the time of the Toronto Purchase translated into modern dollars).

And so now, after years of frustration, the Mississaugas were losing patience. For many, the murder of Chief Wabakinine and his wife was the final straw.

They planned for war, and met with Chief Joseph Brant (Thayendanegea). He was the leader of their allies in the Haudenosaunee Confederacy — and he, too, was furious with the British. Much like Wabakinine, Brant had spent decades fighting at their side, including in the Seven Years' War and the American Revolution. But it was becoming clear their promises meant little. "It grieves me," he once wrote, "to observe that it seems natural to Whites, to look on lands in the possession of the Indians with an aching heart, and never rest till they have planned them out of them."

As his rage mounted, Brant met with American and French revolutionaries in the United States, and there were rumours he and the Mississaugas might support an invasion of Canada mounted by the French and the Spanish.

Peter Russell was terrified. The settlers in Upper Canada now outnumbered the First Nations residents, but not by much — and they were spread thin, with only a few hundred soldiers to protect the entire colony. If the Mississaugas and the Haudenosaunee took up arms, they might very well be able to overpower the settlers. French and Spanish support would make it a foregone conclusion.

Over the course of the next two years, as the threat of an armed First Nations resistance loomed as a real possibility, Russell prepared for war. He raised a militia and ordered hundreds of guns. Two new military block-houses were built at York. Government officials began to travel with armed escorts. Russell ordered his officials to do everything they could to drive a wedge between the Mississaugas and the Haudenosaunee.

In the end, war didn't break out. Even though it meant disobeying his orders from England, Russell finally gave in to Brant's demands, allowing him to sell some of the Haudenosaunee lands along the Grand River. Meanwhile, the strength of the Mississaugas was quickly dwindling. Their food supplies were still being devastated; they were being exposed to terrible new diseases. Soon, they were vastly outnumbered by the colonists.

In the years to come, the settlers would forget any of it had ever happened. The story of the founding of Toronto would be told as the triumph of Loyalists bringing civi-lization to an untamed wilderness and to their grateful First Nations allies. They would forget the betrayal of the Toronto Purchase, forget the blank deed, forget Chief Wabakinine and his wife, forget the night they were bru-tally murdered, and the day their killer was set free.

5

THE TOWN'S FIRST HANGING AND HOW IT WENT WRONG

One night in 1798, John Sullivan and Michael Flannery got drunk. The two friends were drinking whisky at one of the very first taverns ever built in muddy little York. Sullivan was an illiterate Irish tailor. Flannery was known for his habit of reciting Latin proverbs — they called him "Latin Mike."

That night, they drank so much they ran out of money. And when they did, Latin Mike was apparently drunk enough to think it was a good idea to forge a banknote. It was worth about three shillings — a little less than a dollar. Sullivan used it to buy more booze. That was a fatal mistake.

Before long, the forgery was discovered. And while Latin Mike ran for his life all the way to the United States, Sullivan was arrested and thrown in jail.

He was tried, convicted, and sentenced to death.

"Sullivan," the judge intoned, "may all who behold you, and who shall hear of your crime, and of your unhappy fate, take warning from your example.... [I] recommend to you to employ the few days that shall be allowed, of a life spent in wickedness, in humble and fervent prayer to almighty God."

The execution was held at the brand new jail. It was a small, wooden building on King Street (a couple of blocks east of Yonge, where the King Edward Hotel stands now). It was surrounded by a high, spiked fence made of wood and protected by sturdy, iron doors. Inside, there was just enough room to hold three prisoners. Outside, there was a hanging yard.

Sullivan's death was turned into a public spectacle. A crowd of excited townspeople gathered in their finest clothes to watch the tailor die on a Thursday in October.

It was the beginning of a long tradition of capital punishment in Toronto. And there was plenty of corporal punishment, too: petty criminals were flogged in the square at the St. Lawrence Market; some had their hands branded, or even worse, their tongues; others were put in the stocks. But those sentences were all for small offences. There were more than a hundred different crimes that were considered so vile they deserved the death penalty. It wasn't until 1962 — more than a hundred and fifty years after Sullivan's trial on King Street — that Canada's last executions were carried out on the gallows at the Don Jail. By then, hundreds of Canadians had been hanged for their crimes.

But that first hanging wasn't going to be easy. When the time came to kill Sullivan, there was one big problem. Nobody had ever been hanged in Toronto before, so there was no experienced executioner. The city leaders had no trouble with the theory of killing someone for stealing a dollar, but they were having trouble finding anyone who was actually willing to do it in practice. It would be another century before the city got a full-time professional hangman. And in the town of just a few hundred people, no one seemed anxious to volunteer.

Luckily, John Sullivan wasn't the only prisoner in jail that day. He had company in the cells: a fellow by the name of McKnight. He was willing to kill Sullivan for one hundred dollars and a pardon.

It's a difficult job, hanging a human being. Even experienced executioners can have trouble sometimes — that last hanging at the Don Jail went horribly wrong: one of the condemned men had his head nearly ripped off in the process; his neck was torn open, leaving his body swinging by just a few sinews as his blood splattered the floor. And that was with an experienced hangman; McKnight didn't have any experience at all.

His first attempt failed. The rope wasn't strong enough. It snapped when McKnight tried to hang his fellow prisoner, dumping the doomed man to the ground. They would have to try again.

Even Sullivan wasn't impressed. His last words were something along the lines of, "McKnight, I hope to goodness you've got the rope all right this time."

This time, McKnight did.

6
WHATEVER HAPPENED TO PEGGY POMPADOUR?

Russell Abbey was a lovely, elegant home. It stood behind a little fence on Front Street — which, in the 1700s, was a dirt road called Palace Street that ran right along the shore of the lake. From the fine windows of the house you could look out across the bay, to the sun sparkling on the water and the huge flocks of waterfowl that gathered on the lake. Russell Abbey was just one storey high and made of wood, but by the standards of the young town it was a mansion. It would eventually be nicknamed "The Palace."

This was the home of Peter Russell, the interim governor of the province while John Graves Simcoe was away. With the Simcoes gone, Russell Abbey was the centre of social life in the province, where the most important people in York would come to eat, drink, and discuss the politics of the day.

It was also where the Pompadour family was enslaved.

We don't know much about Peggy Pompadour. We do know that she was in her late twenties when Toronto was founded. She had three children: a son named Jupiter and two daughters, Amy and Milly. The Russells enslaved them all. The father of the family worked for them, too, as a paid servant.

John Graves Simcoe hated slavery. Back home in England, he'd spoken out against it as a member of Parliament, giving abolitionist speeches in the House of Commons. He saw no place for slavery in his new province; he was clear about that right from the very beginning. "The principles of the British Constitution do not admit of that slavery which Christianity condemns," he wrote before he became governor. "The moment I assume the Government of Upper Canada, under no modification will I assent to a law that discriminates by dishonest policy between natives of Africa, America or Europe."

But getting rid of slavery wouldn't be easy. There were no slaves in England — a court decision had freed them all fifteen years earlier. But hundreds were "owned" by the colonists in Upper Canada, many brought north to the new province by Loyalist refugees as they fled the revolution in the United States. The British government had actually encouraged the practice, passing a law in Westminster that promised new Canadian settlers they would get to keep their slaves. So if Simcoe wanted to get rid of slavery in the province, he would have to pass a new law to actively abolish it.

To do that, he would need the support of the elected Legislative Assembly as well as the members of his own, hand-picked Legislative Council. Both of those bodies were full of slave owners.

Peter Russell was one of them.

Russell had been born in Ireland, moved to England, and went to school at Cambridge for all of six months before he lost so much money playing cards that he was forced to drop out and join the army. He kept right on gambling, though. His next twenty years were spent travelling around the world: sometimes he was fighting British wars; sometimes he was running away from his creditors. When they finally did catch up with him, he even spent some time in prison.

None of that seems to have kept him from making a good impression on Simcoe. They met in New York City during the American Revolution; Russell had recently finished running a Virginia tobacco plantation into the ground. When Simcoe was put in charge of his new Canadian province, he invited the desperate, debt-ridden Russell to help run it. The compulsive gambler became Upper Canada's first receiver general and auditor general, in charge of financial accountability for the province.

Simcoe also named him to his Legislative Council (which worked a bit like the Senate does today). And Russell wasn't the only slave owner Simcoe chose: at least five of the nine members of the Legislative Council were either slave owners or from slave-owning families. They formed a majority. Simcoe, determined to abolish slavery in Upper Canada, had made it almost impossible to do so.

But he was still going to try. It was the resistance of Chloe Cooley that gave him the opportunity he needed. During the Simcoes' first winter at Niagara, Cooley was living in slavery only a few kilometres away, near Queenston. At the end of that winter, her "master" sold her to someone on the American side of the border, so he tied her up with rope and forced her into a boat to be taken across the river. Cooley, like many slaves, had long resisted her captivity: refusing work, stealing, disappearing for periods of time, generally trying to disrupt the life of her "master" and ensure her enslavement was as much of an inconvenience as possible. Now, she resisted again. As she was unloaded and handed over to her new "owner," Cooley screamed and put up a fierce fight.

Peter Martin, a black Loyalist who had fought on the British side of the American Revolution, watched it all happen. A week later, when Simcoe's Executive Council met for the first time, Martin appeared before them to tell the tale.

Simcoe was appalled, and saw his chance. During the next session of the legislature, he pushed a bill to abolish slavery. But with his government full of slave owners, he was forced into a compromise — the exact thing he had promised never to do. Slavery would not be abolished immediately; instead, it would be gradually phased out. No new slaves could be brought into Upper Canada, but any who were already in the province would spend the rest of their lives in slavery. Their children would be born into captivity, too; they wouldn't be free until they turned twenty-five. Finally, anyone who wanted to free a slave was discouraged from doing so: they would be forced to provide financial security to ensure the newly freed slave wouldn't be a drain on the resources of the state.

The bill was passed just a few weeks before the Simcoes headed across the lake to start their new capital. And so, the foundations of Toronto were laid with the help of slave labour. During the early years of York, there were fifteen black slaves within the borders of the town — and another ten just across the Don Valley.

Peggy Pompadour was in her late twenties when the Act Against Slavery was passed. Since she was already a slave, she would remain a slave. No one seems to know when her daughters were born, but her son Jupiter was a toddler at the time — about the same age as little Francis Simcoe — so he, too, could legally be enslaved for the rest of his life.

At Toronto, the Pompadours spent some of their time labouring at Russell's new farm, Petersfield. (It was outside of town, where Queen Street meets Peter Street today.) But most of their days and nights were spent at Russell Abbey, serving the interim governor, his sister Elizabeth, and the many important guests who came for dinner parties and other social and political events. Young Jupiter would answer the door and welcome them in. His sister, Amy, would wait on the ladies in her striking red turban. The Russells and their guests would dine on a meal prepared by Peggy — given the options in those days, it might have included fresh salmon, beef, venison, or passenger pigeon.

Russell spent three years filling in as governor. He doesn't seem to have been particularly good at it. One historian calls him "timid and vacillating ... Anxious, and more elderly than his years." Another describes him as "easily depressed by minor irritations ... [with] little opportunity and less desire to make a positive imprint upon the province over which he presided so uneasily and so fretfully." About the best anyone has to say about him is that he was "cautious, practical, capable, and painstaking ... [but with] little imagination."

His greatest accomplishment was the expansion of public infrastructure: under Russell, new roads were built, the town was expanded a few blocks west to Peter Street, and the settlement's first church, St. James, was erected on the corner of Church and King (the modest, wooden precursor to the soaring Cathedral Church of St. James, which still stands on the same spot today).

But even his successes opened Russell to criticism. He was notoriously cheap. He wanted to make improvements, but he didn't want to pay for them. It was Russell who commissioned the construction of the jail, but he didn't bother to include any beds, or blankets, or stoves to keep it warm during the winter. On more than one occasion, he refused to pay for work altogether. When he hired Asa Danforth to spend months in the woods building a road toward Kingston, Danforth's men never got the land they'd been promised in return. And when William Berczy's German settlers helped to carve Yonge Street out of the forest, they didn't get all the land they'd been promised, either.

Still, Russell assumed history would remember him fondly thanks to projects like Danforth's new road. "I expect the Gratitude of the People will erect a Statue to my memory for it," he once boasted.

That statue never did get built, but in return for his middling service, Russell was rewarded with a lot of land. First, there was the property in town at Russell Abbey, the farmland of Petersfield, and hundreds of acres on a country estate on the hill above Davenport Road. And he would get more beyond that. Once Simcoe left, Russell found ways of using his new position to his advantage. He notoriously granted himself even more land, found a law allowing him to seize still more from newly arrived immigrants, and even appointed himself as a judge — despite his complete lack of legal experience — so he could collect the salary. Some townspeople began to lampoon him with the saying, "I, Peter Russell, grant to you, Peter Russell," while another joked, "He's called the receiver general because he's generally receiving."

Meanwhile, back at home, he had a family of slaves to wash his clothes, cook his meals, and help turn his farm into a profitable business.

Still, free labour wasn't enough. The Russells weren't happy with the Pompadours — the slaves were fighting back. Much like Chloe Cooley, the Pompadours mounted a resistance to their enslavement: they stole, dragged their feet, and spoke back. The Russells complained about them for years, called them "dirty," "idle," "insolent," and "pilfering." Peggy would disappear for stretches of time. In response, Russell had her thrown into his new jail; Elizabeth refused to let her back into the house. They published a warning in the newspaper: anyone who gave Peggy shelter would be prosecuted to the fullest extent of the law. Jupiter spent plenty of time in jail, too, and once, when the Russells decided that wasn't punishment enough, they bound him and strung him up in the window of a storehouse as a public humiliation.

They spent years trying to break up the Pompadours, searching for someone who'd be willing to buy them. Finally, Russell placed one of the most chilling ads ever to appear in an Upper Canadian newspaper:

TO BE SOLD,

A BLACK WOMAN, named PEGGY, aged about forty years; and a Black boy, her son, named JUPITER, aged about fifteen years, both of them the property of the Subscriber.

The Woman is a tolerable Cook and washer woman and perfectly understands making soap and candles.

The Boy is tall and strong of his age, and has been employed in a Country business, but brought up principally as a House Servant—They are each of them servants for life. The Price for the Woman is one hundred and fifty Dollars—for the Boy two hundred Dollars, payable in three years with interest from the day of Sale and to be properly secured by Bond &c. — But one fourth will be taken in ready Money.

PETER RUSSELL.
York, Feb. 20th 1806.

They never did find a buyer.

By then, Russell wasn't having much luck in his professional career, either. When Simcoe finally officially resigned, Russell fully expected to be named as his permanent replacement. But when the day came, he was passed over. A few years later, when he was overlooked for a second time, he was angry enough to announce that he was moving back to England.

But there was a problem. He had managed to amass an enormous amount of land in Upper Canada: forty square kilometres at the very least. He couldn't find anyone willing to buy it all. And so Russell was stuck in York. He lived out his final years as an old man in the town he was desperate to leave.

We know how Russell died. He was an "important man," so his death was an occasion worthy of notice. It came in 1808, when he was felled by a terrible stroke. The cure — a mustard plaster and a quart of wine laced with crushed deer antler — didn't work, for some reason. He died at the age of seventy-five, taking his final breaths at Russell Abbey. His funeral was attended by many of the most powerful people in the province, including the new governor. He was laid to rest in the family tomb of his good friends the Baldwins, next to Spadina House on their country estate. Years later, the tomb would be moved to St. James Cemetery. Russell's remains are still resting there today, in a shady corner overlooking the Don Valley.

More than two hundred years after he died, Russell is still remembered in the names of Peter Street and Russell

Hill Road. Abbey Lane now runs along the spot where Russell Abbey once stood. The names of some of the city's other slave owners can still be found around Toronto, too. William Jarvis is remembered by Jarvis Street; James Baby's old estate on the Humber River is still called Baby Point today.

But we don't know what happened to Peggy Pompadour — or to the rest of her family. With Russell's death, she and the children were passed down to Elizabeth along with the rest of his "property," but after that, Peggy seems to have disappeared from the historical record. For the most part, the children did, too. We don't know how any of the Pompadours died. Or where they're buried.

Amy is the only one we do know anything about. Elizabeth eventually "gave" her to a friend; soon, she had a son. And many decades later, in the 1870s, when a grizzled old priest named Henry Scadding sat down to write the very first history of the city of Toronto, Amy Pompadour would make the briefest of appearances. Everything we know about her family has come to us filtered through the eyes of others — and this time would be no different. The last glimpse of the Pompadours comes in one of Scadding's own distant childhood memories from the 1820s: a beautiful, tall, black woman with a romantic name walking through the streets of Toronto before she disappears into the unknown.

THE
WAR OF 1812

7
THE BATTLE OF YORK

They appeared out of the gathering darkness, looming above the waves: fourteen warships sailing across Lake Ontario toward Toronto. They were first spotted at dusk from the top of the Scarborough Bluffs, wooden hulls carving through the waves, sails stretching high into the evening sky. From each of the ships flew the red, white, and blue: fifteen stars and fifteen stripes. The American fleet. Not twenty years after Elizabeth Simcoe dreamed of enemy soldiers stalking through the forests of Toronto, her nightmare was about to come true. The War of 1812 was coming to York. The Americans were invading the capital.

That night, as a cannon boomed out the alarm, the town was a flurry of activity. People scrambled to hide their possessions and brace for the invasion. Every man between the ages of sixteen and sixty was expected to take up arms; farmers poured in from the surrounding countryside to join the defence of the town. Three hundred of those amateur militiamen gathered, joining another three hundred professional British soldiers, and maybe as

many as a hundred Mississauga and Ojibwa warriors —
all ready to risk their lives in the battle to come.

As the night began to fade into a clear April day, the
townspeople watched the fleet make its way around the
peninsula, slicing through the calm waters toward shore.
The warships dropped anchor a few kilometres west of
the town (near where the Exhibition Grounds are now).
Then, the first wave of American soldiers descended into
big, flat-bottomed boats and rowed toward the beach.
Many others would follow: there were more than seventeen hundred American soldiers on those ships.

The First Nations warriors were the first ones there
to defend Toronto. They fired upon the invaders from the
edge of the forest as the landing party struggled to reach
the beach and clamber up the steep banks. Soon, those
Indigenous warriors were joined by the first wave of
British troops. The American ships opened fire, hurling
grapeshot at the defenders. It was there on the lakeshore,
amid the crack and hiss of musket fire and the flash of
bayonets, that the Battle of York claimed its first lives.
Dozens were left dead or wounded.

The defenders were badly outnumbered. It didn't take
long for the Americans to establish a beachhead, and then
push their enemy back into the woods. Sharpshooting
riflemen led the way, their green coats blending into the
early spring foliage; they advanced through the forest,
using trees and logs as cover as they picked off their enemies. The red coats of the British made them easy targets.
Many would die in that forest before the morning was
over. As they lay there bleeding in the woods, the last of

their lives ebbing out of them, some would have been able to hear a strangely chilling sound: the American fife and drum corps playing "Yankee Doodle."

All the while, the invaders drew closer and closer to Fort York and to the vulnerable capital beyond.

The War of 1812 had been raging for nearly a year. The Americans and the British had never fully resolved their differences after the War of Independence. In fact, in recent years things had been getting even worse. The United States had a long list of complaints, including the practice of impressment: the British regularly stopped and searched American ships for deserters from the Royal Navy and then forced them to join the fight against Napoleon. Sometimes, they grabbed anyone who seemed like they might be British at all.

Outraged, the Americans finally declared war in June of 1812. The vote in Congress was close, but many were confident that an invasion of Upper Canada would lead to a quick and easy victory. As Thomas Jefferson put it, "The acquisition of Canada this year, as far as the neighborhood of Quebec, will be a mere matter of marching."

There was reason to believe he was right. The military might of the British Empire was distracted by Napoleon. The few men and resources Britain was able to spare for the defence of its Canadian colonies were focused on the larger cities of Lower Canada. Not only was Upper Canada left with feeble protection, some believed the residents of the province would welcome the invaders as liberators. Two-thirds of the population of the province had been born in the United States. It wasn't entirely clear which side they would take when the blood began to flow.

But the summer of 1812 didn't exactly go to plan for the United States. At Fort Detroit, they managed to lose the first major battle of the war without killing a single enemy soldier. The military leader of Upper Canada, Major-General Isaac Brock, teamed up with the leader of his Indigenous allies, Tecumseh, to besiege the fort. The Shawnee chief had united dozens of First Nations to oppose American expansion into their territories — British support for the alliance was one of the reasons the Americans had declared war. But the siege of Fort Detroit ended almost immediately: Brock and Tecumseh bluffed the American general into surrendering on the very first day. They arranged to have Tecumseh's men march by the fort in a loop — making it seem as if he had many more warriors than he actually did. The Americans — terrified by their racist myths about the "savagery" of the First Nations — promptly ran a white flag up the pole. Brock and Tecumseh rode into the fort side by side as victors.

Brock was killed just a few weeks after that, defending Queenston Heights against an American invasion across the Niagara River. But the Americans lost that battle, too, and failed to gain a foothold on the Canadian side of the border before winter set in.

When spring arrived and the ice thawed, the Americans were looking for an easy win. York seemed to be it. The tiny capital made a much more inviting target than Kingston, still the biggest town in the province back then. As the seat of government, York would offer an important symbolic victory and it also contained a tempting prize: near the foot of Bay Street, shipwrights had been building a powerful new warship named in honour of the colony's dead hero. If the Americans could seize HMS *Sir Isaac Brock* and finish building it themselves, they would control Lake Ontario with an iron grip — an enormous advantage that might give them a chance to win the entire war.

But to capture the *Brock*, the Americans would have to go through Fort York.

It was noon by the time the invaders finally emerged from the woods. By then, it had already been a long and bloody day. Dead bodies were scattered through the forest and along the shore of the lake. Even more had died at the defensive battery to the west of the fort (near where the Princes' Gates are today). A chest filled with ammunition had accidentally been detonated. The explosion lifted men off the ground and tore them to pieces. As the smoke cleared, the air was filled with the screams of wounded men and the stench of burning flesh. Fresh corpses lay strewn upon the earth.

But that was just the beginning. Much worse was still to come.

The American commander, General Dearborn, was still safe and sound on board his ship. He was old and seasick, so he'd stayed behind while his troops went ashore. Command on the ground was left to a brigadier-general by the name of Zebulon Pike. He was a famous explorer of the American West; one of the tallest mountains in the Rockies is named in his honour: Pikes Peak.

As Pike and his men came out of the forest, they found themselves in a large field outside Fort York — still a few hundred metres away. The defenders had retreated inside the fortifications under bombardment by the American fleet.

Pike knew he was on the verge of victory. And so, he took a seat on a tree stump to interrogate a British prisoner while his cannons pounded away at the defences. Any moment now, a white flag would appear above the fort. All Pike had to do was to wait.

Inside the fort, the British general knew the battle was lost. But he had no plans to surrender his men. He ordered them to retreat east to Kingston; evading capture, they would be free to fight another day. He was also determined to keep the fort's supply of weapons and ammunition out of enemy hands. Most of it was kept in the grand magazine: a storehouse built into the embankment of the shoreline at the southern edge of the fort. As his troops retreated, the general gave a fateful order: destroy the magazine.

BOOM!

It was one of the biggest explosions anyone in North America had ever seen. The magazine stored thirty thousand pounds of gunpowder, ten thousand cannonballs and thirty thousand musket rounds. The blast could be heard for miles; far across the lake in Niagara, buildings shook and windows rattled. The shockwave swept the American soldiers up off their feet and hurled them twenty metres through the air. Lungs hemorrhaged; intestines burst. A great cloud of debris rose above the fort. Tons of stone, wood and metal were launched high into the sky and far across the field. The wreckage fell back to earth in a deadly rain, tearing through flesh and crushing bone.

"It was more horrible, more awful, and, at the same time, more sublime than my pen can pourtray [sic]," one American soldier wrote. "At first the air was darkened with stones, rafters, and clay. In about half a minute the infernal shower descended and dealt destruction to our column … the ground at the head of it was covered with the dead and dying."

Fort York was in ruins. Inside, many of the defenders had been killed, but it was the invaders who took the full brunt of the blast. Dozens of American soldiers lay dead outside the fort. Hundreds were wounded.

The night before the battle, as Pike sat aboard his ship, he wrote a letter home to his wife. "We are now standing on and off the harbor of York which we shall attack at daylight in the morning: I shall dedicate these last moments to you, my love…. Should I fall, defend my memory and only believe, had I lived, I would have aspired to deeds worthy of your husband."

Now Pike lay dying, crushed by a boulder, his back torn open, his ribs caved in. Some say that as the life ebbed out of him, Pike urged his men on: "Push on, my brave fellows, and avenge your general!" Others say he lived just long enough to hear his men cheer their victory as he took his final breath, or died after being taken back to his ship.

The Americans paid a terrible price, but they had won the day. With the defenders of the capital in full retreat, Fort York was left to the Americans. The Union Jack came down from its flagpole. The Stars and Stripes took its place. The American flag now flew above Toronto.

Negotiations were tense. In the hours after the battle, the two sides met at a house on Front Street to discuss the terms of the surrender. The Americans were furious. To them, the explosion at the fort was treachery, and they felt the British soldiers should have stayed behind to be honourably taken prisoner rather than escaping. They got even angrier when a large column of black smoke was spotted rising from the docks: the British general had ordered HMS *Sir Isaac Brock* burned rather than have it fall into enemy hands. It was all the Canadian negotiators could do to keep the Americans from marching on the town in retribution.

After about an hour of anxious discussion, the two sides finally came to an agreement. Public property was fair game, but the private property of the townspeople was to be protected. That was no surprise: before the attack, the American commanders had told their men that any soldier who plundered from the town would be shot. But in the end the promise meant little. When the time came for General Dearborn to sign the articles of capitulation, he dragged his feet. Instead, he stood by and watched while his men began to ransack the town.

For the next six days, the American soldiers terror-ized York, pillaging, looting and setting fire to public buildings. They broke into homes and businesses and took everything they could find: money and silver, whisky and rum, furniture and clothing, coffee, chocolate, sugar, and tobacco. They stole carpenter's tools and medical instruments. They took piles of books from the library. They even made off with two fire engines and a horse. The invaders loaded their ships full of treasure.

They also made sure to pay a special visit to the home of Major James Givins. He had first come to Canada as aide-de-camp to Simcoe. Now, he was an official with the Indian Department; on the morning of the battle, he stood side by side with the Mississauga and Ojibwa warriors on the beach. To the Americans, that was an especially heinous crime. At the onset of the war, they promised that any white man found fighting alongside First Nations warriors would be executed. As far as they were concerned, Givins was a traitor to his race.

By the time they came for him, he was already long gone. But his wife, Angelica, and their children were still at home. During the afternoon of the battle, she had been hard at work treating wounded men on her dining room table; nearly a hundred years later, you could still see the bloodstains on the floorboards. Now, she could do nothing but watch as the invaders ransacked her home and frightened the children.

Many of the townspeople had already been evacuated: long lines of refugees headed east along the road to Kingston. Those who stayed behind were left to fend for themselves. With the British soldiers gone and the local militia taken prisoner under the terms of the surrender, other local authorities were forced to fill the void.

The most notable was Reverend John Strachan. He was the rector of the town's oldest church, St. James, the spiritual leader of the small town, and the man responsible for the education of all the most respectable young men in the province. He would eventually become Toronto's first Anglican bishop. He was also a diehard Tory who believed passionately in Simcoe's vision of an anti-democratic province deeply opposed to American ideas.

As the invaders pillaged and burned the town, Strachan opposed them at every turn. He berated the American commanders, demanded they finally sign the articles of capitulation, and then did everything he could to hold them to those terms. He made sure the militiamen being held as prisoners in the blockhouse at Fort York were given food and medical treatment. He eventually secured their parole, and helped to carry the wounded to the hospital. He even confronted some of the looters himself, nearly getting shot in the process. And when the Americans returned in July to sack the town again, Strachan would berate them so thoroughly they agreed to return the library books they'd taken the first time.

While the British army abandoned York to its fate, Strachan stood up to the American invaders. It made him a hero in the eyes of many. In the years to come, that reputation would help him to become one of the most influential figures in Toronto — indeed, in all of Canadian history.

But not even Strachan could halt all of the destruction. Before the invaders left, they burned several buildings to the ground, including the Parliament buildings and the governor's residence at Fort York. As partial justification, they claimed they'd found a scalp hanging alongside the speaker's ceremonial mace in the legislature. In the months to come, that image would play an important role in their continuing demonization of the First Nations — and of the British and Canadians who allied themselves with them.

As it turned out, those allies would abandon their pact with the Indigenous nations as soon as it became convenient: at the end of the war, First Nations leaders weren't even invited to the peace negotiations, and the British signed away the promises they'd made to support an Indigenous state free of settler encroachment.

The gruesome Battle of York and the vicious occupation that followed marked the beginning of a brutal new chapter in the war. Those few days in April sparked a bloody cycle of revenge and retribution that carried on until the peace. When the British stormed Washington, D.C., the following year, they would set fire to the White House and the Capitol Building — partially in retaliation for the public buildings set ablaze in York.

When the Americans first invaded Upper Canada, they spoke to the people of the province as if they were family — some of them quite literally were. But the brutal treatment York had suffered at the hands of the occupiers helped to drive a wedge between them. It was hard to see the invaders as liberators when they were burning buildings and looting homes. As the bloody war dragged on, it became clearer and clearer to more and more of the settlers in Upper Canada that they were not, in fact, Americans. They were something else entirely. Something, perhaps, Canadian.

8
THE BLOODY BURLINGTON RACES

This time, they came at dawn. Just a few months after the Battle of York, as a black September night gave way to the light of day, the American fleet was spotted again, far out in the water south of Toronto. In April, they had come to capture one ship. Now, they wanted the entire British fleet.

York was in the middle of an arms race. The Great Lakes were one of the most vital battlegrounds in the War of 1812. Controlling the water meant you could move your troops and supplies wherever you wanted — while keeping the enemy from doing the same. That advantage might decide the fate of the entire war.

Both sides rushed to build the most powerful fleets possible. Some of the biggest warships in the world were being hammered together in the shipyards on either side of Lake Ontario. They had crews of hundreds of men; they bristled with dozens of guns. They turned the lake into the scene of countless horrors. When warships met in battle, the results were so gory that some crews spread sand across their decks to keep them from getting too slippery. Others painted them red so the blood would blend in.

HMS *Sir Isaac Brock* would have been the second-biggest ship on Lake Ontario if it had been completed. And even though the Americans had failed to capture it during the invasion of York, the burning of the vessel had been a terrible blow to British hopes. In the months after, the advantage on the Great Lakes swung dramatically toward the Americans. In early September, they won a stunning victory on Lake Erie. They captured the entire British fleet on that lake, giving them complete control of it. Now, they just needed Lake Ontario: "the key to the Great Lakes." If they won it, they would be able to pull off their grand plan: ship troops down the St. Lawrence River and besiege Montreal.

So now the Americans sailed back toward Toronto, where the British fleet was waiting. This would be a bloody day, with the potential to change the entire course of the war.

The American in charge was Commodore Isaac Chauncey. He was from Connecticut, but had first made a name for himself fighting pirates off the coast of Tripoli. Back in April, he'd been in charge of the American ships invading Toronto. Now, he was commanding his fleet from the deck of a brand new flagship: the USS *General Pike* (named after the American general blown up at Fort York). The *Pike* sailed at the head of a squadron of ten ships, some towed behind the others for extra fire-power. The Americans had bigger guns with longer range than their British counterparts. But their ships were also slower and harder to manoeuvre.

The British squadron was smaller: just six ships. It was commanded by Commodore Sir James Yeo, an Englishman who had been welcomed to Upper Canada as a hero — one of the rising stars of the most powerful navy on the planet. He sailed aboard his own brand new flagship, HMS *General Wolfe* (named after yet another dead general: the one who died fighting the French on the Plains of Abraham). The *Wolfe* was the sister ship of the burned *Brock*, and had been built in Kingston at the same time as the *Brock* had been under construction at York.

As dawn broke over Lake Ontario that morning, the *Wolfe* and the rest of the British fleet were just to the west of York — not far from Port Credit. When they spotted the Americans, they were still about a dozen kilometres away.

The battle got off to a slow start. With all that distance between the two squadrons, Commodore Yeo and his men had enough time to sail over to the harbour at Toronto, sending a small boat ashore with an update. Meanwhile, the Americans patiently stalked their prey: they sailed up to a spot south of the peninsula and waited.

It wasn't until mid-morning that Yeo turned his squadron around and left York, sailing south out into the lake. The Americans followed, chasing the British with the wind in their sails. They were steadily gaining. It wouldn't be long now. Both fleets shifted into single-file lines: battle formation.

It was Yeo and the British who made the first move. A little after noon, the *Wolfe* suddenly swung around, heading back toward the Americans, trying to run by the *Pike* and open fire on the middle of the enemy line.

Commodore Chauncey and the Americans countered. The *Pike* began to turn, too, trying to cut the *Wolfe* off, drawing closer and closer and closer ... until there were only a few hundred metres between them. But until it had fully swung around, the *Pike*'s formidable bank of guns wouldn't be pointing in the right direction. The American flagship was exposed.

The *Wolfe* opened fire. The British guns roared smoke and iron, cannonballs whizzing through the air between the two ships, smashing into the vulnerable *Pike*. One British volley after another tore into it.

Slowwwwwwly, the great bulk of the *Pike* continued to swing around. Now, the might of its broadside was finally facing the *Wolfe*. Fourteen American cannons burst to life: a wall of white smoke and fire.

Back and forth, the two great flagships thundered. Wood burst into splinters. Sails were ripped and torn. Blood spilled onto the decks. On board the *Pike*, a mast snapped, toppling into the sails below.

And then: catastrophe for the British. One of the masts on the *Wolfe* came crashing down, pulling a second mast, sails, rigging, and weights down with it — they tumbled onto the deck and then over the side into the water. Without them, the *Wolfe* was in serious trouble.

At that moment, it seemed as if everything was lost. The *Pike* was closing in, the American sailors were reloading their guns, the end was drawing near. "In the battle for control of Lake Ontario," the historian Robert

Malcomson wrote in his history of the campaign, "this instant may have been the most pivotal." The Americans were about to win the day — and with it, the entire lake. The whole war might follow.

It was the *Royal George* that saved the day. It was the second ship in the British line — and it had finally turned around, too. It rushed into danger, sailing right into the line of fire, putting itself between the Americans and the wounded *Wolfe* and then opening fire. Again and again and again, the *Royal George*'s guns roared, sending a hail of iron death flying into the *Pike*, buying enough time for the rest of the fleet to join the fight. Ships on both sides fired volley after volley, smashing into wood and skin and bone. All was smoke and chaos.

On board the *Wolfe*, the British crew rushed to recover. They dumped their dead overboard, carried the wounded below deck, cut away at the tangle of debris. And they did it all quickly. Fewer than fifteen minutes after the *Wolfe*'s masts tumbled into the water, the ship was ready to go.

But the danger wasn't over yet. Without a full complement of sails, the *Wolfe* was still vulnerable. The fate of Lake Ontario still hung in the balance. So Commodore Yeo turned his flagship around, let the wind fill what was left of the tattered sails, and raced west as fast as he could go. The rest of the British fleet turned and followed. They headed straight for the end of the lake, toward Burlington Bay, toward safety.

It was a decisive moment for Commodore Chauncey and the Americans. Two of the British ships were momentarily exposed — they could be captured. The master commandant of the *Pike*, Arthur Sinclair — great-grandfather of the American writer Upton Sinclair — begged the commodore to forget about the *Wolfe* and take the other ships instead. Capturing even one or two of the British vessels would be a major victory.

But Chauncey had a bigger prize in mind. Immortality was within his grasp; he could taste it. This was the day he was going to defeat the entire British fleet on Lake Ontario. He wasn't going to be distracted. "All or none!" he cried, ordering his fleet to sail west, to chase down the British squadron and defeat them.

The race was on.

For the next hour and a half, all sixteen ships sailed west as fast as they could, speeding across the water south of where Oakville is today.

As the afternoon wore on, a storm gathered. The sky darkened. The waves got bigger. The wind was picking up, blowing in hard from the east, filling the sails of the ships, pushing them ever faster as they raced toward the western end of the lake.

From shore — not just along the Canadian beaches, but also far over on the American side — people strained to follow the movements of the distant ships as they jockeyed for position. Some joked that it was like watching a yacht race. That's how the battle got its name: the Burlington Races.

The *Wolfe* was in rough shape, but the ship was still fast. So was the rest of the British fleet. The Americans struggled to keep up. It was only the *Pike* that managed to stay close enough to keep the British within the range of its guns. They echoed out across the lake, blasting away at the British vessels. But the *Pike* was badly wounded, too. Masts were damaged. Sails were torn. Rigging was cut to pieces. Some of the guns were completely useless. And the ship was leaking: the hull had been hit beneath the waves; there was water coming in below deck. The American sailors scrambled to pump it out as fast as it was coming in.

"This," Master Commandant Sinclair later remembered, "was the most trying time I ever had in my life."

Then, suddenly, the most deadly moment of the entire battle: one of the big guns near the front of the *Pike* exploded. The deck was torn apart in an instant. Iron shards flew in all directions, slicing through wood, sails, and flesh. The deadly debris was flung all the way back to the stern of the ship. More than twenty American sailors were killed or wounded in the blast.

Still, the injured *Pike* and the rest of the American fleet sailed on, chasing the British fleet, cannons roaring. But try as they might, the Americans weren't catching up. They were running out of time. There wasn't much lake left. They were getting closer and closer to Burlington Bay, closer to shore, closer to safety for the British ships.

There are two different stories about what happened next.

The most recent evidence seems to suggest that Commodore Yeo picked a spot to make a stand. He had the British fleet drop anchor near shore — just to the east of Burlington Bay (which we call Hamilton Harbour today). Bunched together with their backs protected by the land, they presented a daunting target. Their cannons were ready. On shore, there were even more friendly guns nearby.

With the British in such a strong defensive position and the *Pike* already badly damaged — maybe even in danger of sinking — Commodore Chauncey realized it was all over. If he fought on, he risked beaching his ships in enemy territory. He'd missed his chance. The American fleet turned and sailed away into the storm.

But that's not the story we've been told for most of the last two hundred years. In the most famous version of the tale, Commodore Yeo and the British fleet kept sailing straight for Burlington Bay. If they did, it was a daring move. The waters at the mouth of the harbour were shallow; the *Wolfe* would be in danger of running aground, stranded and helpless as the Americans swooped in. But at the very last moment, riding the crest of the storm surge, they say the *Wolfe* swept into the bay and to safety. The Americans had no choice but to turn away.

That fabled moment has been immortalized in paintings and textbooks; it was even printed on the historical plaque that stood overlooking the bay until it was updated just a few years ago.

Either way, the British fleet survived.

That night, anchored safely inside the harbour, the tired sailors got to work. In the cold, wind, and rain, they rushed to repair the *Wolfe* and the other battered ships as quickly as possible. The injured men were treated for their wounds. The dead — those who hadn't already been tossed overboard — were sewn inside their hammocks and buried at sea. The work continued all through the next day and into the following night. One man climbing the mast of the *Wolfe* lost his footing and tumbled to his death. And still the crews worked: it would be another two days before the fleet was ready to return to the lake.

Of course, there were more terrible, bloody days to come. Thousands of people died on both sides of the war. Others returned home wounded, many deeply scarred by the things they had seen and done. Just a week after the Burlington Races, Tecumseh — famed leader of the First Nations confederacy — was killed in battle against the Americans. That same day, Commodore Chauncey and his American fleet captured five British ships far on the other side of Lake Ontario. They burned a sixth.

But winter was coming. The sailing season was soon over. The British fleet had survived another year and the Americans still didn't control Lake Ontario. Without free reign on the water, their invasion down the St. Lawrence ended in humiliating defeat.

The very next summer, shipbuilders in Kingston built a new warship, one that changed everything. It took more than five thousand oak trees, two hundred men, and nearly ten months to make HMS *St. Lawrence*. It was by far the biggest thing that had ever sailed on the Great Lakes, boasting more than a hundred guns and a crew of seven hundred. It was bigger even than the flagship Admiral Nelson had used to beat Napoleon's navy at Trafalgar. The *St. Lawrence* was so big and so powerful that the ship's guns never had to fire a single shot. The

Americans immediately gave up trying to conquer Lake Ontario. Commodore Chauncey and his fleet were stuck at home for the rest of the war.

It didn't last much longer. At the end of 1814, the peace treaty was signed. The War of 1812 was finally over. The American invasion of Canada had failed.

9
THE TRUE STORY OF TORONTO'S ISLAND GHOST

On some dark nights, as an eerie mist creeps over the Toronto Islands, they say you can still hear him moaning somewhere in the distance. On others, you might hear him walking up the steps of the old stone lighthouse, even though there's no one there — or see a ghostly light shining up top, even when the lantern isn't lit. Sometimes, you might find his fresh blood spilled on those old wooden stairs. Or even catch a glimpse of him yourself: a spectre stalking through the undergrowth, or wandering the paths around the lighthouse, bloodied and beaten, his arms missing. They say he's the ghost of Toronto's first lightkeeper and that he's searching for pieces of his body hacked off more than two hundred years ago and buried somewhere in the sand.

The story of John Paul Radelmüller came to a bloody end in Toronto, but it began more than six thousand kilometres away — in the royal courts of Europe.

He was born in Bavaria — now part of Germany — in the town of Anspach, not far from Frankfurt. Back then, in the middle of the 1700s, the British royal family were all from Germany. King George II had been born in Hanover; Queen Caroline came from the town where Radelmüller grew up. And even though they were ruling England, the royal family kept close ties to their home-land. Many of their servants were German, too.

That's how Radelmüller ended up in England. He was a teenager when he got a job as a royal servant during the reign of "Mad" King George III: he attended to the king's younger brother, Prince William. But as luxurious as the royal quarters were, it can't have been an entirely easy life. The king was suffering from bouts of severe mental illness and frequently clashed with the prince. At the same time, the prince's son was so unpleasant that even members of his own family called him "The Contagion." After sixteen years serving the prince, Radelmüller finally quit. He headed back home to Bavaria to become a farmer.

But this was 1798. The French Revolution had plunged Europe into decades of chaos and war. Radelmüller's farm was caught right in the middle. He was forced to flee, becoming a refugee. Knowing he would be welcome in England, he returned to the royal court.

This time, he served as a porter to one of the "mad" king's sons: Prince Edward. *The* Prince Edward. The father of Queen Victoria. The prince that Prince Edward Island and Prince Edward County are named after.

Prince Edward was a big fan of Canada. In fact, he's the very first person who ever used the word *Canadians* to refer to both anglophones and francophones. By the time Radelmüller joined his staff, the prince had already spent years living in Quebec and in Nova Scotia; he'd even paid a visit to the Simcoes at Niagara. He was only home in England to recover after falling off his horse. Soon, he sailed back across the Atlantic to Halifax. When he did, he took his new porter with him.

It didn't take long for Radelmüller to fall in love with Canada, too. When Prince Edward fell ill and was forced to return home to Britain, Radelmüller stayed at his side — but he came back to Canada as soon as he got the chance. He landed a position as a steward for the lieutenant governor of Nova Scotia.

Still, he dreamed of becoming a farmer once again. Someone told him the best farmland was far to the west, in the brand new province of Upper Canada. He was determined to make a new life for himself on the Canadian frontier. And no one was going to stop him.

The governor was reluctant to let him go — promising to give him letters of recommendation and then holding them hostage at the very last moment, hoping his trusted steward could be convinced to stay on for another year. But Radelmüller's belongings had already been loaded onto a ship ready to set sail. So he left anyway, making the gruelling five-week trip up the St. Lawrence in the dead of the Canadian winter.

Radelmüller arrived in York on New Year's Day in 1804. He knew nobody. He had no job. No land. No letters of introduction. His life would be far from easy.

But Radelmüller succeeded anyway. First, he headed

north up Yonge Street to Markham, founding a school where he taught English to the Germans who had recently settled there. Before long, he was recognized as their official translator for all government business.

And soon, there would be an even better opportunity.

Simcoe had picked Toronto as the place to build his new capital because it was easy to defend. The natural harbour created by the peninsula had only one way in: through a narrow gap at the western end. (It wasn't until the 1850s that a big storm made a second gap, on the eastern side, turning the sandbar into the Islands.) Simcoe thought that one entrance would be so easy to defend he called the end of the peninsula Gibraltar Point — named after the rocky fortress at the entrance to the Mediterranean.

He also declared that one of York's first buildings should be a lighthouse — to be built right there on Gibraltar Point.

About ten years later, construction finally began. The Gibraltar Point Lighthouse was the very first permanent lighthouse built anywhere on the Great Lakes and the first stone building in Toronto. When it opened in 1808, it towered over the beach right next to the water, stretching about five storeys into the air. It would be the tallest building in the city for nearly fifty years.

At the base, the walls were almost two metres thick, built of limestone shipped north across the lake from a quarry at Queenston — high on the heights at Niagara, which you can still see from Toronto on a clear day. At the top of the lighthouse, a bright lantern shone out as a beacon to ships sailing through the dark waters at night. It burned two hundred gallons of sperm whale oil every year.

Radelmüller, who had done more than enough to earn the trust of the government, was given the job as Toronto's first lightkeeper. He lit the lamp every evening and extinguished it every morning at dawn. He was also put in charge of signalling the city every time a big ship pulled into the harbour. He flew a Union Jack for every vessel arriving from Kingston and the British Red Ensign for ships sailing north from Niagara.

He lived in a small wooden cabin next to the lighthouse and soon, he was joined there by his family. A couple of years into his new job, Radelmüller married Magdalene Burkholder. The wedding was held at St. James Church. Before long, they had a daughter: little Arabella was born.

It was a quiet, peaceful life. At least at first. They say Radelmüller even made some extra money on the side by brewing beer in the German style he'd learned back home.

But it didn't take long for the chaos that had driven the lightkeeper out of Germany to find him far on this side of the Atlantic. Just a few short years after Radelmüller had started his new job as the city's first lightkeeper, Toronto was in the middle of a war zone. The War of 1812 had begun.

The Gibraltar Point Lighthouse was suddenly even more important. Keeping the British fleet safe from the treacherous shoals near the entrance to the harbour was an essential job — one lost ship could turn the tide of the entire war. As the conflict dragged on, Radelmüller played a vital role out there on his lonely sandbar.

Tragically, he wouldn't live to see the end of the war. On Christmas Eve of 1814 the peace treaty was finally signed. But negotiations were held in Belgium, which meant that it would take weeks for the news to cross the ocean and finally reach York. By the time it did, Radelmüller was already dead. He'd been murdered.

It happened after dark on the second day of 1815. The story of that terrible winter night has been told over and over again, passed down from one generation of Torontonians to the next over the course of the last two hundred years. The details are vague; there are many different versions of the tale. But it usually goes something like this:

Radelmüller and his family weren't the only ones on the sandbar. Hunters and fishermen used it, too. Indigenous families occasionally camped nearby. And not far from the lighthouse, there was a new military blockhouse. To this day we still call that spot on the Islands "Blockhouse Bay." It was built during the War of 1812, armed with a gun designed to protect the harbour against the Americans, and occupied by soldiers from Fort York. Those men spent most of their time keeping watch and preparing for an attack, but they were also friendly with the lightkeeper. Sometimes, they'd row down Blockhouse Bay to visit the lighthouse and drink some of Radelmüller's beer.

On that cold January night at the very beginning of 1815, two of those soldiers came by for a visit. They were called John Henry and John Blowman. At first, everything seemed to be going well. They all drank together long into the night. But at some point, Radelmüller decided the soldiers had had enough. He cut them off. And that's when everything went horribly wrong.

The soldiers were angry; they got violent. One took off his belt, the other grabbed a rock, and together they attacked the lightkeeper. Radelmüller ran, bleeding and afraid, scrambling up the steps of the lighthouse in a desperate bid to escape.

The soldiers followed, relentless. They broke down the door and chased him up the narrow wooden stairs to the very top of the lighthouse. That's where the lightkeeper made his last stand: up there, high above the ground as his flaming beacon shone out across the dark lake. There was a final skirmish. Radelmüller was pushed over the railing and fell to his death. It was over. The lightkeeper lay still.

The two soldiers knew they were in deep trouble. The penalty for murder was death. They worked quickly to cover up their crime. They found an axe and used it to hack the body into pieces, severing the limbs. Then, they buried what was left of John Paul Radelmüller, bit by bit, in a series of shallow graves dug in the frozen sand. Their grisly job finished, they ran.

That, it seems, was a mistake. It was more than a little suspicious: disappearing the very same night the lightkeeper did. Within two weeks, the *York Gazette* announced their arrest. "From circumstances there is moral proof of [Radelmüller] having been murdered," the paper reported. "If the horrid crime admits of aggravation when the inoffensive and benevolent character of the unfortunate sufferer are considered, his murder will be pronounced most barbarous and inhuman. The parties lost with him are the proposed perpetrators and are in prison."

It took more than two months for the case to come to trial. When it did, the soldiers were acquitted. There was little evidence. No one had ever found the body. There would be no justice for the lightkeeper.

His soul was doomed to haunt his lighthouse for the rest of eternity.

At least, that's what people like to say. The details, as you might imagine, are more than a little bit sketchy — right down to inconsistent spelling of Radelmüller's name.

It's hard to find a single record of anyone who has ever claimed to have actually seen the ghost. Even the details of the murder itself are hard to verify: the tale was passed down from one generation of lightkeepers to the next. The first detailed record of the story seems to have been written down by Toronto newspaper publisher and historian John Ross Robertson — but that was a hundred years after the killing took place. It was told to him by another lightkeeper at Gibraltar Point — George Durnan — whose family staffed the lighthouse for more than seventy years (from the 1830s right up until 1908). Durnan didn't mention a ghost at all. And while more recent research has uncovered concrete records of the crime, Robertson suspected the murder had never even happened at all. At the time, he was unable to find any record of it in the archives of the *York Gazette*. "There is no doubt that it has been garnished in the telling," he admitted. "It may be a fairy tale."

Decades later, the last of the island lightkeepers — a woman with the wonderful name of Dedie Dodds — spoke to the CBC. "There may be a ghost," she told them, but there were plenty of rational explanations for everything. "The cooing of the pigeons is very eerie on a dark night. And the wind howling through the lighthouse gives you the shivers. When the moon is full, it's reflected back from the top of the lighthouse." Just a few months earlier, even she had been momentarily fooled. "It gave me quite a start."

Still, it made for a very good story. And Durnan did claim to have found a piece of related evidence. He said that one day he went looking for Radelmüller's remains around the spot he'd been told he could find them. There, buried in a shallow grave about a hundred and fifty metres to the west of the lighthouse, he found a coffin. Inside, there was a human jawbone.

It was more than enough to fuel the legend. By the time Dodds became the lightkeeper in the 1950s, the phantom had become part of the myth — and the grisly tale of the haunted lighthouse had become one of Toronto's most beloved ghost stories.

In fact, by the end of that decade, it would earn official recognition. After a century and a half of continuous service, the Gibraltar Point Lighthouse was finally going to be decommissioned. To honour the old building's new life as a historical monument, a new plaque was being erected.

The Ontario Archaeological and Historic Sites Advisory Board decided to include the ghost story as part of the official story of the building. It was the final sentence on the new plaque: "The mysterious disappearance

of its first keeper, J.P. Radelmüller, in 1815 and the subsequent discovery nearby of part of a human skeleton
enhanced its reputation as a haunted building."

That line sparked a heated battle. The Advisory Board
liked it, but the Metro Toronto Parks Committee dis-
agreed. The councillors on the committee were appalled
by the idea that such fantastical nonsense was going to be
officially recognized. One councillor dismissed the story
of Radelmüller's ghost as "a myth ... an old wives' tale"
unworthy of inclusion on a plaque. "I can't see it would
make the place attractive to children," another councillor
worried, completely misunderstanding children. Even
the Metro chairman himself, Fred Gardiner, the politician the expressway is named after, weighed in. "That," he
declared, "would only scare people."

But the Advisory Board refused to back down. The
plaque went up anyway and the story of Radelmüller's
ghost was preserved. Today, you can still find it there on
the side of the lighthouse, giving the people of Toronto a
colourful connection to one of the city's most interesting —
but most easily forgotten — landmarks.

Today, the Gibraltar Point Lighthouse remains standing, the oldest lighthouse anywhere on the Great Lakes.
Some people consider it to be the oldest in all of Canada.
The only older lighthouse is in Nova Scotia — but it has
been repaired and renovated to such an extent that even
Lighthouse Digest suggests that it might not really count
anymore.

For more than two hundred years, the city's first
lighthouse has kept watch over the harbour. It's the oldest

building in Toronto that still stands in the same place where it was originally built. It has borne witness to all of the city's greatest and most terrible moments. It saw the American invasion during the War of 1812. The raging storm that turned the sandbar into the Islands. The arrival of the first steamships and the first trains. It has helped thousands of sailors bring thousands of ships safely into the harbour, carrying countless new Canadians into the city. Once the tallest building in Toronto, the lighthouse has watched the city's skyline grow into a towering wall of steel and glass topped by one of the tallest towers in the world.

It's easy to forget the Gibraltar Point Lighthouse, out there alone on the island. The light was turned off long ago. The cottages where the lightkeepers and their families once lived have now all been demolished. The shoreline has evolved, grown with silt, moved more than a hundred metres away. Even with an 1830s extension taking it another few metres into the air, the lighthouse has nearly disappeared among the trees. It has been swallowed up by the same city it helped bring to life.

But the story of the lightkeeper's ghost helps us to remember — to remember not just the history of that building, but of what the city used to be.

Today, in the early twenty-first century, the guardian of the lighthouse is a volunteer. His name is Manuel Cappel. He too is from Germany, just like Radelmüller. He lives on the Islands, where he also builds bicycles; he used to run the Rectory Café. Torontonians today ask him the very same question they've been asking the island lightkeepers for generations: "Is the lighthouse *really* haunted?"

He gives them the same answer he gives everyone. An answer that couldn't be more true.

"It is," he tells them, "if you want it to be."

DEMOCRACY

10
THE DEADLY DUEL

Four young men stood in a barn overlooking a farmer's field near Yonge and College. It was just before dawn, on a wet July morning in 1817. What is now a bustling downtown intersection was still a country crossroads back then, far outside the growing town. In the sky above the farm, lightning flashed and thunder rolled. The four young men waited for the storm to pass and for the sun to rise.

They had all been born into powerful local families: Jarvis, Ridout, Boulton, Small — some of the most influential founders of the new capital. They were part of a small group of conservative Tories who held most of the power in Upper Canada. They tried to keep the best land and government postings for themselves and imagined they would pass both down to their children. That group was the closest thing Toronto would ever get to the hereditary Canadian aristocracy Simcoe had imagined. They would become known as the Family Compact.

But even within that small group of political allies, there was plenty of jealousy and bickering. Some of them openly hated each other. The Jarvis and Ridout families had been feuding for years. And now, the old grudge was about to turn deadly.

Samuel Jarvis was twenty-five; John Ridout was eighteen. They had hated each other ever since they were children. Now, things had escalated. They were going to try to kill each other in the most dignified fashion possible: a duel.

As the storm passed and the sun rose, the four men headed out into the soggy field. With their seconds looking on, Jarvis and Ridout stood eight paces apart, their pistols at their sides. And then James Small began to count:

One …

Two …

It would prove to be one of the most notorious duels in Canadian history. The consequences of what was about to happen in that field would reverberate through the history of the city — and the history of the entire country — for decades to come. The fatal climax to the old rivalry between two of Toronto's most powerful conservative families would trigger a strange and circuitous series of events that would help turn Canada into a liberal democracy.

But to understand how, it helps to go all the way back to the blood-soaked days of the American Revolution.

In the summer of 1781, William Jarvis got shot. They say it might be the best thing that ever happened to him. Before that, he was just an ordinary soldier, one of the tens of thousands of Americans who stayed loyal to the

British and fought on their side during the American Revolution. But when Jarvis was wounded during that battle in Virginia, he caught the attention of his commanding officer. And that commanding officer just so happened to be John Graves Simcoe.

Up to that point, Jarvis had spent his entire life in the States. He was born in the middle of the 1700s, back in the days when being an American meant you were British, too — and Jarvis liked it that way. He was deeply loyal to the Crown. He was just a teenager when the revolution broke out, but he still signed up for the British army. He spent the next few years fighting against the rebels as a member of the Queen's Rangers.

But Jarvis, of course, had picked the losing side of the fight. He paid a heavy price for that. When he tried to return to his home in Connecticut at the end of the war, he found he wasn't welcome.

One day, while Jarvis and his family were on their way to a picnic, they were attacked by an angry mob. That kind of thing was happening to Loyalists all over the brand new United States. Not long ago, pro-British opinions had been accepted as conventional wisdom; now, they were treason. Jarvis's own sister was attacked over and over again in the wake of the revolution; her home was invaded, her children threatened with bayonets, her husband eventually driven to suicide. While she and tens of thousands of others escaped north to the British colonies in Canada, William Jarvis fled across the Atlantic to England. He spent the next nine years living in London in exile.

He wasn't alone. Thousands of American Loyalists headed for the British Isles, including a young woman by the name of Hannah Owen Peters. She was the daughter of the Reverend Samuel Peters, a slave-owning Anglican preacher so famously reviled that more than two hundred years later he was given his own chapter in a book called *Jerks in Connecticut History*. He, too, had been driven out of his home by violent Patriot mobs. And he, too, went to London. Hannah followed him there.

It was in England that William Jarvis probably met Hannah Peters (although they were both from prominent Connecticut families, so it could have been earlier). And it was in England that they got married.

But soon they would be moving to Canada. While the newlyweds were living in London with Hannah's father, Jarvis was still in contact with Simcoe. And when Simcoe was chosen to be lieutenant governor of Upper Canada, he picked Jarvis to be part of his new government.

William and Hannah packed their bags. They headed back across the Atlantic, where they would eventually become one of Toronto's founding families.

When they arrived at York, they were given some property at Sherbourne and Adelaide, along with one of the hundred-acre "park lots" just outside town (in a strip running between Queen Street and Bloor, where Jarvis Street is now). In return, all William had to do was to move to York with his family, build a road around his property, and be pretty terrible at his government job. It was all made easier by the Jarvises being one of the very few families in town who owned slaves: they kept at least six people enslaved at their mansion and on their country estate.

Having suffered through the horrors of the American Revolution and then the War of 1812, the Jarvis family — like many of the city's founding families — shared Simcoe's fear of what he had called "tyrannical democracy." They believed in his vision for Upper Canada: a province run by a powerful governor with the support of a small group of loyal Tories at the top of a strict class system. Loyal Tories like them. The Tories of the Family Compact.

As far as the Family Compact was concerned, democracy and diversity were dangerous. They imagined their new province should be a safe haven for conservative monarchists, which meant the will of the people would be strictly limited: the elected Legislative Assembly could try to pass all the new laws they wanted, but they were subject to the approval of the governor and his hand-picked Legislative Council.

And while the population of Upper Canada was remarkably diverse right from the very beginning (40 percent of the early Upper Canadian Loyalists were of German descent, for instance), the official culture would be monolithic: stubbornly British and stubbornly Protestant. For the first few decades, with rare exceptions, Anglican ministers were the only clergy allowed to perform marriages. As historian Gerald M. Craig suggests in his landmark history of the province, *Upper Canada: The Formative Years, 1784–1841*, the Family Compact "sometimes seemed to be more British than the King."

William and Hannah were founding members of the Family Compact, but they never quite fit in. They seem to have been truly difficult people to get along with. Even in York — a town rife with petty officials — William and Hannah were notorious. When you read anything about William Jarvis, the same kinds of adjectives keep popping up: "inefficient and careless," "incompetent and corrupt," "incompetent, lazy, selfish, and dishonest." He and Hannah were constantly bickering with the city's other founding families. William once tried to challenge four men to a duel all at the same time; Hannah called the rest of the city's ruling class "a lot of Pimps, Sycophants, and Lyars."

They particularly hated the Ridouts. The two families had been feuding for years. The roots of their rivalry can be traced all the way back to the earliest days of York. William Jarvis was the provincial secretary and registrar; Thomas Ridout was a clerk in the office of the surveyor general. Accusations of incompetence led to some of Jarvis's powers being stripped away and given to Ridout. The two families had been bitter enemies ever since.

They passed that hatred down to their children.

Samuel Jarvis was just a young boy when his parents made the move to Toronto; he and his friends grew up as the city did.

Sadly, young Jarvis would follow in his father's unfortunate footsteps. As a young man, he fought against the Americans in the War of 1812, then relied on nepotism to land a government job. He was settling down to a life of scandal and financial impropriety, just like his dad. And just like his dad, he made a lot of enemies.

John Ridout was one of them.

The Jarvis kids and Ridout kids grew up together. They went to the same school, all attended St. James Church, and were neighbours on Adelaide Street (called Duke Street back then). They were constantly quarrelling. Schoolyard misunderstandings erupted into such passionate arguments that there were stretches of time when the two families wouldn't speak to each other at all.

The feud finally came to a head in the summer of 1817. That July, John Ridout paid a fateful visit to Samuel Jarvis at his office. The exact details of the meeting aren't clear, but it had something to do with a legal case the Ridouts were pursuing against William Jarvis. John was still just a teenager, but he was already working as a law clerk at his brother's firm.

The conversation that day got so heated that Jarvis threw Ridout out of his office in a rage. When they ran into each other on King Street a few days later, they got into a fight. Ridout hit Jarvis with a stick, breaking his hand. Jarvis answered with a punch. A crowd gathered to watch as the two scuffled in the street until they were finally pulled apart.

But they weren't done. With their feelings hurt and two decades of family hatred coming to a boil, Jarvis and Ridout challenged each other to a duel.

Early that Saturday morning, Jarvis, Ridout, and their seconds met on Yonge Street in the dark, and then headed to the field at Elmsley's Farm — a popular venue for duels. As the storm rumbled above them, they took shelter in the barn and waited.

Ridout's second was James Small. The two of them were both still teenagers, but already familiar with death and duels. They were both veterans of the War of 1812. And Small's father — the clerk of the Executive Council — had killed the attorney general in a duel years earlier. William Jarvis had been the foreman on the jury that acquitted him.

Jarvis's second was Henry John Boulton. In his late twenties, he was the eldest of the four: a respectable lawyer soon to become the solicitor general — a post his father had also filled. His younger brother would fight his own infamous duel years later.

When the sun finally rose, it was time. Jarvis and Ridout took their positions and drew their pistols — they stood eight paces apart in the wet grass and waited for the count:

One …

Two …

A shot rang out.

Ridout fired early. And missed.

There was confusion. No one was quite sure what to do, what the rules and honour dictated. But they eventually came to a decision: Ridout would return to his spot so Jarvis could take a free shot.

Some would have missed that free shot on purpose, believing it to be the honourable thing to do. Jarvis did not. The bullet hit Ridout in the shoulder, tore through his neck, severed his jugular, and pierced his windpipe.

According to the coroner's report, Ridout must have died pretty much instantly. But that's not the story Jarvis and the seconds told. They claimed Ridout had lived just long enough to forgive them and absolve them of all responsibility. It didn't work: Jarvis was arrested and charged with murder.

Duels were technically illegal, but they were an ancient tradition stretching back to medieval chivalry. They played an important role in the moral code of Upper Canada; juries tended to acquit anyone who fought a duel fairly. As far as many in the province were concerned, the most honourable and dignified way to settle a dispute was by standing a few metres apart and shooting at each other. Besides, the Jarvis family were important members of the Family Compact. Samuel was acquitted.

But the controversy was far from over. The duel would haunt Samuel Jarvis and the Family Compact for years after Ridout was put to rest, giving their political enemies plenty of fodder. And those enemies were about to get a new leader: a passionate advocate for democracy more troublesome than anyone the Family Compact had ever faced before.

William Lyon Mackenzie. The rebel mayor. He was born in Scotland, ran a store for a while, wrote for some newspapers, gambled a lot, fathered an illegitimate child, and eventually headed across the ocean to Upper Canada in search of a better life. He settled in York in November of 1824 — eight years after the deadly duel — and published a newspaper called the *Colonial Advocate*.

When Mackenzie arrived, he found the Family Compact at the height of their powers. But not everyone in the province agreed with their vision for the province. There was now a growing opposition movement led by the progressive Reform Party.

Reformers believed in democracy. Canadians, they argued, should have the power to make their own laws — without the veto wielded by the British governor and his powerful Legislative Council.

But the Family Compact didn't take kindly to criticism or democratic ideas. Led by Reverend Strachan, hero of the Battle of York, they cracked down on dissent. Those who dared to question the Family Compact tended to end up in jail, or in exile, or left bloody in the streets. Some were even tarred and feathered.

Upon his arrival, Mackenzie immediately joined the chorus calling for reform and quickly became one of the most passionate advocates for the cause, famous for his fiery temperament and for his flaming red wig. He loathed the Family Compact and he used the *Colonial Advocate* to criticize them at every turn. He called some of them demons, some of them jackals, some of them fungus, and Samuel Jarvis a murderer.

To Mackenzie, the duel and the trial that followed were examples of the special treatment the Family Compact regularly gave themselves. Not long after he arrived, Mackenzie published a reference to the duel in which he obliquely implied that Ridout's death was nothing short of cold-blooded murder.

Another of the city's major Reform newspapers, the Irish-Catholic *Canadian Freeman,* took up the cause with a scathing, melodramatic account of the duel:

"John fell," the paper claimed, "crying 'oh! You have killed me, it was foul play.' At that moment, a clap of thunder rent the skies, and lightning flashed, and the rain came down in torrents.... The three then fled to town, leaving the dear youth alone in the agonies of death vomiting up blood."

Jarvis was furious and determined to get revenge. But giving in to his temper would prove to be a terrible mistake.

Mackenzie was actually getting off to a pretty rough start in York. He was having no trouble making a name for himself, but he wasn't having nearly as much success when it came to making money. The *Colonial Advocate* was failing. Mackenzie's debts mounted; his readership did not.

At one point, Mackenzie had to temporarily stop printing the paper altogether. And in the spring of 1826 it seems he was forced to hightail it out of town, fleeing to the United States to avoid his creditors.

That's when Jarvis struck. He rounded up a group of his young Family Compact friends and they headed down to Front Street, to the offices of the *Colonial Advocate,* which was also where Mackenzie lived. The publisher was out of town, but his family wasn't. They hid in the basement as Jarvis and his cronies broke into the office and started trashing the place. Mackenzie's entire operation was destroyed: his printing press broken, his stock of type thrown into Lake Ontario. The attack became known as the Types Riot.

Many in the Family Compact were thrilled. Several prominent members of the older generation were there that day, watching proudly from nearby as the youngsters trashed the office in broad daylight. Two of them were magistrates, tasked with upholding the law, but even they did nothing to stop the riot. Another could barely contain his laughter. As news of the riot spread, one of Samuel's brothers wrote him a letter of congratulations. "I am only sorry," he said, "you did not throw Mackenzie in the bay first and then throw the types and the press on the top of him to keep him under water."

It seemed as if the Family Compact had finally managed to silence one of their most persistent critics.

But in the end, the riot was going to backfire in spectacular fashion. Mackenzie sued the vandals. And even in a court system notorious for ruling in favour of the Family Compact, the newspaper publisher won his case. Not only did his winnings allow Mackenzie to resume publishing his paper, but now it was a bigger, more powerful operation than ever before. The *Colonial Advocate* continued to argue in favour of democracy and against the Family Compact.

Meanwhile, Jarvis was forced to defend himself in pamphlets with catchy titles like "A Contradiction of the Libel Under the Signature of 'A Relative,' Published in the Canadian Freeman, of the 28th February, 1828;

Together with a Few Remarks, Tracing The Origin of the Unfriendly Feeling Which Ultimately Led to the Unhappy Affair to Which That Libel Refers."

Mackenzie would go on to become one of the most famous figures in the history of Toronto. Within a few years, he'd been elected as the city's first mayor and led a failed revolution in the name of Canadian democracy and independence.

Jarvis would be there when Mackenzie's army rose up against the government — he fought for the government side and won. But the victory was short-lived. Soon, democracy would come to Canada anyway and the power of the Family Compact would fade.

By then, Jarvis had already been forced to resign in disgrace from his position as the head of the Indian Department. He, like his father before him, was being accused of corruption and incompetence. In the end, he had to sell off the Jarvis family's estate in order to pay his debts. Their home was demolished to make way for the street that bears their name. Beyond that, Samuel Jarvis is mostly forgotten.

There is, however, one place where you can still find a reminder of his infamous duel: St. James Cathedral, which stands on the same spot where the Jarvis and Ridout kids used to go to church more than two centuries ago. At the entrance on King Street there's a gravestone mounted on the wall. It reads: "In memory of John Ridout ... Filial affections, engaging manners and nobleness of mind gave early promise of future excellence ... but a Blight came and he was consigned

to an early Grave on the 12th day of July 1817, aged 18.
Deeply lamented by all who knew him."

11
THE BLUE DEATH

York was changing quickly. By 1832, it was no longer a tiny little town, alone in the woods. During William Lyon Mackenzie's first decade in town, the population skyrocketed from sixteen hundred to nearly ten thousand. From those first few blocks around the St. Lawrence Market the town had spread all the way west to Bathurst Street. And with a new lieutenant governor, John Colborne, aggressively encouraging immigration, there were more people arriving all the time.

They were met by a disgusting mess. There was no sewer system or running water. People dumped their garbage wherever they liked. They emptied their toilet buckets into the road. King and Yonge and Queen Streets were a muddy soup of excrement and filth. There were no sidewalks, either; you'd just wade through it and track it into your home.

Francis Collins complained about the mess in his *Canadian Freeman* newspaper. He was one of the great Reform heroes: the publisher of the melodramatic account of the Jarvis-Ridout duel, he'd once spent months in jail for criticizing the Family Compact too harshly. He wrote about "stagnant pools of water, green as a leek, and emitting deadly exhalations." He called the water in Lake Ontario "carrion-broth." Townspeople used the lake as a dump. In the winter, Collins reported, "All the filth of the town — dead horses, dogs, cats, manure, etc. [was] heaped up together on the ice, to drop down, in a few days, into the water."

That was York's drinking water. Soon, it would kill Collins. And his wife. And his brother. And hundreds more.

It all started in India, five years earlier and more than twelve thousand kilometres away. It began in the spot where the Ganges meets the Bay of Bengal, one of the most fertile places on Earth. The river widens out into an endless expanse of swamps and streams, of lush mangrove and bamboo forests. There are tigers, elephants, leopards, and pythons. And there's also cholera. It has been in the water for as long as anyone can remember. Millions upon millions of deadly bacteria lay dormant in the silt and come alive in the monsoon season when the conditions are right.

But, of course, in 1826 they didn't know that's what was happening. The science of disease was still in its infancy. All they knew was that people were dying, and the cholera was beginning to spread.

It was slow at first. People started to die farther up the river. And then all across India, wherever the trade routes led. It took a year to get to China and another to get halfway across Russia. But when it hit Europe and the Middle East, things sped up. Three thousand Muslims died on the pilgrimage to Mecca in 1831. Thirty thousand deaths were announced in Cairo and Alexandria. There would be a hundred thousand dead in Hungary. And in France. Bodies piled up in all the cobblestoned capitals of Europe.

Death struck without warning. One survivor, who fell suddenly ill while walking down the street, said it was like being "knocked down with an ax. I had no premonition at all."

Heinrich Heine, a German poet, was in Paris when the plague swept through a masked ball: "Suddenly the gayest of the harlequins collapsed, cold in the limbs, and underneath his mask, violet blue in the face. Laughter died out, dancing ceased and in a short while carriage-loads of people hurried from the Hotel Dieu to die."

The deaths came so quick, they ran out of coffins. All over the world, corpses were being tossed into mass graves by the thousands.

In England, they were shipping in cholera directly from the source. The British East India Company had been gradually conquering India for more than a hundred years. When they shipped tea back home, they scooped bilge water up from the Bay of Bengal, carried it halfway around the world, and dumped it into the Thames. More than six thousand people died in London; more than fifty thousand across the United Kingdom.

Ireland was hardest hit. In places like Dublin, Limerick, and Cork, terrified refugees packed into ships and set sail for North America. They crowded together in squalor, sharing cholera-ridden water and cholera-ridden piss-pots for weeks on end. By the time they reached the Canadas, some ships had already lost dozens on board to the disease.

Officials in Lower Canada, where the ships arrived first, did their best to screen passengers and quarantine anyone who showed signs of the sickness, but it didn't seem to do much good. Cholera devastated Quebec City that summer, killing more than two thousand people. In Montreal, doctors rushed through the streets all day and night. The apothecaries stayed open around the clock. The army fired blank artillery shells at nothing — a desperate attempt to drive the cholera out of the air. More than a thousand died in a single month.

As cholera marched west, York braced for the horror. Lieutenant Governor Colborne declared a day of "Public Fasting, Humiliation, and Prayer" in an attempt to stave off the disaster. The government formed a Board of Health, led by the most famous doctor in town: the staunch Reformer William Warren Baldwin.

Baldwin's Board of Health had a doctor check all new arrivals before they left their ships. They washed buildings and outhouses with lime. They shut the bars at ten. But it was no use. Eleven thousand immigrants came to York in the spring and summer of 1832. Many of them were already sick. By the end of June, it had begun.

The disease was terrifying. Cholera bacteria are resilient; they can survive the acids in your stomach and make it all the way to your small intestine. There, they swim over to the intestinal wall and begin to produce a toxin. It sucks the water out of the rest of your body and forces you to expel it in an endless stream of watery diarrhea. You can spew out twenty or thirty litres in a day (provided you last that long), clear liquid with chunks of your intestine in it. You vomit, too. A lot. You lose so much fluid that your hands go wrinkly. Your eyes sink back into your head. Your skin changes colour — that's why they call it "The Blue Death."

And then, you die. It happens *fast*. You can go from healthy to dead in just a few hours. And all that excrement your loved ones have tossed into the street or into the drinking water is filled with the next generation of bacteria ready to do the same thing all over again.

For the rest of that summer, York was filled with people dying sudden, grotesque deaths. Hundreds more got sick and thousands fled to the countryside in terror. The Board of Health tried to fight back, but they didn't really understand what they were fighting. They asked everyone to burn tar and sulphur in their yards to drive it away. They told people to hide under blankets at night with the windows closed. To cut back on vegetables and drink lots of coffee. To avoid brandy and opium. To switch from cotton socks to wool ones. They rounded up all the drunks from the streets and threw them in jail or into the stocks. Doctors debated the cause of the disease — many mistakenly blamed it on miasma: sickly vapours drifting into town from the vast Ashbridge's Marsh at the mouth of the Don River (where the Port Lands are today).

Even the good advice — to get rid of standing water,

take a bath every day, clean up the garbage, go to the hospital if sick — was being ignored. Officials couldn't force anyone to do anything, since the Board of Health had no real power. And Colborne, who wanted to protect his authority and ensure no one interfered with his open immigration policy, refused to give them any.

Nine deaths were reported in the first week of the outbreak. Twenty-four in the second. The numbers went up quickly from there. By the time fall came to York and the plague finally died out, estimates suggest there were at least two hundred fresh corpses in town. One out of every twenty people who stayed in the city was dead.

The people of York were scared. The plague might have died out in the town, but it was still wreaking havoc in cities around the globe. Cholera could easily return to the muddy streets of York. The town needed to prepare. The outbreak had clearly shown the current system wasn't working; some degree of political reform was desperately needed in order to clean up the town and to allow the authorities to quickly and effectively respond to emergencies. The lack of local power over local affairs had deadly consequences. Now, even the Family Compact could see the lieutenant governor needed to share some of his power.

Scared by the plague and overwhelmed by the soaring population, the Tory-dominated, Mackenzie-hating, democracy-bashing legislature voted to turn the Town of York into the City of Toronto. There would be a city council elected by the people. There would be a mayor and a new Board of Health. They would all have real power: they could introduce taxes, pass bylaws, and make sure those bylaws were enforced. And they wouldn't have to ask the lieutenant governor first.

The city's inaugural municipal elections were held in the spring of 1834. The Reform Party won. They picked William Lyon Mackenzie to be the very first mayor of Toronto.

Mackenzie's year in power is best remembered for helping Toronto to establish its own new, Canadian identity. Mackenzie's time in office gave the city its own motto — "Industry, Intelligence, Integrity" — and its own coat of arms, which mixed British imagery (like three golden lions and the Union Jack) with local imagery (like a beaver and the figure of a First Nations chief). As the town was turned into a city, the old British name of "York" was abandoned in favour of the older, Indigenous name "Toronto." There would be no more calling the place "dirty little York" to avoid confusion with New York or the city of York in England. "This city," as one politician put it, "will be the only City of Toronto in the world." It was distinctive, more historically appropriate, and had a much more pleasing ring to it. As one Reform leader claimed, "Toronto for poets — York for men of business."

But Mackenzie wasn't just the mayor. He was also picked as the head of the new Board of Health. Most of the municipal government's time was spent cleaning up the city. They put in sidewalks. They made it illegal to let pigs run free in the streets. Citizens weren't allowed to toss their refuse into the road anymore. Regular garbage pickup was introduced. There were new regulations about how to dispose of corpses.

Sadly, the new measures weren't enough. Toronto was still a pretty gross place, and doctors still had little idea how cholera was really being spread. There wasn't much they could do to fight the wave of disease that arrived with the thousands upon thousands of new arrivals who were still pouring off ships at the waterfront. Too many of those ships were pulling into Toronto Bay flying a yellow flag from their mast — a warning there were cholera victims on board.

The outbreak that summer would be even worse than the first. Hundreds died — maybe as much as 10 percent of the population.

Most of the city's wealthiest citizens fled to their country estates north of Queen Street and up onto the escarpment above Davenport Road, but the greatest of Toronto's leaders — Reformers and Family Compact Tories alike — stayed behind to battle the disease. Some of them, like Francis Collins, would die. The garbage carts became ambulances, and then death carts. Mackenzie volunteered as an attendant. John Strachan did his part too. They would both load the dead onto the death carts, taking many of the victims to be buried en masse in a pit beside St. James Church. It was dangerous work. Mackenzie fell ill, nearly died, and was lucky to survive.

They're still there today, those victims, maybe as many as six thousand of them according to the highest estimates, buried together in the ground beneath St. James Park.

The second outbreak in Toronto did peter out eventually. But in some parts of the world, the pandemic raged on for years. Millions died. It would take another worldwide outbreak before a doctor in London made the first major breakthrough: in 1854, Dr. John Snow mapped out the cases in Soho and tracked the source to a water pump. For the first time, people realized that contaminated water was the problem. Still, there would be another four cholera pandemics after that one, the most recent in the 1970s. Cholera is easy to prevent: just don't drink any water with feces in it and you'll probably be okay. But more than a hundred thousand people still die from it every year because they just don't have that option.

Toronto would never suffer a cholera outbreak like that again. To fight it, the Family Compact and the Reformers found more common ground than you'd expect. The Tories had helped to create a new city government with real democratic powers. And the Reformers had shown that while they might not support all centralized authority, they did believe in the power of good, strong government.

But they still had fundamentally different visions for the future of the country. Things were going to get much worse before they got better.

Mackenzie had spent years looking for peaceful ways to achieve meaningful democratic reform, but his victories had been few and far between. He was running out of patience. Just two years after the end of his term as mayor, Mackenzie would turn to violence. Rebellion was brewing in Toronto.

12
REVOLUTION! ISH!

Robert Moodie was the first one shot. He was a retired army officer, nearly sixty years old. He'd fought against Napoleon and against the American invaders during the War of 1812. He was a Tory. And he was worried.

Even far to the north of Toronto, near Richmond Hill where he lived, it was clear there was a rebellion brewing. William Lyon Mackenzie hadn't been hiding his plans. Tensions had been rising all year. Now, on the first Monday in December, scores of men could be seen marching down Yonge Street, heading south toward the capital. The time had come. If all went according to their plan, the rebels would overthrow the colonial government and replace it with republican democracy.

Something had to be done. That afternoon, a few Tories met at Colonel Moodie's house, where they wrote a letter warning the governor about what they'd seen. They sent a local tavern owner south to deliver it, but he didn't make it far: he was quickly captured by the rebels. The Richmond Hill Tories would have to try again.

This time, Moodie volunteered to carry the letter himself. He and a few others loaded their pistols, grabbed their horses, and set off down Yonge Street as fast as they could.

They made it nearly all the way down to Eglinton Avenue before they ran into trouble. There, the rebels were gathering at Montgomery's Tavern before marching on the capital. Barricades blocked the road. Mackenzie's men were stopping everyone, and taking Tories prisoner.

But the old colonel wasn't going to be stopped without a fight. Moodie charged right at the rebels. He galloped past the first barricade, but before he could get by the second, they grabbed his horse by the bridle.

"Who are you, who dares to stop me upon the Queen's highway?" he demanded, firing his pistol above the rebels' heads to drive them off.

They stood their ground and fired back.

Moodie slumped over in his saddle. "I am shot — I am a dead man," he moaned. And he was right. The rebels carried him into the tavern. Two hours later, he was dead.

The rebellion had begun.

It was 1837. William Lyon Mackenzie was fed up. He'd spent more than a decade looking for a peaceful way to bring democratic reform to Upper Canada. He wrote passionate editorials, led protests, made speeches, organized committees, collected signatures for petitions. He ran for office and was elected to the Legislative Assembly and then again as the first mayor of Toronto.

None of it worked. The Family Compact blocked him at every turn. They denounced him in their own newspapers, trashed his business, and destroyed his printing press. They burned him in effigy, pelted him with garbage, and beat him bloody in the street. The Tories in the Assembly voted to throw him out of the legislature over and over again even as his constituents voted him back in with overwhelming majorities — sometimes unanimously.

And yet through it all, Mackenzie still believed in the British system. He even sailed to England to spend a year meeting with colonial officials in London. For the first time in decades, the British Tories were out of power and the more liberal Whigs were in; they were fighting their own battle for reform. At one point, Mackenzie stayed up for six straight days and nights listing his grievances for them, writing furiously, switching from one hand to the other when the first cramped up. He drove himself to the point of exhaustion, convinced the British would listen to reason if only they truly understood what was happening in Canada.

But even that failed. In the end, the only real change the Whigs did introduce unintentionally made things even worse: they fired the lieutenant governor and replaced him with a ruler who would prove to be even more inflammatory.

Sir Francis Bond Head had something of a Toronto connection — his wife had been friends with the Simcoes growing up; she was expected to marry Francis Simcoe until he died at Badajoz — but even more important, everyone thought he was a reformer. That's why the Whigs picked him.

On his month-long journey across the Atlantic to take up his new post as governor, he studied Mackenzie's list of grievances — all five hundred and fifty-three pages of them. When he finally rode into Toronto, triumphant banners welcomed him as "FRANCIS BOND HEAD, A TRIED REFORMER." His very first act was to appoint leading Reformers to his Executive Council.

But Sir Francis Bond Head was no reformer. To this day, some people think the Whigs must have confused him with his cousin and appointed the wrong person. Once in power, he quickly took the side of the Family Compact. He praised them for their "industry and intelligence" while dismissing Mackenzie as "an unprincipled, vagrant grievance-monger." He had no intention of listening to his Executive Council; after just three weeks, all the councillors resigned in protest — even the Tories. When the Legislative Assembly backed them up, Bond Head dissolved the legislature and called an election.

It would prove to be one of the most corrupt elections in Canadian history. There were bribes, threats, and riots. Polling stations were purposefully placed in Tory neighbourhoods; returning officers were hand-picked for their conservative sympathies. Bond Head — who was supposed to be neutral — openly campaigned for the Tories; he called the election a battle between "the forces of loyalty, order, and prosperity" and the "selfish and disloyal." The Tories won in a landslide.

For Mackenzie, it was the final straw. In London, he'd met many of the Radicals and Reformers behind the British democracy movement. They believed the

Canadian colonies should be independent from Britain; if the government refused to listen, they believed violence was an acceptable solution. As the situation in Toronto deteriorated, those ideas were making more and more sense to Mackenzie. By 1837, he was convinced: it was time for revolution.

"Canadians," he wrote, "Do you love freedom? ... Do you hate oppression? ... Then buckle on your armour, and put down the villains who oppress and enslave your country ... Up then brave Canadians. Ready your rifles and make short work of it."

With crops failing, an economic depression gripping the continent, and Bond Head in power, plenty of Upper Canadians were willing to listen. Hundreds of protesters came to Mackenzie's rallies. Farmers polished up old muskets. Blacksmiths forged new pikes. Training drills were held in the countryside.

And they weren't alone: Toronto wasn't the only Canadian city in the grips of a struggle for democracy. Very similar things had been happening in Montreal. Lower Canadians had their own version of the Family Compact (the Château Clique), their own reformers (les Patriotes), their own fiery leaders (like Louis-Joseph Papineau and Wolfred Nelson), and their own list of grievances (the Ninety-Two Resolutions). When the British government rejected every single one of their complaints and banned public meetings, les Patriotes responded with the biggest rally they had ever held. Six thousand people were there as Nelson roared, "The time has come to melt our spoons into bullets!" Within weeks, he was leading a makeshift army of volunteers through the countryside outside Montreal. They even won their first battle.

The government in Montreal asked Bond Head for help. He responded by sending every single soldier he had. Toronto was essentially left undefended.

This was it: Mackenzie's big chance. He declared independence from Britain, drafted a new constitution, and sent word to his followers: they would meet at John Montgomery's tavern (which was on Yonge Street just north of Eglinton — a few kilometres north of the city back then). From there, they would march down Yonge, head over to City Hall, seize the weapons stored inside, capture Bond Head, and establish a new Canadian republic.

On the first weekend in December, they began to arrive. There were hundreds of them: farmers and black-smiths and clerks and craftsmen. On Tuesday, December 4, 1837, they would march on Toronto.

Robert Moodie was the first one shot. But he wasn't the first to die. While Moodie was still bleeding slowly to death at Montgomery's Tavern, Captain Anthony Anderson would be shot and killed on the spot.

Anderson, too, had fought against the American invaders during the War of 1812, and he and his wife had been married by Reverend Strachan. But Anderson was no Tory. He believed in Mackenzie's vision of a demo-cratic Canada. He spent the autumn training rebels in North York. Now, he was expected to play a leading role when the army marched on Toronto.

The night before the attack, he and Mackenzie led a patrol south toward the city. But they weren't the only ones travelling through the dark.

Far to the south, in the heart of the capital, Colonel James FitzGibbon had spent his day preparing for the attack. He had long played a central role in the history of Upper Canada. He was yet another hero of the War of 1812: the soldier Laura Secord famously ran to warn of an American attack. It was FitzGibbon who had been the one to separate Samuel Jarvis and John Ridout when they brawled in the street before their deadly duel. And he had also once saved Mackenzie's life from an angry Tory mob. Now, he was about to play an even bigger role in Toronto history.

As the date of the rebel uprising approached, FitzGibbon found himself in charge of the city's defences. Bond Head refused to believe the threat of a rebellion was real, but FitzGibbon trusted the troubling updates from north of the city: of rebels staging military drills; of blacksmiths working day and night to forge enough weapons for an army.

So while Bond Head sent all of his soldiers away to Lower Canada, FitzGibbon got to work behind his back, making preparations for the defence of the capital. He ran training drills with militia volunteers. He wrote a list of every loyal Tory he could think of and went from door to door warning them to keep their guns loaded and at the ready. He developed a warning system: at the first sign of an attack, they'd ring the bells of St. James Church and Upper Canada College. He assigned a group of his men to protect City Hall every night, along with the precious weapons stored within.

Now, on the eve of the revolution, FitzGibbon was hearing reports of the rebel army gathering on Yonge Street. The attack was coming. That night, he rushed through the streets of Toronto, trying to convince the city's reluctant Tories to take up arms. He wouldn't sleep at home that night; he was worried the rebels would come to kill him in his bed. Instead, he set up shop at the new Parliament buildings on King Street.

Before turning in for the night, he, too, headed out with some men on a scouting mission. One of those who joined him was John Powell. Powell was a leading judge and politician: a devout Tory and a staunch member of the Family Compact. It was Judge Powell who let Samuel Jarvis off scot-free after the duel with Ridout — only about a year before Jarvis married Powell's daughter. It was exactly the kind of conflict of interest that helped drive Mackenzie to rebellion; now he would be the first to draw rebel blood.

When FitzGibbon turned for home, Powell and a friend ventured farther north, drawing ever closer to the rebel army. They didn't get far before they came across four riders in the dark. At first, they thought they were fellow Tories — but, in fact, it was Mackenzie and Anderson with their patrol.

Mackenzie caught Powell and his friend by surprise and took them prisoner. He made sure the Tory judge wasn't carrying any weapons by asking him politely if he was carrying any weapons — and then took his word as a gentleman.

Powell lied. While Mackenzie carried on, Captain Anderson took custody of the prisoners and headed back to the tavern. On the way there, Powell pulled out the pistol he was carrying, shot Anderson in the back, and made his escape. The bullet severed Anderson's spine. He died instantly.

For the rest of the night, Toronto was in chaos. Powell hurried back downtown to warn Bond Head; Bond Head rushed to get his family on a steamer out of town and then ran around in an ineffectual panic. While he was busy doing that, the students of Upper Canada College rushed to ring the school's bells in warning, but their headmaster sent them back to bed. When FitzGibbon tried to ring the bells of St. James, no one could find the keys to the bell tower. He was about to break down the door with an axe when the keys were finally found. In the end, the alarm was answered by a couple of hundred men; they grabbed their guns and hurried to King Street to guard City Hall and the Parliament buildings.

Then, they waited.

When dawn came the next morning, the rebels were feeling more than a little discouraged. This was supposed to be the day of their glorious revolution, but things weren't going to plan. As they prepared to march south, they could hear the bells ringing in the city below; they'd lost the element of surprise. The news from Lower Canada was dispiriting: the rebels there were being crushed; that very day, martial law was being declared in Montreal. The general who was supposed to lead Mackenzie's assault — a Dutchman named Von Egmond who had fought both for *and* against Napoleon — had yet to arrive. In his place, Captain Anderson was supposed to lead them, but now he was dead. Mackenzie's next pick, Samuel Lount, was a blacksmith who didn't feel up to the challenge of leading an entire army.

So when the rebels — five hundred strong now — finally did start marching down Yonge Street just before noon, it was Mackenzie who was at their head, riding a white horse and wearing as many jackets as he could possibly squeeze into, apparently trying to make himself bulletproof. Many who marched with him that day agreed: he was behaving even more erratically than usual.

It was a long, slow march. They'd only made it to St. Clair Avenue before Mackenzie had them stop for lunch. He went to the postmaster's house and forced the postmaster's terrified wife to make a meal for his troops. Some of his men never bothered marching any farther south than that — they just hung out on the lawn eating boiled beef and drinking whisky.

Then came emissaries from Bond Head. The government was trying to stall the rebels by getting them to talk about a truce. But since they had to send men whom the rebels wouldn't shoot, they chose Robert Baldwin and John Rolph — two of the few Reformers the Family Compact could tolerate. Little did they know that Rolph was secretly in cahoots with Mackenzie. He'd been passing information to the rebels. In fact, if the revolution succeeded, Rolph had already agreed to serve as the first provisional president of the Republic of Canada.

Rolph warned the rebels they should hurry; the government was still disorganized. But Mackenzie didn't really listen: he paused again near Bloor Street to burn down the house of a Tory who had once crossed him. Then he tried to burn down Rosedale, the country house of the sheriff — yet another member of the Jarvis family. Lount was only just barely able to talk Mackenzie out of it.

It was already dusk by the time the army neared College Street. It was there, for the very first time, that the rebels faced off against the government's defenders. Ignoring Bond Head's orders, FitzGibbon had sent Sheriff Jarvis and twenty-six other men to hide behind some shrubs and ambush the rebels. It worked. They fired a volley into the rebel ranks. They even hit a couple of them. And then, as the front line of rebels returned fire, the loyalists all ran away as fast as they could. Sheriff Jarvis called after them to stand and fight, but it was no use.

Luckily for them, the rebels had just as little experience in battle. When the front line of their ranks dropped to one knee to reload their guns in the dark, the men behind them assumed they'd all been shot. So they ran away, too.

Most historians seem to think that if the rebels had kept marching south into the city, they'd have captured it that night. But it may have only been the beginning of a bloodbath. Once the government's army in Lower Canada was finished with the rebels there, they could easily have marched west to attack Mackenzie in Toronto.

We'll never know what might have happened. Instead of marching south into the city, most of the rebels headed back north to regroup at Montgomery's Tavern. Some kept going all the way home.

The day after that, the rebels didn't do much. Mackenzie led some men out to rob a stagecoach and a tavern to help pay the bills, but having failed in their first attempt, the rebels decided to wait for Von Egmond before launching another assault.

For the loyalists, the day was much more productive. Reinforcements arrived. They came from Hamilton, Pickering, Niagara, Peel, and a host of other nearby towns. By the following morning there were more than a thousand of them — enough to crush the rebels. So that's what they decided to do.

It was a clear, bright day in an unusually warm December. The loyalist muskets and cannons glinted in the sun. Bond Head climbed up on his white horse in his white uniform and led his army north. It was commanded by some of the city's most familiar faces. John Strachan rode at Bond Head's side. Samuel Jarvis led a group on one of the flanks. Colonel FitzGibbon led another. Even Bond Head's aide-de-camp was a future mayor.

As the army marched up Yonge Street, loyalist citizens cheered them on. They leaned out their windows waving flags. A military band joined the troops, with the drone of bagpipes filling the air.

Up at Montgomery's Tavern, the rebels were far from ready to fight. Von Egmond had finally arrived that morning, took one look at his men, and declared Mackenzie's plan to immediately attack the city "stark madness." Mackenzie almost shot him for that.

Instead, they sent a farmer, Peter Matthews, off with some men to burn a bridge over the Don River as a decoy. It didn't work. Bond Head's army kept coming. Soon, the rebels could see the metallic gleam of their enemies' guns as they crested the hill down at St. Clair.

When they reached the spot where Mount Pleasant Cemetery now stands, the government's cannons let loose with their first volley. The cannonballs crashed harmlessly through the woods. They were still too far south. But soon, they would be close enough.

It had taken years for the resentment between radical Reformers and the Family Compact to come to a head, but the Battle of Montgomery's Tavern lasted just fifteen or twenty minutes. The second volley smashed through the tavern's dining room window and brought down three chimneys. Men scattered and poured out of the building. The government troops surged forward and opened fire with their rifles and muskets. A few rebels were hit. A few would die. Most ran away.

The government had won the day. The rebels had lost. Democracy would have to wait.

As Bond Head's men began to loot the area, the governor ordered the tavern burned to the ground. It marked the beginning of a dark time for Toronto democrats. In the wake of the rebellion, Bond Head and the Family Compact would crack down on dissent with renewed brutality. Anyone who was suspected of democratic sympathies became a target. Even some who had never supported the rebels were denounced as traitors.

The Reform movement was left in tatters. The next mayor of Toronto would be John Powell, hailed as a hero for shooting Captain Anderson in the back.

The rebellion was over, but there were more deaths to come. The fallout from Mackenzie's uprising would be claiming lives for years.

Many of the rebels — both in Upper and Lower Canada — were arrested and thrown into foul prison cells. Von Egmond caught a case of pneumonia in his; the illness took his life. Others were exiled without trial, forced to leave their friends and family behind. Some were sent across the border to live in the United States, or shipped all the way to Bermuda. Many found themselves transported to the other side of the world: to do hard labour in brutal Australian penal colonies. Some of those rebels would die from the harsh conditions they were forced to endure there.

Back home, the blacksmith Samuel Lount and the farmer Peter Matthews were both tried, convicted, and sentenced to hang. Lount's wife personally delivered a petition with thousands of signatures and begged the chief justice to spare her husband's life. But her pleas were ignored — the judge had fought with the loyalists.

The two rebels were brought to the gallows in Court House Square at eight o'clock in the morning on an early spring day. When Sheriff Jarvis went to collect them, even he broke down in tears. "We die in a good cause;" Lount told his fellow prisoners on his way to face his death, "Canada will yet be free." The crowd watched as the sheriff placed the hoods over the heads of the condemned men, and slipped a noose around their throats. Then the trapdoors opened and the ropes snapped their necks.

"The spectacle of Lount after the execution was the most shocking sight that can be imagined," Mackenzie later wrote, although he wasn't there to see it himself. "He was covered over with his blood, the head being nearly severed from his body, owing to the depth of the fall. More horrible to relate, when he was cut down, two ruffians seized the end of the rope and dragged the mangled corpse along the ground into the jail yard."

At least one report suggested Lount's daughter was so distraught by the sight that she soon died of grief.

The new governor refused to allow the families to bury the two dead men — he worried a public funeral might encourage unrest. Instead, the rebels were quietly buried in Potter's Field, the pauper's cemetery on the corner of Yonge and Bloor, laid to rest in a simple grave beneath a modest, flat gravestone. Later, they were moved to the Necropolis cemetery in Cabbagetown, where you can still find them today. The simple stone is still there, but the grave is far from forgotten. Six decades after the executions, a towering, fifteen-foot column was erected next to their grave, and a plaque was added a century after that.

As for Mackenzie, he managed to escape, fleeing the scene of the battle. Just a few years earlier, he'd been the city's first mayor; now he was Toronto's most wanted fugitive. Bond Head offered a £1,000 reward for his capture. Mackenzie was smuggled through the countryside by his supporters, pursued by angry gangs of loyalists. He ran all the way south to Niagara, getting rowed across the river just a few minutes ahead of the men who had come to capture him. He was lucky to escape Canada with his life. He would spend the next decade living in exile.

But he wasn't done yet. Just a few days after his harrowing escape across the border, Mackenzie and his supporters seized an island on the Canadian side of the Niagara River — Navy Island, just above Niagara Falls — and declared themselves to be the provisional government of the new Republic of Canada. They even had their own flag and currency. They used their island foothold and support from sympathizers in the United States to launch a series of border raids against the colonial government.

They called it the Patriot War. It dragged on for another year. There were battles and skirmishes near Windsor, near Prescott, on Pelee Island, and at other sites along the border. More than a hundred more men died in battle before Mackenzie's war was done. More would be hanged for treason. And still more sent to Australia to die in the prison camps.

Finally, it was all over. The Family Compact had won. It seemed as if their deeply conservative, anti-democratic vision for Canada would determine the future of the country.

But with the radicals thoroughly routed, the moderates were about to take control of the Reform movement.

And they were going to accomplish what Mackenzie's revolution never could.

13
THE GRISLY GRAVE OF ROBERT BALDWIN

On a cold winter night in 1859, four men descended into the earth beneath the grounds of Spadina House. They ventured down into the Baldwin family tomb, where the body of Robert Baldwin — one of the architects of Canadian democracy — had been put to rest a month earlier. They found his coffin there in the dark and prepared to crack it open. They had come to defile his corpse.

Baldwin was born into the first generation of Toronto settlers; the city was still just a tiny, muddy town when he took his first breaths in 1804. His mother gave birth to him in the very same house where William Lyon Mackenzie's printing press would later be trashed by Samuel Jarvis and his friends.

Baldwin was younger than those rabble-rousing youth of the Family Compact, but in many ways he had a very similar childhood. He was born into one of the most influential families in the new capital. His father, William Warren Baldwin, would leave a lasting mark on Toronto as a physician, lawyer, architect, and politician. He was the same doctor who had tried to save the life of his good friend Peter Russell with a cure of crushed deer antler and red wine. He was there during the American invasion in 1813, tending to the city's wounded defenders while his family was evacuated. And he was there again during the cholera outbreak in 1832, head of the Board of Health. He built the original Spadina House on his country estate on the hill overlooking Davenport Road, and carved Spadina Avenue out of the woods to the south of it so he'd have a clear view all the way to the lake. Baldwin Street, he named after himself; Phoebe Street, he named after his wife. He was one of the architects of Osgoode Hall, and he helped to establish the city's first library. After Russell's death, he and his family moved into Russell Abbey and tended to Russell's troubled sister Elizabeth. After her death, the Baldwins inherited the vast Russell estate, making them wealthier still. When it came time for young Robert to go to school, he was sent off to study under the Reverend John Strachan, just like the children of the Family Compact.

But when it came to politics, William Warren Baldwin was far from conservative. He was a staunch Reformer. And Robert would follow in his father's footsteps. The Baldwins were nowhere near as radical as Mackenzie: they didn't want independence from Britain; they didn't believe in armed revolution. But they did passionately support the idea of Canadian democracy. They believed Canadians should have control over their own affairs. Ultimately, government ministers shouldn't be responsible to the British governor, they argued, but to the elected representatives in the legislature — to Parliament, and therefore to the Canadian people. They called the idea *responsible government*.

Now, in the wake of the rebellion, with the most radical Reformers dead or in exile, the moderate Robert Baldwin would find himself leading the democracy movement in Upper Canada. He would spend the next decade fighting for responsible government. And he would do it while struggling with severe depression.

Elizabeth Sullivan was just fifteen years old when she fell in love with her cousin. Robert was four years older, a promising law student with a passionate heart and a love of romance novels; he shared her feelings deeply. But the young love got off to a rough start: their family disapproved of the incestuous match. The very same month that Robert was called to the bar, young Eliza was bundled up and sent off to live with relatives in New York City; their parents hoped the time apart would cool the budding romance.

It didn't work. During her exile in Manhattan, Eliza received a stream of heartsick love letters and poems from York. Robert missed her dearly, longed for her return, and dreamed of her at night. They agreed that on the first evening of every month, they would both be thinking of each other at the same time, so they could feel connected despite all the miles between them.

The forced separation lasted more than a year, but their love didn't fade. And so, finally, the family gave up.

Eliza was allowed to return home and their parents reluctantly agreed to a wedding, a subdued affair held at St. James Church.

The newly married couple settled first into Spadina House and then into an elegant brick home on the corner of Front and Bay. While they raised their children Robert entered politics, defeating Sheriff Jarvis in his first election. It was a blissful life. "I wish everyone was as happy as I am," Eliza wrote.

But tragedy struck with the arrival of their fourth child. Eliza's labour was difficult; she was forced to have a caesarian section. The baby survived but the operation left Eliza with a life-threatening infection. Months later, she was still suffering the ill effects. She headed back to New York City to recuperate, leaving Robert to fulfill his duties and pursue his career, deeply worried for his wife.

Eliza never did recover. Nearly two years after the end of her pregnancy, she returned home to Front Street to spend her final days with the man she loved. She passed away quietly in the winter of 1836. She was buried at Spadina House in the family tomb.

Her death shook Robert to the core. Baldwin would suffer from severe bouts of depression for the rest of his life, centred on his painful memories of his dead wife. During the years he was fighting to lay the foundations of Canadian democracy, there were days he couldn't leave the house. His nights were haunted by terrible dreams; he lost so much sleep he nodded off in Parliament. The memory of Eliza was with him always. He carried her letters with him wherever he went, her room was kept as a shrine only he was allowed to enter, and every year on the anniversaries of their wedding and her death, he roamed the streets of Toronto visiting the landmarks of their relationship — from their home on Front Street all the way up to Spadina House, where she lay waiting for him in the tomb.

It began like so many of the most exciting moments in Canadian history: with a government report.

The British were worried. They wanted to understand what the hell was happening in Canada: why the rebellions broke out and how to avoid more violence in the future. So the Whig government enlisted the most progressive politician they could find and sent him across the Atlantic to investigate.

Lord Durham was so liberal they called him "Radical Jack"; he spent the summer of 1841 touring the Canadian colonies, speaking with Tories, Reformers, and Patriotes alike — including Robert Baldwin and his father.

By then, the young Baldwin had already spent years at the centre of Upper Canadian politics. Bond Head had arrived in Toronto just two weeks after Eliza died — and Robert was plunged into the political crisis that followed while he was still raw in mourning. He was one of the Reformers named to the governor's Executive Council; when all the councillors quit three weeks later, many suspected Baldwin was the architect of the protest. On the day Mackenzie's rebel army marched down Yonge Street, Baldwin was one of the moderate Reformers sent to negotiate with the rebels — which he did in good faith, not knowing that it was a ploy and both sides were already determined to fight.

Now, he and his father used their meeting with Durham to strongly advocate for the idea of responsible government.

Radical Jack listened. The Durham Report listed responsible government as one of its most important recommendations.

The British weren't convinced. When they got the report, they ignored the part about democracy and focused instead on the most racist of Durham's recommendations: they combined Upper and Lower Canada into one province so francophone voters in Quebec would be drowned out by the anglophone majority.

But in the new united Province of Canada, Baldwin saw his chance: an alliance with the francophone reformers. Together, they could outvote the Tories and force the British into accepting Canadian democracy.

In Quebec, the new moderate leader of les Patriotes — Louis-Hippolyte LaFontaine — was facing violent opposition from the Tories. Armed conservative mobs blocked francophone voters from getting to the polls. So Baldwin invited LaFontaine to run for election in Toronto. He won by a landslide. The victory sent a powerful message, helping to cement the alliance: a francophone Catholic reformer from Montreal had won a seat in Protestant Tory Toronto.

Just a few years later, Baldwin and LaFontaine were swept into power with a huge majority — now they had their mandate. The government they led is remembered as "The Great Ministry." In just a few short years, they laid much of the groundwork for the Canada we know today. They introduced an independent judiciary, the jury system, and a system for appeals. They made sure that everyone — not just the rich — had access to the courts, and that anyone — not just the rich friends of Tory politicians — could be appointed to the civil service. They opened Canadian ports to ships from all over the world and helped to build the country's first railways. They introduced public education and took the religious King's College away from Bishop Strachan and turned it into the secular University of Toronto. They even won amnesties for many of the old rebels, including William Lyon Mackenzie. The rebel mayor was finally allowed to come home to Toronto, after more than a decade in exile.

But none of that was as important as what they would pull off in the spring of 1849. That's when democracy finally came to Canada.

The Rebellion Losses Bill shouldn't have been controversial. It was simply going to pay damages to people in Lower Canada (Canada East) whose property had been destroyed during the rebellions. That seemed fair: when the Tories were in power, they'd already done the same thing for people in Upper Canada (Canada West).

But that's not how the Tories saw it. Lower Canada was full of francophones — and as far as the Tories were concerned, francophones could never be loyal British subjects. They weren't "real" Canadians at all. Paying them for damages was as good as paying the rebels themselves.

And so, the debate that raged in Parliament that spring was about more than just one bill — it was about two fundamentally different visions for the future of Canada: one, a monolithic British state; the other, a multicultural society. "The spring of 1849," as the philosopher John Ralston Saul has argued, "was the defining moment for modern Canada."

The debate over the bill was vicious. The Tories claimed the payments would be "an open encouragement to rebellion." They declared the Reform Party was "dangerous, criminal and subversive of order ... under the dominion of French masters." If Baldwin and LaFontaine had their way, Canada would be "ruled by foreigners."

The Tories filibustered as long as they could: every hour of every day they were on the floor of the legislature in the new capital of Montreal, denouncing the bill, playing for time while conservative newspapers printed inflammatory headlines. Anger among Tory supporters grew.

They called on the governor general — Lord Elgin — to do what the appointed governors had always done when they were backed into a corner: step in on the side of the conservatives and dissolve Parliament, snuffing out the bill. "The Tory party," Elgin wrote in a letter home to England, "are doing what they can by menace, intimidation and appeals of passions to drive me to a coup d'état."

Instead, Elgin did nothing. The Rebellion Losses Bill passed. Now all it needed was his signature. If he signed the bill, it meant the British were recognizing Canadian authority over Canadian affairs. It meant responsible government. It meant democracy.

Then, nothing. For nearly two whole months, Elgin refused to make a move: he literally just stayed home at the governor general's residence outside Montreal. But in the meantime, dozens of other bills were passed by Parliament. They needed signatures, too. One way or another, the governor general was going to have to decide.

It was on a Wednesday in late April that Lord Elgin finally climbed into his carriage and headed into the capital. He pulled up to the Parliament buildings around four o'clock in the afternoon. He was escorted upstairs, where he signed every single one of the bills waiting for him. Including the Rebellion Losses Bill.

The violence began immediately. By the time Elgin got back outside, hundreds of angry conservatives were already waiting for him. He climbed into his carriage under a hail of insults, eggs, and rocks. That night, a Tory mob burned down the Parliament buildings; some members of the legislature barely escaped with their lives. In the days to come, rampaging Tories attacked the houses of leading Reformers. There were gunfights in the streets of Montreal. "The city," according to Baldwin biographer Michael S. Cross, "was on the verge of civil war."

The unrest reached far beyond the borders of Montreal. As news of Elgin's decision spread, there were protests, riots, and death threats all over the Province of Canada. In Toronto, angry Tories took to the streets and burned Reformers in effigy. The mayor called in troops to keep things from getting out of hand.

"I wish they would catch old Elgin & string him up," Samuel Jarvis's son wrote in a letter to his mother, "as a caution to other traitor Governors."

But Baldwin and LaFontaine refused to be drawn into a violent clash. While some called on the politicians to order their troops to open fire on the crowds, the Reform leaders exercised restraint, knowing chaos was part of the Tory plan; it would only encourage the British to step in and undo all the progress they had made. In time, the unrest died down. The Reformers had won.

The struggle took nearly fifty years. Countless Canadians — in Toronto and across the country — had died fighting for democracy. They had been hanged for it, rotted in jail for it, been banished from the country they loved. But now, without firing a shot, Baldwin and LaFontaine had won. The new system was far from perfect: it would, for instance, be many decades before women won the right to vote and more than a century before Indigenous people in Canada could cast a ballot without sacrificing their status under the Indian Act. But it was a beginning: the head of the British government in Canada had just acknowledged the people of Canada as the true rulers of the country.

Canada *was* a democracy.

Baldwin didn't last much longer. He had never been a natural politician. He was an introvert: quiet and reserved. He mumbled his way through his speeches. His skin was pale and his eyes dull. He was tall but stout and always hunched over. They said he carried himself with "a funereal bearing." Politics had always been a struggle.

Things got even harder after his father died: William Warren Baldwin fell ill on Christmas Eve of 1843, lingered on for a couple of weeks, and then passed away. His death came at a trying moment for his son: the Reformers had just lost an election; as Toronto's Tories celebrated with an enormous bonfire, responsible government seemed a distant dream. Baldwin's depression grew even deeper. There were headaches. He was known to burst into tears in public. Soon, he was thinking of quitting politics altogether.

That day finally arrived just two years after the victory over responsible government. William Lyon Mackenzie was back in Parliament by then; the rebel mayor united a radical faction of Reformers against Baldwin and nearly won an important vote. Baldwin was only forty-seven, but he decided the moment had come. He rose to his feet in the legislature and gave one final speech announcing his retirement. When he sat back down, he had tears in his eyes. LaFontaine announced his own departure later the same day.

Baldwin's health crumbled quickly after that. He shut himself away in the house at Spadina, dedicating himself more fully to his dark obsession with his dead wife. His eyesight faltered. His hands trembled. His mind began to fail. He complained of a "disagreeable rumbling noise in [his] head" and that his "organs [were] too powerful." He was gripped by thoughts of his own death: his chance to be reunited with his dear Eliza.

He took his final breaths at Spadina House in the winter of 1858. The crowd who came to his funeral was one of the biggest Toronto had ever seen.

It was weeks later that the note was discovered in the pocket of one of his vests. A list of his final requests: among them, he asked to be buried with Eliza's letters and a brooch she'd given him as a gift. Their coffins should be chained together. And his corpse should be cut open — given the same abdominal wound as the caesarian section that had slowly killed his wife. He was very clear: even if the letter wasn't found until after his body was buried, he wanted his family to honour his wishes.

And so, on that January night in 1859, Baldwin's son, his brother, and his brother-in-law all descended into his tomb. They brought a doctor with them, armed with a scalpel. There in the cold and the dark, they fulfilled his grisly requests.

Today, the Baldwin family tomb has been moved from Spadina to sit beneath the grass of St. James Cemetery. A century and a half after Robert Baldwin was laid to rest, he still sleeps beneath the ground in Cabbagetown, one of the fathers of Canadian democracy, chained to the bones of the woman he loved.

THE
BOOMING
METROPOLIS

14
BLACK '47 IN THE ORANGE CITY

You'll find them standing along the river in the dock-lands of Dublin: a group of haunting statues. There are six of them, all made of green bronze. They are tall and terribly thin; their cheeks have wasted away, their eyes have sunk back into their heads. They look tired and scared, clutching a few precious belongings to their chests as they shuffle along the quayside; one carries a body slung over his slender shoulders. They are all rotting away, starving and sick. Behind them, a gaunt dog struggles to keep his feet. They were sculpted by the Irish artist Rowan Gillespie, commissioned to stand in Dublin as a reminder of the horror that befell Ireland more than a century and a half ago.

In the spring of 1847, the first Catholic bishop of Toronto found himself standing near that very same spot. Michael Power had travelled to Europe to meet with the pope, visiting Ireland on his way home. He arrived in Dublin during the darkest moment in Irish history. The Great Famine had begun.

The blight arrived in Ireland just three years earlier, but it spread quickly, devastating the staple crop of potatoes. In a country where the average man ate fourteen pounds of potatoes every day, the blight meant wholesale devastation. As the crop failure continued year after year, people began to die of starvation. Others, weakened by malnutrition, were easy prey for the typhoid epidemic that was sweeping across the island.

A million people would die in Ireland before the Great Famine was over. Another 2.5 million fled.

In Dublin, Bishop Power watched as thousands of refugees crowded the docks, waiting to board their ships. More than a hundred thousand of them would sail across the Atlantic that summer, bound for Canada in a desperate bid for survival.

Even as they left the terror of the Great Famine behind, the starving refugees were subjected to new horrors. As they crowded onto the ships in Dublin and in other Irish ports, they were stuffed into the holds below deck, locked away in unimaginably inhumane conditions. Hundreds of people were crammed together for weeks on end, given little to eat or to drink. Many of them fell deathly ill: hidden away in their clothes were the lice that carried the deadly salmonella bacteria that cause typhoid fever. The disease spread like wildfire through the ships, taking advantage of the passengers' weakened condition. They were, as one refugee described it, "dying like rotten sheep thrown into a pit." On some ships as many as a third of the refugees died before they ever saw Canada, their corpses thrown overboard to the sharks. The death toll was so high they called them "coffin ships."

Those who did survive the crossing were screened as soon as they arrived in Canada, and anyone who showed signs of illness was sent into quarantine. The island of Grosse Île, near Quebec City, had first been turned into a quarantine station in order to deal with the cholera epidemic in 1832; now it would be the final resting place for thousands of the famine's typhoid victims.

Those who were still healthy enough to continue the voyage were packed onto steamships — "like pigs," according to one witness — that chugged up the St. Lawrence toward the Great Lakes. "The poor creatures ... were crowded together like herring in a barrel," the *Globe* reported, "and many had difficulty gasping for a breath of fresh air." As the refugees moved west, deeper into Canada, they sparked typhoid outbreaks wherever they landed: Quebec City, Montreal, Kingston ... getting ever closer to Toronto.

The city knew what was coming. The newspaper accounts were chilling. And as soon as Bishop Power had seen the scale of the devastation in Ireland with his own eyes, he'd written a letter home: his warning was read in every Catholic church in and around the city, describing the horrors to come and calling on the people of Toronto to help. He rushed home as soon as the weather allowed, steaming up the St. Lawrence as the spring ice melted, arriving home just ahead of the first wave of refugees so he could help prepare the city.

But the scale of what did come to Toronto that summer was beyond what anyone could have imagined. More than thirty-eight thousand Irish refugees would pour into the city in just a few months — twice the entire population of Toronto.

They began to arrive at the beginning of June: hundreds of them spilled off the ships that pulled into Toronto Harbour. By the end of the month, there were sometimes four steamers a day unloading refugees at Rees' Wharf (near the foot of Simcoe Street, where the Convention Centre stands today). Some hadn't survived the final leg of the journey, dying under the hot summer sun on the short trip down the lake from Kingston. Dead bodies were found among the living. The stench of the ships was so strong, it sent officials on the dock staggering backward. The refugees were herded off the steamers like cattle, kept in line by constables armed with sticks.

As they disembarked at the wharf, the refugees were screened again. A quarter of them were already sick. They were bundled onto wagons and shipped the two blocks up John Street toward the Toronto General Hospital for treatment. But there were far more patients than the building could handle; as the refugees overwhelmed the wards, sixteen fever sheds were built on the grounds. The hospital stood on the northwest corner of King and John; today, that same spot is home to the glitz and glamour of the Toronto International Film Festival headquarters, but in 1847 it was where dying Irish refugees spent their final moments in agony.

Typhoid begins with a high fever. Over the first few days, it gets progressively worse. There might be headaches, nosebleeds, abdominal pains. Rose spots might begin to appear on the patient's skin. Eventually, the victims are too weak to stand. In the end, intestines begin to hemorrhage and develop holes. Excrement seeps out into the abdomen and the body beings to attack itself. It's a painful way to die.

More than a thousand refugees would pass away in Toronto that summer. Some were Protestant; they were buried in St. James Cemetery. Most were Catholic. They were given wooden coffins and carried in horse-drawn hearses across King Street to the other side of the city, where they would be buried on the grounds of St. Paul's Church. Residents along the route complained of the terrible smell as the corpses were transported across town. On one day in August, a hearse hit a rut; coffins were tossed into King Street and broke open, spilling dead bodies into the road. Two had been stuffed together into a single box, sparking a scandal and fears that authorities were pocketing funds.

While some Torontonians fled the city in fear of the plague, doctors and nurses spent long hours in the fever sheds, fighting to save lives. There was little they could do: antibiotics had yet to be invented; they relied on ineffective cures like brandy, wine, milk, and smoke. Every minute they spent with their patients, they were putting their own lives at risk. Inevitably, they, too, began to fall ill. Some of them would die the same horrifying deaths as their patients.

Bishop Power was visiting the fever sheds every day, comforting patients, praying with them, giving the dying the last rites. Four priests assisted him; every single one of them fell ill that summer. Soon, the bishop joined them. Power showed the first signs of the fever near the end of September. Within days, he was confined to his bed, unable to write or to eat. On the first day of October, at the new rectory for his half-built St. Michael's Cathedral, Bishop Power breathed his last.

Most of the famine refugees didn't settle in Toronto. They weren't welcome. The vast majority of them were Catholic; Toronto was still deeply Protestant and deeply suspicious of Catholicism — as the battle over responsible government was showing. And while the power of the Family Compact might have been fading, the city's relationship to Catholicism wasn't going to get any better: the Orange Order would come to dominate Toronto politics for the next hundred years.

The Orange Order had begun in Northern Ireland, born of the sectarian violence that still plagues cities like Belfast to this day. From the very beginning, it was designed to be staunchly British, fiercely Protestant, and profoundly anti-Catholic. It was named in honour of King William of Orange: the Dutch prince who was invited to invade Britain in the late 1600s and seize the crown from the Catholic King James in order to permanently establish Protestantism as the kingdom's official religion.

It didn't take long for the Order to cross the Atlantic and find a home in Toronto — another staunchly British city filled with Irish Protestants who shared bitter memories of the violence back home. The organization quickly became a major force in the Upper Canadian capital. Orangemen filled positions of influence and kept Catholics out of them. For nearly a century — until 1954 — almost every single one of the city's mayors was an Orangeman.

Every July, the streets of Toronto would be filled with Orange parades: members of the local lodges marched with painted banners celebrating religious victories from days gone by. On the date of the biggest parade, July 12, city employees were given the day off so they could attend. Catholic families tended to stay indoors; they kept their children close.

Before long, people were calling Toronto "The Belfast of Canada." And the nickname was well earned. It was "the most Irish of all North American cities" — with a higher proportion of Irish-born residents than even Boston or New York. The struggles of Ireland were regularly played out on the streets of Toronto. Violence between Protestants and Catholics became an increasingly familiar sight in the city. Riots were sparked by parades, religious processions, public meetings, speeches, elections.... Orange thugs began to play an important role at the polls, using threats and violence to keep Catholic voters away and Reform Party candidates from winning. The Baldwins repeatedly tried to ban the Order and failed.

More than once the violence turned deadly. At times, it verged on outright war. In 1866, an army of Irish Republicans — the Fenian Brotherhood — invaded Canada in an attempt to pressure the British into leaving Ireland. The first monument ever erected in Toronto remembers those who fought and died opposing the Irish invaders at the Battle of Ridgeway. It stands near Queen's Park.

In the wake of the Great Famine, the situation became even worse. For the most part, Torontonians of all religions came together in aid of the refugees: private citizens donated money to the relief efforts; the government helped new arrivals find jobs and land. But the refugees were discouraged from settling in Toronto itself. Anyone healthy enough to travel was forced to keep moving as soon as they got off the ships: to Hamilton, to Niagara, to London, or into the farmland surrounding the city.

Still, about two thousand did stay. Over the next few years, the percentage of Catholics living in Toronto nearly doubled. And anti-Catholic violence rose in response.

Many in the city saw the Irish as an inferior people. As far as those bigots were concerned, the famine had confirmed their racist beliefs. Those opinions were echoed in the highest levels of the British government — even by the head of the famine relief effort. "The judgement of God sent the calamity to teach the Irish a lesson," he said, "that calamity must not be too much mitigated.... The real evil with which we have to contend is not the physical evil of the Famine, but the moral evil of the selfish, perverse, and turbulent character of the people."

During the hunger, the British government purposefully limited their relief efforts in fear the aid would make the Irish dependent on charity. At the same time, many wealthy landlords seized the opportunity to evict starving tenants and increase the future profitability of their lands. The British response helped make the famine much more deadly than it otherwise would have been — and then they used the scale of the catastrophe as evidence of Irish inferiority.

In the years to come, racism against Toronto's Irish Catholics became one of the defining features of life in the city. "Irish beggars are to be met everywhere," the *Globe* complained, "and they are as ignorant and vicious as they are poor. They are lazy, improvident, and unthankful; they fill our poorhouses and our prisons, and are as brutish in their superstitions as the Hindoos [*sic*]."

In the second half of the 1800s, sectarian riots between the city's Protestants and Catholics became even more common than they had been before. There were dozens of them. Even the Catholic bishop got stoned by a mob. Violence became so common that the St. Patrick's Day parade was banned for more than a century: it wasn't held again until 1988.

Meanwhile, the Order tightened their grip on power. The Orange domination of Toronto would continue well into the 1900s. It wasn't until after the Second World War, when large numbers of immigrants began to arrive from all over the world, that the Orange lodges lost their power. As the city became a modern, multicultural metropolis, it was forced to let go of its fiercely British identity.

Today, Ireland Park stands on the Toronto waterfront. It's tucked away behind the old silos at the foot of Bathurst Street, near the island airport. You'll find them standing there next to the harbour: a group of haunting statues. There are five of them, all made of green bronze — just like their cousins in Dublin. They are tall and terribly thin; their cheeks have wasted away, their eyes have sunk back into their heads. One has collapsed to the ground, unable to carry on any farther. They all look tired and scared. But at the front of the group, one of the statues has his arms raised in elation toward the skyline of the modern city: this is Toronto; they have arrived.

15
ABRAHAM LINCOLN'S SHAWL

The bullet hit Lincoln in the back of his head. It was a tiny thing: a little lead ball barely a centimetre across — not much bigger than a pea. It was flattened by the impact when it struck the bone near the base of the president's skull, but it didn't stop there. The momentum carried it deep into his head, pushing a small piece of bone forward through his brain. It carved a hole through the mind of one of history's great leaders — slicing through the neural pathways of the man who oversaw the end of American slavery and the North's victory in the Civil War — before it finally came to rest in the white matter behind his right eye.

The president slumped over in his chair. His wife, Mary Todd Lincoln, was sitting next to him; she screamed.

The assassin was still right there, standing behind Lincoln's chair: he was the famous actor, John Wilkes Booth. As one of the president's guests tried to stop him, Booth slashed away with his knife, cutting the man's arm, and then made a daring escape. He leaped from the president's box directly onto the stage of Ford's Theatre, breaking his ankle as he landed in the middle of a scene. He shouted something, a slogan — some heard "*Sic Semper Tyrannis*": thus always with tyrants — and then limped away quickly before the audience had time to realize what was happening.

Lincoln was still alive. But even as a doctor rushed to his side and examined the bullet hole, it was clear the president wouldn't last much longer. "His wound is mortal," the doctor announced, "it is impossible for him to recover." There was nothing left to do but to find a comfortable place for Lincoln to spend his final hours.

The White House was only a few blocks away, but even that trip was considered too much for him, so they carried him across the street to a boarding house. Long into the night, they watched him slowly die, keeping solemn vigil through those dark hours. They came from all over the city: Lincoln's friends, family, and supporters. There were doctors and senators and cabinet members and close confidantes. A few dozen were drawn to the house that night to pay their final respects.

One of them was an unlikely friend for an American president in the 1800s: the very first black doctor ever licensed to practise medicine in Canada. His name was Dr. Anderson Ruffin Abbott.

Abbott's parents fell in love on the banks of the Mississippi River. His father was a steward on a steamboat; his mother was a maid, looking after a couple of young children on a trip south from Boston. It was sheer luck that brought them together: walking along a dock one day, Wilson Ruffin Abbott was struck by a cord of falling wood and seriously injured; Ellen Toyer nursed him back to health. Soon, they were married. They settled down together in Mobile, Alabama, where they ran a general store.

At first, things went relatively well. The store was a success; they had enough money to buy a few properties around town, including a nice riverfront home. But life in the South was far from easy for anyone with dark skin. In Mobile, all "free blacks" were forced to register with the government; they had to provide a bond signed by two white men guaranteeing their good behaviour and then wear a badge to prove they'd done it. The Abbotts' commercial success and their protests against the racist law made them an obvious target for local bigots. Just a few years after their wedding, they were sent a chilling warning in an anonymous letter: a mob was coming for them.

That night, Wilson Ruffin Abbott watched as their store was trashed and burned to the ground. By then, his family was already escaping on a steamer to New Orleans; he followed the next day. From there, they headed north to New York City. And finally, frightened by the racism they found even in the northern states, they fled across the border into Canada.

By the time the Abbotts arrived in Toronto in the middle of the 1830s, there were no slaves left in the city — the gradual phase-out that John Graves Simcoe had started decades earlier was finally complete. (In fact, slavery had recently been abolished across the entire British Empire.)

There was still plenty of anti-black racism in Toronto, but it paled in comparison to what could be found south of the border, where there were many more deeply discriminatory laws and regulations.

The Abbotts would play a leading role in the life of the city for decades to come. They ran a tobacco shop on King Street, found success in real estate, and helped to establish a new church. When Mackenzie's army gathered on Yonge Street, Wilson Ruffin Abbott was there, taking up arms against the rebels at the Battle of Montgomery's Tavern as a volunteer in the militia. A few years later, he ran for office and won a seat on city council. He would eventually become an important member of the Reform Party.

The Abbotts raised their son to follow in their illustrious footsteps. Anderson Ruffin Abbott was born during the year of the rebellion, and was still just a few months old when his father marched up Yonge Street. His parents made sure he got the best possible education, including a few years at Oberlin College in Ohio, the very first American college to accept black students. Then, he came back home to study medicine at the University of Toronto.

It was an education he would put to good use.

Abbott grew up watching his parents work hard in the fight against slavery. Back in Alabama, they'd done what they could, using profits from their store to buy the freedom of several slaves. In Canada, they continued that work, buying freedom for even more people, supporting the Anti-Slavery Society of Canada, and founding the Queen Victoria Benevolent Society to help black women arriving in Toronto as refugees.

When Lieutenant Governor Bond Head sparked a riot by ordering that an escaped slave should be sent back to his American "master," it was the Abbotts who gave the man refuge in their home until things calmed down. They did everything they could to ensure Canada would be a more welcoming place for black Americans fleeing the oppression of the United States. Thanks in large part to the Abbotts and other prominent black families in the city, Toronto was quickly gaining a reputation as a relatively safe haven for escaped slaves — an important destination at the end of the Underground Railroad.

Their son was eager to do his part, too. And he would soon get his chance. The very same year Anderson Ruffin Abbott left medical school, the American Civil War broke out south of the border. A couple of years later, President Lincoln issued the Emancipation Proclamation, legally freeing all of the slaves in the Southern states. Up to that point, Lincoln had always denied it, but now there was no doubt: the Civil War was a war against slavery.

The Canadian provinces, as part of the British Empire, were officially neutral. But that didn't stop tens of thousands of Canadians from heading south to join the war — most of them on the Union side. Thousands of them were black Canadians determined to do their part to end American slavery forever. Some estimates suggest that more than 13 percent of all the black residents of Canada West left the province to join the Union war effort.

Dr. Abbott was one of them. Within weeks of the Emancipation Proclamation, he was making his own preparations to head south. That summer, he would travel to Washington, D.C., to join the Union cause as a surgeon under contract to the Yankee army.

"I am a Canadian," he later explained, "first and last and all the time, but that did not deter me from sympathizing with a nation struggling to wipe out an inequality." It was, he said, "a struggle between beautiful right and ugly wrong — it determined whether civilization or barbarism should rule, whether freedom or slavery should prevail upon this continent."

It was the summer of 1863. Washington was overflowing with people. Just a few years earlier, it had been a sleepy government town. Now, it was the lively hub of the entire Union war effort. As the war dragged on, the population was skyrocketing. Dozens of new military forts, depots, factories, and warehouses sprang up all over town. Soldiers were everywhere. Countless refugees streamed into the city — tens of thousands of them were newly escaped slaves, drawn to the capital by the promise of a new, better life.

Some of them never found it. To handle the influx of fleeing slaves, Lincoln's government was opening refugee camps across the country, but at some the conditions were so terrible that freed slaves were asking to go back to their old "masters." Several of the camps opened in Washington; the first was Camp Barker, built on a patch of marshy ground just a couple of kilometres north of the White House. In the camp's first six months, 10 percent of the refugees there died — an average of five a day.

As Camp Barker's administrators struggled to make improvements, they decided to put a new doctor in charge of the camp's small medical facility. The new head of the Freedmen's Hospital would be the very first black doctor ever put in charge of a hospital anywhere in the United States. His name was Dr. Alexander T. Augusta. And he just happened to be Abbott's mentor.

Dr. Augusta was born in Virginia, but when he tried to enroll in medical school, he discovered that his applications to American universities were all being rejected because of the colour of his skin. So, in the end he headed north instead. He studied at Trinity College at the University of Toronto. (Today, the college grounds have become Trinity Bellwoods Park.) When he graduated, it was as the first black student to graduate from medical school in Canadian history.

He, too, played an important role in the life of the city: he ran his own practice, opened a pharmacy on Yonge Street (one door south of Elm), supported the Anti-Slavery Society, and set up a charity to donate books and school supplies to black children. When Abbott was looking for an experienced surgeon to show him the ropes, it was Dr. Augusta who agreed to take him on as a student.

Just days after Lincoln issued the Emancipation Proclamation, Augusta wrote the president a letter from Toronto asking to join the Union Army as a doctor. After initially being rejected by a racist examination board, he was eventually commissioned as the army's first black surgeon. A few months later, he found himself in Washington running the Freedmen's Hospital.

Still, even as a major in the army, Augusta faced a torrent of racism. Something as simple as taking public transit could turn into a life-threatening ordeal.

His refusal to give up his seat on a streetcar in Washington led to him being kicked off the vehicle entirely. His subsequent complaint led to the first laws banning discrimination on the city's transit system. And when he rode the streetcar in Baltimore — a northern city, but one that still clung to slavery for a year after Lincoln outlawed it in the South — he was nearly killed for it. This time, he was viciously attacked; the assailants tore the major's stripes from his uniform. His face was bloodied by a punch and he was pursued through the streets by an angry mob of hundreds before he was finally able to make his escape from the city — and that was only after a group of soldiers came to his aid, drawing their revolvers on the crowd.

Once, while examining new black recruits, Abbott was pelted by a hail of rocks. On another occasion, white doctors serving under him demanded to be transferred. One of them wrote a letter of complaint to a senator: being forced to serve under a black man, the assistant surgeon wrote, was "grave, unjust and humiliating."

But no matter how much racism he was subjected to, Augusta refused to be intimidated. "He had," Abbott once said of his mentor, "the bulldog tenacity of temperament which cannot be deterred by fear."

Abbott would need some of that determination himself.

In July, he left Toronto bound for D.C.; he was going to join Dr. Augusta at the Freedmen's Hospital. Augusta's wife, Mary, was travelling down with him. But on their way to Washington, they had to catch a connecting train in New York City. They arrived in the Big Apple at dusk on one of the most dangerous Friday nights in the history of the city. Lincoln had just instituted a draft. New Yorkers were furious, and they were about to turn their violent rage on their black neighbours.

While the two travellers from Toronto were waiting for their ten o'clock train, a man bumped into Mary Augusta, pretending to be drunk, using it as an excuse to launch into an aggressively racist rant. A large friend soon joined him. Things were getting dangerous. When they saw their chance, Dr. Abbott and Mary Augusta ran for their lives.

They were relatively lucky. They were able to escape, fleeing through the darkened streets and then lying low in an oyster bar until it was time to catch their train. Many others in New York City that weekend weren't as fortunate. On Sunday, the anger against the draft sparked the biggest riot in American history. By the time the authorities regained control days later, more than a hundred black New Yorkers had been killed.

But Abbott, thankfully, was safely in Washington by then, where he took his place at the Freedmen's Hospital. Eventually, Abbott would take over for Augusta as surgeon-in-chief. And in time, two more black doctors from Canada West came south to serve under him. Abbott spent two years at Camp Barker, fighting an uphill battle against death and disease. Many of those who stumbled into camp were in terrible shape: newly freed slaves weakened by a lifetime of abuse at the hands of their "masters," or soldiers suffering from the savagery of war. Even on good days, the hospital was overcrowded; it spilled out from the main building into leaky tents pitched on the damp, marshy ground. There weren't enough supplies. There wasn't enough food. Clean water was so hard to find that the doctors couldn't always rinse their instruments between surgeries, never mind properly cleaning them.

Sometimes, things were even worse. Abbott once described the horrors he witnessed on the nights after big battles were fought. An endless parade of horse-drawn ambulances poured into hospitals all over Washington, delivering a deluge of the dead and wounded. On those nights, the doctors rolled up their sleeves and worked themselves to the point of exhaustion, hour after hour until the sun rose, covered in blood and gore as they sawed away at limbs and stitched bodies back together, trying desperately to keep their suffering patients alive. At times, there were so many wounded soldiers flooding into Washington that all sixteen of the city's hospitals were overwhelmed — authorities scrambled to find extra space; patients were treated on the floor of the Senate and the House of Representatives. And still the wounded came.

"I have never worked so hard," one of the other Canadian surgeons wrote in a letter home, "had so little rest, and felt so tired as I do now."

The Civil War would prove to be the bloodiest war the United States had ever fought. Three hundred thousand people died before it was over. Month after month, the blood kept flowing. But ever so slowly, the Union was winning.

Finally, just before Easter 1865, Richmond fell. The Confederate capital was in Yankee hands. Days later, the rebel general Robert E. Lee surrendered. The war was over.

Washington burst into celebration. For nearly a week, the people of the capital took to the streets. They danced and drank and sang. Dr. Abbott joined them, marvelling at the city draped in light and decoration, and "the intense feeling of joy which thrilled the heart of the nation."

Even six days later, on Good Friday, the party was still going strong. That night after dinner, Abbott went to see the festivities being held in honour of the secretary of war, watching as the cheerful procession made its way toward the secretary's house. The torches carried by the crowd were, he said, "like a fiery serpent winding its sinuous course through the streets and avenues of the city." Bands played. The secretary gave a speech. And when it was all over, Abbott headed to a friend's house to keep the party going.

But it didn't last much longer. Abbott and the other revellers were just about to break into song — the first few happy chords rang out on the piano — when there was a knock at the door. Someone had come to give them the terrible news.

Abraham Lincoln had been shot. The party was over.

Abbott knew Lincoln. They had first met more than a year earlier — at the White House on New Year's Day. It was Dr. Augusta's idea that he and Abbott should attend the annual New Year's levee, a purposefully bold suggestion:

he was determined to break yet another colour barrier by becoming the very first black guests in the history of the event.

"The White House was a blaze of light," Abbott later wrote. "Soldiers were guarding the entrance. Carriages containing handsomely dressed ladies, citizens and soldiers were continually depositing the elite of Washington at the entrance of the porch. Music was wafted to our ears from the marine band which was stationed in the Conservatory. Ushers, lackeys, waiters, messengers were scurrying here and there attending to guests."

When Abbott and Augusta walked in, both dressed in their striking blue Union uniforms, they created quite a stir. The Washington elite gawked at them through their monocles and lorgnettes, some curious, some welcoming, some openly hostile. The two doctors did their best to act as if the attention wasn't bothering them — they pretended to take an intense interest in the paintings on the walls — but it wasn't easy.

"I felt as though I should have liked to crawl into a hole," Abbott admitted. "But as we had decided to break the record we held our ground. I bit my lips, took Augusta's arm and sauntered around the room ... Wherever we went a space was cleared for us and we became the centre of a new circle of interest."

Lincoln was thrilled. Some of his guests might have had their reservations, but when the president spotted the doctors on their way in, he was quick to welcome them, eager to shake their hands. When his son, Robert Todd Lincoln, interrupted to express his own doubts, the president brushed him off. It was the first day of a new year and the first anniversary of the Emancipation Proclamation. It was about time for things to change.

After that, it's not entirely clear how much Abbott and Lincoln kept in touch. But many sources say they became friends — after Lincoln's death, the *New York Weekly News* went so far as to call Abbott "one of his warmest friends." At the very least, they had one very good friend in common.

Elizabeth Keckley had been born into slavery in Virginia, but she bought her own freedom and moved to Washington before the war began. In the capital she worked as a seamstress, making dresses for some of the city's most powerful women. She quickly found herself among those at the very top of society, working as the personal stylist to Mary Todd Lincoln. Soon, she was the First Lady's closest confidant.

Keckley was also very good friends with Mary Augusta. Back in Toronto, the doctor's wife had run her own dress-making shop on York Street (between Adelaide and Richmond) — it was the only business in the city owned by a black woman. So when she came south to join her husband in D.C., she and Keckley had plenty to talk about.

Now, as President Lincoln lay dying, his distraught wife wanted her close friend by her side. She sent four messengers out into the night looking for the seamstress. One of them, presumably knowing Keckley was friends with Abbott and the Augustas, came knocking on Abbott's door.

By then, it was late: about two in the morning. Abbott was fast asleep. It had already been a long night. In the hours since the president was shot, Abbott and his friends had ended their party, heading out into the streets to see if they could learn anything more about the fate of the president. When they got to the house of the secretary of state — whose throat had been cut in a second, coordinated attack by one of Booth's accomplices — they found an upset crowd quickly turning into an angry mob. The mood in the city was turning sour, even dangerous. Innocent bystanders were accused of being part of the plot; some wanted to hang them.

"For the first time during my stay in Washington," Abbott later admitted, "I was troubled with a feeling of uncertainty regarding my safety.... The night had become very dark, and Washington streets at that time were ... but dimly lighted with gas, and the dark shadows of alleys, areas, and porches affording convenient lurking-places for garroters, murderers, assassins, and thieves."

But Abbott's night wasn't over yet. He offered to escort Keckley on her way to Lincoln's bedside. They pushed through the throngs of mourners outside the White House — assuming the president was there — and then finally headed to the boarding house across from Ford's Theatre.

As they approached the boarding house, they were stopped by a cordon of soldiers. But a note to the soon-to-be-widow got them inside. Mary Todd Lincoln couldn't even bring herself to stay in the same room as her dying husband; Abbott said she was "lying in an adjoining room prostrate with anguish."

Meanwhile, in a small bedroom on the first floor, the president rested, naked beneath his sheets, lying diagonally across the mattress as the life gradually ebbed out of him, his tall frame too long for the tiny bed. His chest rose and fell with laboured breathing, his pulse weak, his expression calm and still. Soon after being shot, his right eye had begun to swell; his face darkened into a deep bruise. As his limbs went cold, those at his bedside did what they could to keep him warm and comfortable: plenty of blankets; hot water bottles; mustard plasters for his chest. And then, they waited.

At twenty after seven the next morning, all the church bells in Washington began to ring. Abraham Lincoln was dead.

Lincoln's funeral would be a massive, three-week spectacle of mourning spread across more than a dozen cities. It would begin at the White House, where the president's body lay in state. Twenty-five thousand people came to see him there. Dr. Abbott was one of them, paying his respects in the very same room where he and Augusta had defiantly stared at the paintings during the New Year's levee. The following day, the president's body was moved to the Capitol Building for the funeral service. As his coffin was carried through the streets, the bells of all the churches and all the fire halls rang out. Cannons thundered a salute once every minute. Thirty marching bands played funeral dirges with muffled drums. All the buildings were draped in black.

After Washington, Lincoln's body would tour another dozen cities in seven states. Huge crowds gathered along the tracks as the funeral train carried him to Philadelphia, New York, Buffalo, Chicago.... In Baltimore, people filled the streets as the president's coffin was carried through the city in a solemn procession. At the head of seventy-five thousand troops, Dr. Augusta was proudly riding in his Union blue uniform — given a place of honour in the same city where he'd nearly been killed for riding a streetcar just two years earlier.

Mary Todd Lincoln missed it all. She was too upset to attend her husband's funeral, refusing to leave her room in the White House, turning away all visitors except for her closest loved ones. "I shall never forget the scene," Elizabeth Keckley remembered in her autobiography, "the wails of a broken heart, the unearthly shrieks, the terrible convulsions, the wild tempestuous outbursts of grief from the soul."

Eventually, though, the new widow would have to leave the White House. Before she did, she made sure those with a special connection to her husband were presented with a posthumous token of his affection. Abbott received Lincoln's famous shawl.

Lincoln had worn it often on chilly nights when he went to meet with the secretary of war. But long before the war started, the shawl had already become a powerful symbol of just how divided the nation was, and how much racial hatred had to be overcome. The southern states were outraged when Lincoln won the presidential election. They quickly announced their intention to leave the union, and rumours of assassination were everywhere. On his way into Washington for the inauguration,

Lincoln's security team took every possible precaution. They convinced the president-elect to wear a disguise. He slouched to hide his height, donned a hat and an overcoat, and finally pulled a plaid shawl over his shoulders. He hurried through the train station — briefly startled by a congressman who recognized him despite the thin disguise — and rushed to the safety of his hotel room. Even there he wasn't free from the threats: he found a letter waiting for him — a hateful, racist screed, which ended by calling him the n-word.

Four years later, the danger had finally caught up with him. But not before he and countless others had won the fight against American slavery. Now, his shawl would be heading to Toronto, the treasured possession of one of the thousands of black Canadians who had rushed south to join that fight.

Back home in Canada, Dr. Abbott would continue to dedicate his life to the causes he believed in. He fought for black rights and against segregated schools. He worked at the Toronto General Hospital and taught medicine to a new generation of students. And he became one of the earliest advocates for the importance of remembering Toronto's past, joining the city's first local history group: the York Pioneers & Historical Society. Abbott was especially passionate when he was telling the story of black Canadians in the Civil War — a story he could see was already being forgotten in his later years, as a new century dawned and the horrors of the First World War approached.

"I am now an old man," he said in those later years, "and as I grow older, I appreciate more highly the part (though humble) I took ... in securing the humblest citizen ... whether he lives under the protecting folds of the red cross of St. George, or the glorious star spangled banner, the blessings of peace, civil and religious liberty, and in giving to the world a higher conception of the value of human liberty."

16
CANNONBALL

Bases loaded. Bottom of the eighth. This was it: first place was on the line. Toronto and Newark came into that Saturday afternoon battling for the lead in the International League. With only a couple of weeks left in the 1887 season, every win was vitally important. And with just one inning left in their second game of the day, the Toronto Baseball Club was losing to Newark by three runs.

That's when Ned "Cannonball" Crane came to the plate. He was the ace of the Toronto pitching staff — big and tall and impossibly strong. He once threw a ball more than four hundred feet — a world record; impressive even by today's standards — and he could throw a ball faster than anybody else could, too. He was one of the game's first big power pitchers. He combined the blistering speed of his fastball with breaking pitches that he called "snakes": twisters, in-curves, out-curves, and a "deceptive drop ball" that baffled opposing hitters. It was a deadly combination. He won thirty-three games for Toronto that year — more than any other pitcher has ever won on *any* Toronto team.

He could hit, too. Crane was one of the best hitters in the whole league that year. His .428 batting average is still considered to be the best by a pitcher in professional baseball history. (If he'd hit that in the Major Leagues, it would put him sixth on the all-time list — for *any* position.) On the days when Crane wasn't pitching, he was in the outfield or at second base so they could keep his bat in the lineup.

On that Saturday afternoon in September, Crane had already done more than his fair share. Toronto and Newark were playing a doubleheader: two games at Toronto's new stadium at Queen and Broadview, on a spot overlooking the Don Valley.

It was Toronto's first baseball stadium. Originally known as the Toronto Baseball Grounds, it would soon be nicknamed Sunlight Park in honour of the nearby Sunlight Soap factory. Spectators could walk in off Queen Street or ride up in their carriages and park their horses on the grounds. Admission was a quarter — plus an extra dime or two to sit in the best seats in the house. The sheltered grandstand had enough room for more than two thousand people, and there was standing room for another ten thousand beyond that — not that much smaller than the Air Canada Centre's capacity today. A sellout meant that one of out every ten Torontonians was at the ballpark that day. And the stadium had never seen attendance like this. Those two games against Newark drew a record-setting crowd.

In the first game, Crane pitched all nine innings, keeping the Newark hitters at bay while the Toronto bats smashed their way to victory. The final score was 15–5.

But there was still one more game left to win. And Toronto had already used up their ace. The scheduled pitcher for the second game was a fellow by the name of Baker — and as the time for the first pitch drew near, he was out on the field warming up, just as everyone expected.

Then, a surprise: as the Toronto team took the field to start the second game, Baker didn't head toward the pitcher's box. Instead, it was Cannonball Crane who came back to take his spot in the middle of the diamond.

A reporter from the *Globe* was there: "As soon as it was made clear that Crane was to pitch the second game, hundreds leaped to their feet and cheered frantically, a mighty whirl of enthusiasm took everybody within its embrace and an astounding volume of sound shook the stands and swept down toward the city and out over the grounds like the march of a tornado."

Cannonball Crane was going to pitch two games in one day.

Still, even with Crane in the pitcher's box, the second game didn't get off to a good start. Toronto fell behind and stayed there. It wasn't until the eighth inning — behind by three runs — that they rallied to load the bases, bringing Cannonball to the plate with a chance to play the hero.

That's exactly what he did. The slugger hit a double, clearing the bases. Three runs scored. The game was tied.

As they headed into extra innings, Crane kept pitching. He held Newark scoreless in the tenth. And then again in the eleventh. He had now pitched twenty innings in a single afternoon.

In the bottom of the eleventh, Crane came to the plate with a chance to play the hero yet again. He crushed a pitch high into the sun above the Don Valley: deep ... deeeep ... gone. A walk-off home run. Toronto had won both games. According to the *Globe*, as Crane rounded the bases "the mighty audience arose and cheered and stamped and whistled and smashed hats ... the frantic fans dashed on to the field and carried Crane aloft as his foot touched home."

The team's owner — a stockbroker by the name of E. Strachan Cox — headed over to the scoreboard. He wrote a message for the crowd:

"CITIZENS, ARE YOU CONTENT? TORONTO LEADS THE LEAGUE."

The team was now in first place — and they would stay there for the rest of the season, winning every single game for the rest of the year. By the time it was all over, they'd won sixteen in a row. Toronto had its very first baseball championship.

It was the first of many. The Toronto Baseball Club eventually morphed into the Toronto Maple Leafs (decades before the hockey team took the same name); they won nine more International League pennants before they were sold and moved to Kentucky in the 1960s. Some of those Maple Leafs teams are still considered to be among the best minor league teams ever to play the sport.

Sadly, Toronto's big hero wouldn't be back for the 1888 season. Instead, Cannonball signed with the New York Giants, helping them to win the National League pennant and then the "World's Series" — the precursor to the

World Series. He threw a no-hitter that year, and became one of the very first pitchers to wear a glove while fielding.

But that season was the beginning of the end. Things began to unravel for the pitcher almost as soon as he left Toronto.

At the end of that first season with the Giants, Crane was invited to join Spalding's World Tour. The biggest stars in baseball signed up for a trip around the world, showcasing the sport to other countries. They played games on the grounds of the Crystal Palace in London, outside the Villa Borghese in Rome, in the shadow of the Eiffel Tower while it was still being built, and at the foot of a rumbling Mount Vesuvius ... plus Australia, New Zealand, Ireland, Scotland, Samoa, the Arabian peninsula, Ceylon ... After they played a game on the sands of the Giza Plateau, they had contests to see who could throw a baseball over the Great Pyramid or hit the Sphinx in the eye.

The problem was that when the players weren't on the field, they were drinking, gambling, and partying their way around the world. They say that Cannonball had gone his entire life without ever having had a single drink — right up until the days just before the tour began. "Crane," one newspaper reported, "did not know what the taste of liquor was like until he made the trip around the world. He got his start drinking wine at the banquets tendered the American tourists."

And as Cannonball quickly discovered, he liked to drink. He liked it a lot.

It was an issue right from the very beginning of the tour. On Crane's first night, in San Francisco, he got so trashed that he couldn't even play the next day. The day after that, he did manage to drag himself out onto the field, but his pitching performance was a complete debacle: he gave up twelve runs to a minor league team from Oakland. They hadn't even left the United States yet and Crane was already a mess.

He spent much of the tour serving as a sluggish umpire with a hangover and heatstroke instead of actually playing in the games. At some stops, he never even got off the ship — choosing instead to get drunk on board with his tiny, troublemaking pet monkey, entertaining his fellow passengers by breaking into song. At one point, he had a standoff with soldiers at the French-Italian border when they insisted he should pay an extra fare for his simian companion.

The Giants repeated as World's Series champions the next year. Cannonball was back in the pitcher's box, serving as their ace, winning four games in the series. But as he continued to drink, his weight ballooned and he lost his effectiveness as a pitcher. His final year in the majors was a disaster: a 6.98 earned run average over twelve games. He was released by the Giants (twice), signed by Brooklyn, and then released by them, too. Things were spiralling out of control.

People in Toronto still loved him, though. In 1895, he returned to play for the Toronto Baseball Club. But he wasn't the same. After an uninspiring beginning to the season, he was released for what the *Toronto Evening Star* called "alleged sulkiness on the field." The team across the lake in Rochester then signed him and gave him another shot, but Crane didn't even show up for his first game with them.

He made his final appearance at Sunlight Park in the summer of 1896. He was playing for Springfield now. The Toronto fans gave him a warm welcome as he came out onto the field, but it was a bittersweet reunion. By then, Crane weighed nearly three hundred pounds. His glory days were far behind him. He was no match for the Toronto bats.

There was a time, as the *Globe* remembered, when Crane's name had "inspired dread among all other players.... But that is but a hazy memory. The once mighty name has lost its magic. It no longer inspires dread and fear.... He essayed to pitch for Springfield against Toronto over the Don yesterday afternoon, and he made a sorry exhibition of himself.... It would be painful to go into the details of the game." Soon, Springfield gave up on him too.

Finished as a player, Cannonball tried to find work as an umpire. But even that was a failure. At thirty-four years old, he was unemployed and alcoholic, his wife and child had left him, and he was slipping into depression.

"Crane sank deeper into the bottle as his prospects and money quickly ran out," according to the Society for American Baseball Research. "He became despondent, freely talking about his troubles and the grim outlook for his future wherever he went."

Cannonball wouldn't live to see the end of that 1896 season. On a Saturday in mid-September — almost nine years to the day since his glorious doubleheader in Toronto — he spent the afternoon getting drunk in his room at the Congress Hall hotel in Rochester. He hadn't paid his bill in ages. When he went downstairs, the owner warned him that if he didn't fork over the seventy dollars he owed, he would be forced to give up his room. Crane promised to settle his bill. And then he headed back upstairs.

There was a bottle of chloral waiting for him.

The next morning, the maid couldn't open the door. A bellboy climbed up to peer through the transom to find Cannonball laid out on his bed. Dead. The official coroner's report described it as an accidental overdose. But everyone assumed it was suicide.

The next morning, he was remembered on the front page of the Toronto newspapers. His life had come to a tragic end, but thanks to those two games in the thick of a pennant race one Saturday afternoon in September, the name of Cannonball Crane lived on. He'd become an indelible part of Toronto sports lore, mentioned over and over again in local newspapers over the course of the next century — remembered fondly for bringing the city its very first baseball championship.

17
A BRIEF HISTORY OF THE PIGEONS OF TORONTO

Pigeons have been living with people for as long as any-one can remember. They were among the first animals humans ever domesticated — back in the days of prehistory. Pigeons are already there in some of the oldest records we have: Egyptian hieroglyphics, Mesopotamian tablets from five thousand years ago, the epic of Gilgamesh.... Julius Caesar and Genghis Khan used them to send messages during battle. The ancient Greeks used them to announce the results of the first Olympic Games. The Greeks *and* the Romans *and* the Phoenicians all used them as a symbol of the goddess of love. White doves, which are really just white pigeons, are still a symbol of peace today.

The domestic birds were selectively bred over thousands of years into a kaleidoscope of colours and characteristics. But they're all descended from wild rock doves. The species has been around for about twenty million years — so, about a third of the way back to the dinosaurs (when *we* were still living in trees). They evolved in Asia before spreading to Europe and Africa and they're still around today. They all look pretty much like your standard template pigeon: blue-grey with black stripes on their wings and iridescent purple-green necks. They live on sea cliffs and on mountainsides, and thanks to their super-powers they can almost always find their way back home. Scientists think pigeons might be able to sense the Earth's magnetic field. And they're crazy-smart, too: you can train them to recognize the letters of the alphabet and their own reflection in a mirror. One scientist taught them to tell the difference between a Monet and a Picasso. They're smart enough to use landmarks to find their way home.

That homing instinct is what made pigeons such a useful species to domesticate: if you want to send a message, you can just take a pigeon to the place you want to send the message from and then let the bird fly home with it. They can cover thousands of kilometres. They're fast, too: they can get up to almost a hundred kilometres per hour over short distances. That's faster than a cheetah.

Some of those domestic pigeons never did fly home, though. Instead, they went feral. Back on the other side of the Atlantic, they've been doing it since the days of antiquity. In towns and in villages and in cities, they found tall buildings and temples and cathedrals that were a lot like the sea cliffs and mountainsides they were originally evolved for, using them to roost and nest. They also found lots of food. Pigeons can eat all sorts of things. And unlike most birds (or mammals, for that matter), both female and male pigeons can turn that food into a kind of regurgitated milk for their baby squabs. They grow up quick and they multiply fast. They can start pumping out babies when they're just six months old and can do it over and over and over again. When conditions are right: six times a year.

They also, more adorably, mate for life.

It was the French who first brought them to the Americas. In 1606, a ship docked in Nova Scotia at the colony of Port-Royal, which had just been founded by Samuel de Champlain. On board were the very first rock doves ever to be shipped across the Atlantic. Champlain figured the birds would bring a touch of European civilization to New France — and make good meat pies. When he founded Quebec City a couple of years later, a pigeon-loft was part of the original settlement. As Europeans spread out across the continent, domestic pigeons — and their feral descendants — went with them.

But they weren't alone. North America already had lots of pigeons before the Europeans arrived. There were passenger pigeons by the *billions*.

When Samuel de Champlain first arrived, they were everywhere. In his diary, he describes them as "infinite." At their peak, there were flocks of millions of them flying all over the eastern half of the continent, including what we now call southern Ontario. Their nesting grounds covered vast stretches of forest. A single tree could hold a hundred nests; branches buckled and cracked under the weight while droppings covered the ground like snow. In the spring and in the fall, they would migrate in enormous numbers. One naturalist near Niagara-on-the-Lake watched a flock head south into the United States for fourteen straight hours. They formed a column a kilometre and a half wide and five hundred kilometres long. And that was nothing. Sometimes, they could blot out the sun for days.

Passenger pigeons were bigger than their rock dove cousins, with longer necks and longer tails. People called them "graceful" and "dashing." Their colour was a little bit like a mourning dove's or a robin's: brownish-blue-grey on top with a pinkish-red breast. "When they flew to the east of you so that the sun shone on them there was a perfect riot of colour as they passed," the *Owen Sound Daily Sun Times* wrote, "the sheen of their plumage in the evening sun was such that no words could be found to describe nor a painter to paint it. The flash of brilliant colour and the wonderful whirr of their wings in flight as they passed within a few yards can never be forgotten."

One of the most stirring descriptions of the birds comes from Chief Simon Pokagon of the Potawatomi. He wrote about them in a newspaper called *The Chautauquan* in 1895:

> If the Great Spirit in His wisdom could have created a more elegant bird in plumage, form, and movement, He never did.... I have stood for hours admiring the movements of these birds. I have seen them fly in unbroken lines from the horizon, one line succeeding another from morning until night, moving their unbroken columns like an army

of trained soldiers pushing to the front. At other times, I have seen them move in one unbroken column for hours across the sky, like some great river, ever varying in hue; and as the mighty stream, sweeping on at sixty miles an hour, reached some deep valley, it would pour its living mass headlong down hundreds of feet, sounding as though a whirlwind was abroad in the land. I have stood by the grandest waterfall of America and regarded the descending torrents in wonder and astonishment, yet never have my astonishment, wonder, and admiration been so stirred as when I have witnessed these birds drop from their course like meteors from heaven.

He called them "the most beautiful flowers of the animal creation of North America."

In Toronto, the birds most famously congregated on the banks of Mimico Creek in Etobicoke. They would rest there before making the flight south across the lake. In fact, that's how Mimico got its name: it's derived from the Mississauga word *omiimiikaa*, which means "abundant with wild pigeons."

It wasn't just Mimico, though. The birds were all over town. In 1793, Elizabeth Simcoe described flocks of passenger pigeons so thick you could tie a bullet to a string and knock them down with it. There are stories of enormous flocks flying up the Don Valley every spring, soaring over the Islands, and spending the night in the Beaches. In Don Mills, people remembered a flock that once took an entire morning to fly by. In Cabbagetown, they remembered one that took days. Children were paid to shoot at them, to scare them away from farmers' fields. In Mimico, they said you could kill a dozen birds with a single shot.

When a flock passed through Toronto in the 1830s, hunters went on a killing spree. "For three or four days the town resounded with one continued roll of firing," a writer later remembered, "as if a skirmish were going on in the streets." At first, the authorities tried to control the slaughter, but soon they gave up: "a sporting jubilee was proclaimed to all and sundry."

The area around Sherbourne and Bloor became known as the Pigeon Green, where hunters would wait for the birds to descend into the valley — bringing them within easy firing range. In the city's early days, passenger pigeons were a staple of the Torontonian diet. They were fried, roasted, stewed, and turned into soups and pies.

The hunting of passenger pigeons became a major industry. The flocks had always been harvested by the First Nations, but now the slaughter was waged on a massive scale. At some sites in the United States, tens of thousands of birds were killed every day for months on end: shot, trapped in giant nets, poisoned with whisky, burned in trees set on fire to drive newborn squabs out of their nests. Entire railway cars were packed full of them and shipped away to be sold as meat and mattress stuffing. You could buy them nearly everywhere, including the St. Lawrence Market.

The hunts took a staggering toll. So did the logging industry, which grew by leaps and bounds in the 1800s, destroying the ancient forests where the pigeons lived. All over eastern North America, the birds were being wiped out at a breathtaking pace. In just a few short decades, they went from being quite probably the single most populous bird species on Earth to the brink of extinction. Some estimates claim there were a quarter of a million birds dying every day.

Many people refused to believe what was happening. As the number of passenger pigeons plunged, concerns about overhunting were dismissed by critics as "groundless," "absurd," and "without foundation." Even some people who did admit the population was crashing refused to believe humans were responsible. They came up with alternative theories: some said the birds had all drowned in the ocean or in Lake Michigan; some said they'd flown away to Australia, or died in a forest fire, or froze to death at the North Pole.

By the end of the 1800s, the birds had almost completely disappeared from the wild. The Toronto Gun Club had to start shipping them in from Buffalo for their annual hunt. By the time the Ontario government finally got around to protecting them in 1897, there were barely any passenger pigeons left to protect.

The last two to be killed in Toronto were caught in the fall of 1890. Ten years later, someone said they saw five of them fly over the Islands. That was the very last time a passenger pigeon was ever seen in Toronto. In 1914, the last member of the species — a twenty-five-year-old named

Martha — toppled off her perch at the Cincinnati Zoological Garden. Passenger pigeons were officially extinct.

By then, rock doves had taken over Toronto.

In the early 1900s, domesticated pigeons were still being used in much the same way they'd always been used. Every year at the Canadian National Exhibition, pigeon owners raced thousands of birds. At the Royal Winter Fair, they awarded prizes to the best-bred — they still do. Some were used as game for hunting. Others were used to fight in the world wars: the Canadian Army enlisted pigeons to deliver messages just like the ancient Romans did thousands of years ago. It was a pigeon called Beach Comber who brought back the first word of the disastrous landing at Dieppe. They gave the bird a medal for it.

The feral descendants of those domestic pigeons took to the skyscrapers and bridges of Toronto just like they'd done in cities all over the world. You can see them flying above the city's muddy downtown streets in archival photographs from more than a century ago. Most of them are many generations removed from their captive ancestors; they've reverted to the blue-grey colouring of wild rock doves. But some are still white or pink or brown or speckled or spotted, the genetic heritage of their domestic great-grandparents.

Still, not all of Toronto's wild pigeons are rock doves from the far side of the ocean. There's one native species that still calls the city home — the closest living relative of the passenger pigeons. These birds used to be called turtle doves, or rain doves, or Carolina pigeons. Today, we call them mourning doves because their gentle hoots sound like a person crying.

They were here when the first Europeans arrived, too, but in much smaller numbers than passenger pigeons. Instead of dense woods, they preferred open spaces. As the forests of the passenger pigeons disappeared and were replaced by farmers' fields, mourning doves prospered. Today, there are something like four hundred million of them: they live all over the warmer half of the continent.

Some scientists hope those mourning doves will soon be rejoined by their extinct cousins. The Great Passenger Pigeon Comeback project is using cutting-edge genomics in an attempt to bring the species back from the dead. To find the passenger pigeon DNA they needed, they turned to Toronto. The Royal Ontario Museum boasts the largest collection of passenger pigeon specimens in the world. If all goes to plan, the DNA from those Toronto birds will be used to bring the species back to life and to reintroduce it into the wild, helping to restore forests to their natural cycles. If the ambitious project succeeds, it may just be a matter of time before passenger pigeons fill the skies above Toronto once again.

18
THE TOOTH

I t's easy to miss. It's far from the most impressive-looking artifact in the room. It spends its days sitting in a glass case at the Royal Ontario Museum surrounded by the bones of dinosaurs and other prehistoric beasts, including mammoths, sabre-toothed cats, and giant sloths. It's just a few inches long: a curved fragment of fossil. But for a tooth, it's huge — and it tells a remarkable story about Toronto from a long, long time before the city was founded.

The tooth was found more than a century ago in the Don Valley. It's thought one of the workers at the newly opened Don Valley Brick Works must have found it and passed it along to the city's most celebrated mustachioed geologist: Arthur Philemon Coleman. In the late 1800s, the U of T professor studied the earth at the new brickyard extensively, becoming the first geologist to realize the importance of the cliff that stands on the northern edge of the site.

Layer by layer, the exposed earth shows traces of the last two ice ages coming and going — the rocks, dirt, and boulders tell of the enormous glaciers that covered the land in ice, melted away, and then returned over and over again. It's the only place in the region where you can see all of that history laid out in front of you: a record of the last 135,000 years written into the land.

The tooth wasn't the only fossil in that cliff. Coleman and his team uncovered the remains of many animals who lived in Toronto during the relatively warmer periods when the ice receded. At various times, the place where the Evergreen Brick Works now stands was home to mammoths, mastodons, and muskoxen. There were giant bears. Massive, ancient bison. Woodchucks and white-tailed deer. Prehistoric stag-moose, bigger even than moose are today, with immense sets of antlers.

At the very bottom of the cliff, the fossils are from an even more distant time. The Don Valley is one of the places where the shale bedrock beneath the city is exposed. It's 450 million years old, filled with the fossils of the strange marine creatures who swam through the waters of Toronto when the city was covered by an enormous inland sea. Trilobites. Sponges. Coral. Huge, tentacled cephalopods, some three metres long, ancestors of today's octopuses and nautiluses.

It must have been in one of the layers right near the very top of the cliff that the tooth was uncovered. It belonged to one of the last ice age residents of Toronto, an aquatic beast who lived in the area about 24,000 years ago, just before the glaciers covered the land for one last time.

The giant tooth belonged to a giant prehistoric beaver.

The giant beaver was one of the largest rodents ever to have walked the earth. It could grow to be as much as seven feet long and weigh more than two hundred pounds: the size of a black bear. Its teeth were six inches long, but scientists aren't sure if they were used to chop down trees as beavers do today — giant beavers probably ate aquatic plants — and there's no evidence they built giant dams, either. Their tails were likely quite different from their modern cousins' too: longer and thinner. And they had shaggier hair.

They may have spent even less of their time on land than modern beavers do. They stuck to the swamps, swimming through marshland, feeding on aquatic reeds and long grasses. They'd been living like this, in the wetlands of North America, for two million years. But their days were numbered: as the last ice age ended, many giant beasts went extinct, including the giant beavers.

A.P. Coleman imagined what might have happened when the prehistoric beavers of Toronto died, their carcasses drifting to the bottom of an ancient ancestor of the Don River, bones scattered along the riverbed, one precious tooth left in the mud to fossilize, waiting patiently in the earth for 24,000 years.

As the 1800s came to a close, Toronto was already home to nearly two hundred thousand people, and more were arriving all the time. The city needed new buildings. New buildings needed new bricks. New bricks were made with clay. And one of the best sources for clay was discovered in the very same place where Coleman's prehistoric wetlands once stood. That's how the Don Valley Brick Works was born, turning clay into red and yellow bricks of such a high quality that they won gold medals at the Chicago World's Fair. A lot of Toronto's historic buildings are made of Brick Works bricks. Much of the city has been quite literally built from the mud of the swamps where prehistoric beasts once roamed.

Today, the Brick Works is no longer an industrial site. Instead, it has been returned to its roots: a mixture of wetlands, forests and fields. Native species of plants and animals have been reintroduced and allowed to thrive — some of them are the very same species that would have been there in the days of the giant beaver. If you get lucky, you might even spot one of the new residents: a modern, normal-sized beaver, swimming around the wetland where 24,000 years ago its giant beaver cousins did the very same thing.

19
THE CROOKED KNIGHT
OF CASA LOMA

Once upon a time, a knight called Sir Henry built himself a castle. It was magnificent, kitschy, and big. So big, in fact, that it was the biggest home anyone had ever built for themselves in the entire history of Canada. It had ninety-eight rooms. Thirty bathrooms. Twenty-five fireplaces. An elevator, a central vacuum system, and space for an indoor swimming pool. An oven so big you could cook an entire cow in it. A library with thousands of books. Plus stables, secret passages, a tunnel, a fountain, a shooting gallery, and three bowling alleys. It was built by three hundred construction workers at a cost of millions of dollars over the course of three years. It was all made possible because Sir Henry Pellatt wasn't just a knight, he was also one of the richest and most powerful business tycoons in the country. And one of the most notoriously crooked, too.

Sir Henry was born rich. His father had been one of the most powerful stockbrokers in Canada. When he retired in the late 1800s, his son inherited the business. By then, Pellatt was already an extremely well-connected young man. He'd gone to Upper Canada College, made a name for himself as a teenager by setting the world record for running the mile, and joined the prestigious Queen's Own Rifles military regiment. Plus, he was a member of all the most important gentlemen's clubs — including the Albany Club on King Street, the official Conservative party hangout.

Armed with his contacts and his dad's business, Pellatt built an even bigger fortune. He invested heavily in stocks for the Canadian West, made money off the railways, and got interested in electricity just as Edison and Tesla were about to change the world. By the time he turned thirty, Pellatt had a monopoly on all of the electric streetlights in Toronto.

If Sir Henry had his way, that was only going to be the beginning. When he and a couple of other businessmen built the first hydroelectric dam on the Canadian side of Niagara Falls, it looked like they were going to have a monopoly on all of the hydroelectric power in Ontario for a long, long time to come.

As the 1800s turned into the 1900s, Pellatt had a fortune of $17 million dollars. He was the head of more than twenty companies and on the board of a hundred more. He was listed as one of twenty-three men who controlled the entire Canadian economy. Some people say he controlled a quarter of it himself. Decades after the defeat of the Family Compact, much of the power and influence in Canada was still controlled by a precious few.

And much like the Family Compact before them, Pellatt and his colleagues were notorious for their shady business practices. Sir Henry lied to his investors, lied to his creditors, lied to the boards of directors of his own companies. He cooked books. Committed fraud. Claimed nonexistent profits. He deployed a wide variety of tricks to artificially inflate the value of his investments. When the federal government launched a royal commission to investigate this kind of unwelcome behaviour in the life insurance industry, Pellatt was specifically singled out for his practices. When his father died, Pellatt even took money from the inheritance of his own siblings.

One day, his lies would catch up with him — and when they did, Pellatt would take the life savings of thousands of innocent people and one of Canada's biggest banks with him. But before that happened, he spent money like crazy. He bought all the fanciest new products, collected art and horses and cars. He had a beautiful home on Sherbourne Avenue and a country estate north of the city. He gave generously to the charities he believed in and even helped organize the first Canadian chapter of St. John Ambulance.

But Pellatt especially liked to lavish money on his favourite militia. He'd joined the Queen's Own Rifles as a teenager, and eventually worked his way up to be commander of the unit. They fought, killed, and died in the name of Canada and the British Empire. They'd been there at the Battle of Ridgeway, fending off the Fenian invaders. They'd been sent to the Prairies to help quash Louis Riel's Northwest Rebellion. More recently, they'd gone all the way to South Africa to fight in the Great Boer War.

For the regiment's fiftieth anniversary, Sir Henry threw a massive week-long party at the Canadian National Exhibition. Every night there was a two-hour spectacle celebrating the military history of Canada: twelve hundred performers, two military bands, sprawling sets, and elaborate costumes. Ten thousand people came to see it. Pellatt's wife, Lady Mary, presided over the festivities in diamonds, rubies, and a gold crown.

That wasn't all. A few years later, as the First World War approached, Pellatt took the entire 650-man regiment to England for military manoeuvres. He paid for the whole thing himself — even brought all the horses along — and took great pride in showing the English that the Canadian military was willing and able to fight for the Empire. Just a few years later, many of those same men would be making the trip across the Atlantic once again, this time to fight and die on the Western Front.

The trip to England and the show at the CNE were both hailed as great successes. Although a couple of people did die (a soldier was killed by typhoid; an actor was impaled on the pommel of his saddle), the dark moments were overshadowed by the good. The highlight came during the trip, when Pellatt got to meet the future King George V at Balmoral Castle. It was one of the greatest moments of his life.

Pellatt, like generations of Canadian conservatives before him, was a big fan of the monarchy. When Queen Victoria celebrated her Diamond Jubilee, Pellatt went to England with some of the Queen's Own Rifles to be part of the honour guard. He even got a signed photo. When

King George was crowned, not only did Pellatt go, they say he had a commemorative medal made for nearly every single child in Toronto. His efforts were rewarded: in 1905 he talked his contacts into getting him knighted. One day, Sir Henry dreamed, he would be given a hereditary title to pass down to his son — and the Pellatt family would officially join the ranks of the British Empire's aristocracy.

And, like any self-respecting British aristocrat, Sir Henry wanted to live in a castle.

He bought himself some of the most prestigious land in the city: everything from Davenport up to St. Clair and from Bathurst to Spadina, where Toronto's oldest ruling families had once built their country estates on the hill overlooking the city. He would build his new opulent home right next door to Spadina House.

Pellatt developed part of the land as housing, but kept the rest for his castle. To build it, he hired Toronto's grandest architect: E.J. Lennox, the same man who designed Old City Hall, the King Edward Hotel, and the west wing of Queen's Park. Lennox came up with a design that combined Pellatt's favourite elements from his favourite castles: a medieval pastiche of architectural ideas from all over Europe, especially from Balmoral, the British monarchy's summer home in Scotland where Pellatt had met King George.

To top it all off, Sir Henry gave his castle a Spanish name: Casa Loma, the house on the hill.

Pellatt hoped to host royalty at his new home, so he wasn't going to spare any expense. Masons were shipped in from Europe; stones for the wall were hand-picked by Lennox himself. Wood was ordered from all over the globe and carved by master craftsmen. Even the horses' stalls in the stables were made of mahogany, the floors of Spanish tile. The fixtures in the bathrooms were gold. The lighting and telephone systems were state-of-the-art. The gardens and greenhouses were filled with rare and exotic flowers. The Simpson's department store was hired to find all of the most lavish art, furniture, wine, and treasure — Pellatt wanted to quickly assemble the kind of historic collection those old British families had built over the course of a few centuries, and he was willing to pay millions of dollars to do it.

Of course, not everyone in Toronto had that kind of money to burn. There was plenty of poverty in the city. Just a couple of kilometres away, at the foot of Casa Loma's hill, people were living in tarpaper shacks. And in the distance, in the shadow of the spire of Old City Hall (which Pellatt could see from his window), poor immigrant families were squeezed together in the squalor of the Ward — the slum that used to stand where Nathan Phillips Square is now. Slumlords forced tenants into overcrowded, ramshackle housing, rife with disease. Many families still lived without running water or even a drain. Those lucky enough to find work were likely to be working painfully long hours for low wages at dangerous factory jobs, in a city thick with coal smoke.

So, as you might expect, income disparity was a controversial issue during the twenty years that Pellatt was planning, building, and living in his castle. Newspaper headlines were full of stories about injustice and of the clashes between the working and ruling classes. The *Titanic* sank with poor passengers left to drown. The Bolshevik Revolution brought Communism to Russia. The trenches of the First World War made a mockery of class distinctions. Meanwhile, unions were getting stronger and more power-ful than ever, making demands like a minimum wage, safer conditions, and an eight-hour workday. Unionists were denounced as radicals, sometimes beaten by the police, even killed. In Winnipeg, when workers put together the biggest general strike in Canadian history, Mounties charged into the crowd on horseback, swinging clubs and firing their weapons. Two strikers were killed and hundreds more were injured. They called it Bloody Saturday.

Thanks to his service in the Queen's Own Rifles, Sir Henry was no stranger to the violent side of labour rela-tions: the only time he ever saw action was back in his younger days when the QOR were called in to break a railway strike in Belleville. The regiment advanced on the workers with their bayonets drawn. Two strikers were stabbed and two soldiers were hit in the head by flying rocks. After it was all over, the men of the QOR were pre-sented with medals made out of the rails the workers had pulled up. Pellatt wore his on his dress uniform for the rest of his life.

And that wouldn't be the last time Sir Henry got caught up in the debate over private profit and the public interest. In fact, he played a central role in one of the big-gest fights about it that Toronto has ever seen.

This was back before he started building Casa Loma. The dispute was about the hydroelectric dam he and his friends were building at Niagara Falls. It was a big deal: an engineering marvel, a beautiful design by E.J. Lennox, and vast potential for profit. But as the dam was being built, the public was getting fed up with private monopolies. The government didn't provide a lot of the public services it does today — and the private companies that did provide them had a reputation for using their monopolies to drive up prices while letting the quality of the services plummet.

As the *Globe* put it in the year 1900: "The twentieth century will be kept busy wrestling with millionaires and billionaires to get back and restore to the people that which the nineteenth century gave away.... The nineteenth century shirked its duty, humbugged and defrauded the common people, playing into the hands of the rich."

Many were beginning to suggest that hydroelectric power should belong to the people, not to Pellatt's private corporation. The champion of the idea was Adam Beck, the former mayor of London who was now a Conservative MPP. "The gifts of nature are for the public," he declared. And he pushed the Conservative provincial government to agree. "It is the duty of the Government to see that development is not hindered by permitting a handful of people to enrich themselves out of these treasures at the expense of the general public."

While Beck was leading the charge at Queen's Park, William Peyton Hubbard was doing the same thing a couple of blocks down the street at City Hall. He was the son of escaped slaves, close friends with Dr. Anderson Ruffin Abbott, and had gotten into politics after saving George

Brown from drowning in the Don River. He was one of the first black politicians elected in any Canadian city, sitting on Toronto's city council for a couple of decades, even stepping in as acting mayor more than once. He and Beck both argued in favour of what they called "public power."

Pellatt and his friends fought back. They claimed Beck's idea was the worst kind of socialism. Since they had built the dam, they should profit from it. Otherwise, British investors would be scared away. (They then tried to get the British investors to promise that they *would* be scared away.) Pellatt even asked King Edward VII to intervene — but without any luck. The businessmen were eventually so desperate they tried to bribe one of the newspapers who opposed them: they offered $350,000 to the *Toronto World* if it switched sides and started arguing against public power instead of for it. It didn't work.

None of it worked. The Conservative government at Queen's Park agreed with Beck. Premier James Whitney got up in the legislature and declared that "water-power at Niagara should be as free as air and, more than that, I say on behalf of the Government that the water-power all over this country shall not in future be made the sport and prey of capitalists, and shall not be treated as anything else, but as a valuable asset of the people of Ontario."

That's how Ontario Hydro was founded. It became the biggest publicly owned corporation on the continent. (It would survive all the way to the 1990s — until the government of Premier Mike Harris split it into pieces and sold some of them off to private owners.) Eventually, the provincial government would buy out the company

Pellatt and his friends had founded. And with William Peyton Hubbard leading the way, Toronto soon signed on to the new public power grid with a dazzling ceremony at Old City Hall.

Beck was knighted for his public service and Toronto City Council built a monument in his honour. (It's still there today: a bronze statue in the middle of University Avenue just south of Queen.) In the years that followed, City Hall would take on more and more of the public services that private companies had been providing — it was one of Pellatt's hydroelectric partners who lost the streetcar contract, allowing the city to create the Toronto Transit Commission.

Sir Henry's business empire had taken a blow, but he was still one of the most extravagantly wealthy men in the country. And he would be for a while. In fact, he soon started construction on Casa Loma, and he lived there for a decade before everything finally fell apart.

In that time, he and Lady Mary turned the castle into a social hub. They threw some of the most lavish parties in the city's history: garden parties, curling parties, hockey parties, dinners with a hundred guests. And they threw parties for their favourite public causes, too. The Queen's Own Rifles were regular guests. So were the Girl Guides of Canada — Lady Mary had been drafted into being their first chief commissioner (in part because she was wealthy and influential, in part because of her traditional views on womanhood and the vote). Pellatt would even fulfill his dream of hosting royalty: the Prince of Wales, who would go on to briefly become King Edward VIII before he abdicated his throne and left it to his stuttering brother, visited Casa Loma not just once, but twice.

Pellatt was still hard at work in those years defending his business empire. He fought with the federal government when it took over his airplane factory during the First World War. And when the *Wall Street Journal* accused Sir Henry of making an exorbitant profit in selling shells to the army, the prime minister forced Pellatt to make a public denial. He waged a battle with the municipal government over his property taxes, too. They'd gone up after he built his castle, so he took the city to court. His lawyers argued that Casa Loma was so big and so expensive that it actually drove the value of the property *down* — that Pellatt was a fool to have built it. (Meanwhile, he'd already mortgaged it for four times what the city claimed it was worth.)

Still, it wasn't until 1923 that everything finally came tumbling down. Here's how it happened:

Pellatt had borrowed a *lot* of money from a lot of different sources. One of them was the Home Bank of Canada. It had been founded in Toronto back in the 1850s by the city's second Catholic bishop, the man who took over from Bishop Michael Power. The idea was that it would give poor Irish-Catholic immigrant families a place to invest and get loans in Orange Toronto. But over the course of time, the bank had become more and more secular, less and less charitable, and more just like a regular bank. Now, it had branches all over the country — more than eighty of them (including one on King Street just west of Yonge, designed in part by E.J. Lennox).

Tens of thousands of working-class people had put their savings into the bank — Toronto Catholics and farmers in the Prairies more than anybody else.

Sir Henry, on the other hand, was in the habit of taking money *out* of the bank. It was run by a couple of friends of his: a Conservative senator and his son, both of them from the Queen's Own Rifles. They, too, relied on controversial business practices: happy to lend their customers' money to their friends without making sure those friends could pay it back. They gave Pellatt more money than anyone else — millions and millions of dollars, cooking their books to back some of his dubious investments. In return, they were supposed to get a cut of his profits.

But those profits never came. Pellatt was pulling his usual tricks, but this time they didn't work.

For instance: he used a lot of the money to buy some land northwest of Bathurst and St. Clair. Then, he sold that land to himself at an inflated price. That way, he could use the inflated value of the land as collateral to borrow even *more* money to buy even *more* land. But when the First World War broke out, people stopped buying land. And when it ended, the economy didn't recover right away. So, when the bank was finally forced to ask Pellatt to pay the loans back, he couldn't. All he had was a bunch of land and stocks that weren't worth anything near what he claimed they were worth. Plus, a giant castle and a load of debt. He owed the Home Bank two million dollars and that was just one debt of many. He was in trouble. And so was the Home Bank.

Pellatt desperately schemed and stalled and skimmed money — he even dumped some of his most questionable stocks on the staff at Casa Loma — begging for more time, but eventually that time ran out. The fraud was uncovered. On a Saturday morning in the summer of 1923, a blunt notice was hammered into the beautiful wooden door of the Home Bank branch on King Street: "BANK CLOSED. PAYMENT SUSPENDED."

And just like that, everyone's money was gone.

Tens of thousands of Canadians lost their life savings. One customer even died of a heart attack at a public meeting held at Massey Hall to discuss the issue. Ten bank officials were arrested. One had a nervous breakdown. Some people say the senator's son — who had once survived an armed bank robbery and a bullet through his lungs during the Great Boer War — killed himself because of it. Others go as far as to link the bank's collapse with the rise of populist political parties out West — farmers on the Prairies were furious at the eastern bankers who had lost the farmers' life savings.

In the end, the federal government, now run by Mackenzie King's Liberals, launched a royal commission to investigate the collapse. Corruption was uncovered. New rules were proposed. Conservative ministers from the previous government were grilled about a suspicious bailout they'd given the bank. Eventually, laws were changed to outlaw some of Pellatt's dirtiest tricks. And a new inspector general of banks was appointed to make sure those new laws were obeyed. About ten years later, on top of all the new regulations, the Bank of Canada was created to help control the country's banking system. Not a single Canadian bank has failed since.

Pellatt, meanwhile, managed to save himself — legally, at least. Before the collapse, he moved his assets around so he could never be sued for it. And he put Casa Loma in his wife's name so it couldn't be seized. His days as a titan of industry were over, though. His fortune was gone; his reputation ruined.

And so, Sir Henry was forced to move out of Casa Loma. The castle was much too expensive to run: it took a million and a half pounds of coal to heat it every winter and tens of thousands of dollars to keep it staffed. He and Lady Mary moved into an apartment on Spadina, but she died soon after that — of a broken heart, they like to say.

For Pellatt, it was downhill from there. He remarried, but when his new wife died of cancer he bitterly accused her of having known she was sick all along — that she'd "bamboozled" him into marrying her. He moved into one apartment after another, each getting progressively smaller. When the Great Depression struck, Pellatt couldn't afford the castle's property taxes anymore. Ten years after the collapse of the Home Bank, the City of Toronto took over Casa Loma.

Sir Henry was an old man by then. The last few photos of him are heartbreaking. He was thin and frail, almost blind from cataracts. He walked with a cane. He doesn't look anything like the imposing figure who spent forty years as a financial giant. He looks like a tired old man. Defeated. And very mortal.

The knight of Casa Loma spent his final days living with his chauffeur's family at their modest home in Mimico, down by the lake in the west end. He didn't have many friends or family left to care for him, but his niece and her mother would come by to read to him and listen to his stories. He consoled himself by retelling tales from the old days and with the few mementos he had left: his signed photo of Queen Victoria, his invitation to King George's coronation, a seating plan for the dinner at Balmoral.... He did still have his knighthood, too — the city hadn't forced him to formally declare bankruptcy, so he got to keep it. And there was one last fancy dinner at the Royal York Hotel: a reunion of the Queen's Own Rifles for his eightieth birthday, including a telegram of congratulations from King George's wife, Queen Mary. Sir Henry was moved to tears.

He died two months later, in his chauffeur's arms.

The Queen's Own Rifles gave him a full military funeral. It was held at St. James Cathedral, still standing on the same spot where the city's most powerful Anglicans had come to pray, get married, and say goodbye to their dead since the days of the earliest settlers — the old stronghold of the Family Compact, where John Strachan's bones are buried beneath the chancel. Thousands came to pay their respects to the man who built Toronto's famous castle. And as they remembered the old knight, the tallest church spire in the country towered above them: the soaring copper peak marking the spiritual Canadian heart of Sir Henry's beloved empire.

THE
GREAT WARS

20
THE GROUP OF SEVEN ON THE WESTERN FRONT

"What war?"

A.Y. Jackson was far from home in the summer of 1914, high among the peaks of the Rocky Mountains. He was there to paint. This was back in the earliest days of the Group of Seven, years before they began to use that nickname. Jackson was still new to the group; the others had only recently convinced him to join them in their efforts to change the Canadian art world forever — and with it, the way Canadians saw their own country.

Even before they met Jackson, the other artists in the group admired him. His style was deeply influenced by his studies in Paris, living at the heart of the Impressionist revolution before it reached Canada. The group saw Jackson's work — a painting called *The Edge of the Maple Wood* in particular — as the example they wanted to follow.

So they offered Jackson a deal. One of the members of the group had quite a bit of money: Lawren Harris wasn't just a talented artist, he was also an heir to the Massey-Harris farming equipment fortune. Jackson would get free room and board for a year if he agreed to move from Montreal to Toronto and do nothing but work on his art. They even had a brand new building to put him up in: the Studio Building in Rosedale, specifically built for artists.

He accepted. But in those early days, the group's paintings were terribly controversial. Established critics dismissed them in much the same way Van Gogh, Matisse, and Picasso had been dismissed. "The Hot Mush School," they called them. "A horrible bunch of junk." "The figments of a drunkard's dream." "Daubing by immature children." "A spilt can of paint."

Still, not everyone agreed with those critics. Some people were thrilled by the way Jackson and the others were using vivid colours and Impressionist techniques to capture what they saw as the spirit of the Canadian landscape. When the Canadian Northern Railway built a new line through the Rockies, they commissioned Jackson to travel with their construction camps as they worked along the Fraser River. That's how he made his first trip to the West.

While he was in the Rockies, Jackson would leave the camps for days on end, hiking into the mountains with a guide. "We took many chances," Jackson remembered later in his autobiography, "sliding down snow slopes with just a stick for a brake, climbing over glaciers without ropes, and crossing rivers too swift to wade, by felling trees across them."

It was at the end of one of these "scrambles" that he heard the news: back at camp, an engineer was waiting for him. "What do you think about the war?" he asked the painter. It was the first Jackson had heard of it.

As the military might of Europe shifted into gear, Jackson kept painting. Most people thought the war would be over soon; there didn't seem to be any pressing need for the artist to join the fight. Instead of heading back to Toronto, where young men were lined up outside the Armouries on University Avenue waiting to enlist, Jackson headed straight from the Rockies to Algonquin Park. There was someone waiting for him there.

Tom Thomson was one of the most promising young artists in Toronto. But Thomson found that fact hard to believe. He had a steady, paying gig at Grip Ltd., a downtown design firm where many of the Group of Seven artists worked. He was known as the most accomplished outdoorsman of them all; it was Thomson who first fell in love with Algonquin Park and introduced it to the others. But he lacked their confidence when it came to his art. He worried that if he quit his day job, he wouldn't be able to make a living off his paintings. And so, as part of Jackson's deal to get a free year in the Studio Building, the others also asked him to take Thomson under his wing. The two artists would share a studio on the top floor. While Thomson taught Jackson about life in the bush, Jackson taught Thomson about painting.

The two met in Algonquin that autumn for their first sketching trip together. They roughed it in the bush: living in a tent, travelling by canoe, and working on birch panels small enough to be carried through the wilderness. That fall, they made sketches that would lead to some of their most famous work. Jackson's *The Red Maple* was a result of that trip. So was Thomson's *Northern River*.

Meanwhile, six thousand kilometres away, young men were facing a very different reality. "There was a war on too," Jackson later wrote, but "in Algonquin we heard little about it and hoped it would soon be over."

Of course, it wouldn't. The war on the Western Front had kicked off with a big, fast German drive into France and an Allied counteroffensive that pushed them far back. But now that quick, dramatic war of sweeping movement — the kind everyone had been expecting — was settling into a gruelling stalemate. That September, in order to avoid being driven back any farther, the Germans dug the very first trenches. The French soon followed suit. By the time the artists got back from Algonquin, it was already becoming clear that this would be a new, more horrifying kind of war. And not a short one. "When we reached Toronto," Jackson wrote, "we realized that we had been unduly optimistic, that the war was likely to be a long one, and that our relatively carefree days were over."

He tried to get back into the swing of things at the Studio Building, turning sketches like *The Red Maple* into full canvases. "But I could not settle down to serious work. The war made me restless." With his free year at the Studio Building coming to an end, Jackson decided to head back to Montreal and join the army.

As it turned out, it would still be a few months before he finally signed up. The news from Europe shifted again and it seemed, again, as if it might be a quick war. Jackson seized the opportunity to take another sketching trip, this time to one of his favourite spots in rural Quebec.

But in April the Germans successfully deployed a deadly new weapon for the first time: chlorine gas. In Belgium, near the town of Ypres, a thick cloud of poison yellow smoke descended on trenches full of French, Moroccan, and Algerian troops. Six thousand people died in the first few minutes: suffocating, lungs burning, frothing at the mouth, cut to pieces by German guns. The Germans attacked and drove the Allies back to a spot near the village of Saint-Julien, where Canadians rushed to plug the hole in the line, holding urine-soaked handkerchiefs over their faces as feeble protection against the deadly fumes. Three-quarters of them would die, too, but they would hold the line and keep the Germans at bay. That was just the beginning of a long, bloody battle — the same one that would inspire another sometime Torontonian, John McCrae, to write "In Flanders Fields."

"At the railway station one morning I heard the first news of the Battle of St. Julien," Jackson wrote. "I knew then that all the wishful thinking about the war being of short duration was over."

Finally, he saw a recruitment poster:

YOU SAID
YOU WOULD GO
WHEN YOU WERE
NEEDED
YOU ARE NEEDED
NOW!

It "ended any doubts I had about enlisting," he said. A few months later, he was on his way to the front lines.

Yet while Jackson was willing to fight, he was far from being seized with a patriotic lust for battle. His letters made that perfectly clear. "I'm a Social Democrat," he wrote to his sister from the battlefields of Belgium, "and don't believe in war." He scorned the wealthy, Empire-loving Canadians who glorified the war from the safety of home while the poor were forced to fight it. "I don't think I ever in my life took so little pride in being British," he wrote in a second letter. "The rough neck and the out of work far outnumber the patriot. Volunteers by pressure ... when you hear all the bosh talked and written about our precious honor, Christian ideals, etc. it just about makes you sick ... people who entrust their national honor to men they would not allow to enter their houses in times of peace are not worth fighting for."

When Jackson first signed up, Harris had offered to buy him a commission as an officer (and all the preferential treatment that came with it). But Jackson refused, preferring to earn his rank through experience. "This Canadian army," he wrote, "would be a far finer machine to my mind if all class distinctions were done away with, and officers lived under exactly the same conditions as the men."

It was early in 1916 that Jackson ended up in the trenches just outside Ypres, not far from the spot where the Battle of Saint-Julien had raged a year earlier. It was a bombed-out, blood-soaked mess. "The flag waving was over," he wrote. But he did see some haunting beauty in the desolation. "Flanders in early spring was beautiful, as was Ypres by moonlight and the weird ruined landscapes under the light of flares or rockets."

That summer, the Germans launched an attack against the high ground held by the Allies outside the town. Jackson was there "crawling along a trench in Sanctuary Wood, and an aeroplane circling overhead like a big hawk, signalling to the artillery who were trying to blow us up. It was a day of glorious sunshine and only man was vile, in general, individually they were magnificent."

Once the Germans had pushed the Allies off the high ground it was up to the Canadians to counterattack — the first time the country's army had ever been given such a task. It was, according to the official British history of the war "an unqualified success." The Canadian forces developed new methods for fighting this new kind of brutal war — changing, for instance, the number and timing of artillery barrages before they went over the top, so the Germans wouldn't know when they were coming.

Now, a century later, a museum stands on that spot, still run by the grandson of the farmer who owned the land. Nearby, a monument has been erected as a memorial to the Canadians who died there. Some of the craters and the trenches where they fought are still there, too, preserved by the museum. In Toronto the battle is remembered every year with a parade at Fort York.

Jackson survived the barrages, the attack, and the counterattack, but it was hard for anyone to last very long in that devastated place. A week later, during a German bombardment, he was wounded. It got him in the hip and the shoulder.

He was taken to a hospital in France and then to England to recover. That's where he was when he got a letter delivering tragic news from Canada.

When Jackson left Toronto to enlist, Tom Thomson had stayed behind to paint. He had a medical condition that kept him out of the army. But at that point, *his* free year in the Studio Building was over, too, and without someone else to help make rent, he was forced to move into the shed out back instead. He spent the warmer months away on sketching trips in the northern bush, while he spent the snowy months holed up in the shack on the slopes of the Rosedale Valley, deeply immersed in his work. There, he would paint some of the most famous canvases in Canadian history, works like *The Jack Pine* (now in the National Gallery) and *The West Wind* (now in the Art Gallery of Ontario).

All the while, he worried about the war. The shed, as rustic as it was, was still only a few blocks away from the intersection of Yonge and Bloor, where he watched as thousands of soldiers marched by on their way to war. The military was all over the city. And Thomson had friends on the other side of the Atlantic to worry about, too. "I can't get used to the idea of Jackson being in the machine," he wrote to another artist in the group, "and it is rotten that in this so-called civilized age that such things can exist."

But while Jackson would survive to see the end of the war, Thomson wouldn't be so lucky. During the summer of 1917, he took another trip to Algonquin. It would be his last. The accomplished outdoorsman disappeared on a canoe trip and was found eight days later, floating dead in Canoe Lake, decomposing with fishing wire wrapped around his leg. At the time, he was still barely known outside the small group of artists in Toronto. But over the course of the next few decades, his fame grew — and so did the legend of his death. Some say he was murdered, some that he took his own life. Still others claim he must have fallen over drunk while standing to pee from his canoe. Conspiracy theories and myths abound. A century later, Thomson is celebrated as one of the most famous Canadian artists ever and his suspicious death is one of the country's most infamous mysteries.

For Jackson, it was a very personal tragedy. "I could sit down and cry to think that while in all this turmoil over here ... the peace and quietness of the north country should be the scene of such a tragedy," he wrote in a letter home. "Without Tom the north country seems a desolation of bush and rock. He was the guide, the interpreter, and we the guests partaking of the hospitality so generously given."

In his autobiography, Jackson remembered, "The thought of getting back to the north country with Thomson, and going farther afield with him on painting trips after the war was over, had always buoyed me up when the going was rough. Now I would never go sketching with Tom Thomson again."

* * *

It must have been rock bottom. Thomson was dead and Jackson was recovering from his wounds at the worst possible time: the Allies were getting ready for a big offensive. Soon, Jackson's unit — already miserable to the point of mutiny — was going to be sent back to the front lines outside Ypres, to be cut down at the long and muddy Battle of Passchendaele, where hundreds of thousands of men would die. Jackson was already reaching the end of his tether — he'd been worn down by the war; friends worried he couldn't take much more of it. Passchendaele might very well be the end for him.

His life was saved just a few days later. He was digging a latrine when an officer interrupted him. There was a new project they wanted him to join.

The man behind the idea was Lord Beaverbrook: a Canadian entrepreneur turned British politician and newspaper baron. He was determined to make sure there would be a historical record of the Canadian contribution to the war. So he used some of his own fortune to establish the Canadian War Records Office. Part of his plan was to hire artists to capture the Canadian experience. Eventually, there would be almost a hundred and twenty of them, producing nearly a thousand paintings by the time it was all over. Jackson was one of the very first asked to join the cause. He would paint more canvases for the War Records Office than any other artist.

Now, instead of a gun, his main companion was a sketchbook.

It was challenging work — and not just because he was trying to make art in the middle of a war zone. In the past, battles had tended to be fought by men standing in fields in straight lines; they wore brightly coloured uniforms; artists were commissioned to glorify their exploits. Now, they were hidden away in trenches, being torn apart by distant machine guns, or blown to pieces by a rain of artillery. The traditional approach wasn't going to work anymore. "What to paint was a problem for the war artist," Jackson admitted. "There was nothing to serve as a guide. War had gone underground, and there was little to see. The old heroics, the death and glory stuff, were gone forever; there was no more 'Thin Red Line' or 'Scotland For Ever.'"

Instead, Jackson chose to paint landscapes, much as he did back home in Canada. These places, though, were more dead than alive, dreadful and haunting, ravaged by the most destructive war in human history. In Jackson's paintings, individual soldiers are dwarfed by the scale of the devastation around them. In *Gas Attack, Liévin*, vast, poisonous clouds stretch across a dark horizon, lit by green flares. In *House of Ypres*, riders on horseback disappear into the ghostly wreckage of the town. In *Springtime in Picardy*, soldiers blend into the ruins of a French farmhouse.

Even as an official war artist, Jackson didn't shy away from letting his political beliefs shine through in his work. In a painting he called *A Copse, Evening*, there is no copse at all, just a few blasted tree trunks scattered across the wretched, muddy ground; the evening's dull yellow sky is cut by vicious searchlights.

"Do the mothers and wives think it hard to know that their men are dead?" one critic wondered in response to the work. "Let them look at this picture … and know that it is lucky for them … that they do not know how and with what thoughts their men *lived* for some time before they escaped from a *Copse, Evening*. It was not death they dreaded. Sometimes that was welcomed."

Jackson wasn't the only Group of Seven artist in Europe. Fred Varley enlisted, too. And he, too, ended up working for the Canadian War Records Office, producing paintings that were even more disturbing than Jackson's.

"I tell you, Arthur," Varley wrote home to the group's Arthur Lismer, "your wildest nightmares pale before reality. You pass over swamps on rotting duckboards, past bleached bones of horses with their harness still on, past isolated rude crosses sticking up from the filth and the stink of decay is flung all over. There was a lovely wood there once with a stream running thro' it but now the trees are powdered up and mingle with the soil."

While Jackson painted menacing landscapes, Varley's most striking work was more directly focused on the human suffering caused by the war. In *German Prisoners*, exhausted POWs trudge along a muddy road. In *Some Day the People Will Return*, a cemetery has been blown apart, coffins in pieces, crosses askew. In *The Sunken Road*, German corpses lie in the dirt, barely distinguishable from the twisted earth beneath them. As Jennifer Morse of *Legion Magazine* once put it, with Varley "we can't really see where the land begins or the death ends."

The most famous of his war works is a bleak painting of a broken wheelbarrow filled with dead bodies. Behind it, gravediggers are at work in the muck beside a row of pale crosses. Varley was even bolder than Jackson in making his political views clear. He called the work *For What?* Today, it's in the collection of the War Museum in Ottawa.

As the war entered its final months, Varley shared something of his experience in a letter home to his wife:

> You in Canada ... cannot realize at all what war is like. You must see it and live it. You must see the barren deserts war has made of once fertile country ... see the turned-up graves, see the dead on the field, freshly mutilated — headless, legless, stomachless, a perfect body and a passive face and a broken empty skull — see your own countrymen unidentified, thrown into a cart, their coats over them, boys digging a grave in a land of yellow slimy mud and green pools of water under a weeping sky. You must have heard the screeching shells and have the shrapnel fall around you, whistling by you — Seen the results of it, seen scores of horses, bits of horses lying around, in the open — in the street and soldiers marching by these scenes as if they never knew of their presence — until you've lived this ... you cannot know.

Meanwhile, back in Canada, other future members of the Group of Seven were recording the war on the home front. Franz Johnson was hired to paint the Royal Flying Corps training program in Ontario, while in Halifax Lismer was capturing the images of warships in the harbour.

Before too long those subjects would include vessels returning home to Canada filled with soldiers on their way back to friends and family. The war, after four long, agonizing years, was finally over. Jackson joined Lismer there, painting the return to peace. In one of his final war works, *Entrance to Halifax Harbour*, you can barely even tell it's a war painting at all; the only sign is a few camouflaged ships in the distance.

The war would never quite leave him. You can find echoes of the Western Front in the works both Jackson and Varley painted upon their return. Their macabre experiences in Europe influenced the way they saw Canadian landscapes. They sought out the stormiest skies and bleakest trees for years to come.

Still, their darkest days were behind them. With the war over and Thomson gone, Jackson returned to the top floor of the Studio Building in Toronto, and reunited with the other artists in the group. The war work he and Varley had painted was finally earning them the kind of praise Canadian critics had been reluctant to give the group. A memorial exhibition of Thomson's work, which Jackson helped to organize, met with the usual disdain from the older critics; the fight within the art world would last for at least another decade. But the tide was finally turning.

Canada had a new sense of itself in the wake of the First World War, and for the first time since Confederation, Canadians seemed ready to support artists who wanted to capture the unique essence of their own country. Now Jackson and the others were attracting the attention of younger artists. They were selling their work to the National Gallery. Their war paintings won glowing reviews from the British press. Soon, they would have their first group show together at the Art Gallery of Toronto (now the Art Gallery of Ontario).

The year after they returned from the war, they decided to publicly declare themselves as a new movement with a new name. They called themselves "The Group of Seven." And they were going to do exactly what they promised to do: change Canadian art forever.

21
THE NIGHT OF THE DROWNING NURSES

One black night in the summer of 1918, HMHS *Llandovery Castle* was steaming through the waters of the North Atlantic. The ship was far off the southern tip of Ireland, nearly two hundred kilometres from the nearest land. It was a calm night, with a light breeze and a clear sky.

The ship had been built in Glasgow and was named after a castle in Wales, but now it was a Canadian vessel. Since the world had been plunged into the most terrible war it had ever seen, the steamship had been turned into a floating hospital. It was returning now from Halifax, where it had just dropped off hundreds of wounded Canadian soldiers.

On board were the ship's crew and medical personnel, including fourteen Canadian nurses. They were just a few of more than two thousand Canadian women who volunteered to serve overseas as nursing sisters — nicknamed "bluebirds" because of the light blue dresses they wore under their white aprons and veils. They spent those bloody years healing wounds, saving lives, and comforting those who couldn't be saved.

As the ship sliced through the water, big red crosses shone out from either side of the hull, bright beacons in the dark. The trip was almost over. Soon, they'd be in Liverpool.

But they weren't alone in those waters. Beneath the surface of the waves, a German submarine lurked. The *U-86* wasn't planning on letting the *Llandovery Castle* ever reach land again.

When the war broke out, the women of Toronto rushed to do their part. As train after train left Union Station filled with men heading to the Western Front, women got work on the home front. Thousands took jobs at munitions factories across the city. Others volunteered for the local Red Cross or spent long hours knitting and sewing supplies for the soldiers in the trenches. They staffed recruiting stations, went door to door to raise money, and filled countless other vital roles. Many became nurses.

As hundreds of wounded men began to return from the front, Toronto's hospitals were overwhelmed. Temporary facilities were opened in public buildings, all of them needing staff and volunteers. One of those workers was Amelia Earhart. While in town visiting her sister, she'd been overwhelmed by the sight of wounded soldiers on the streets of the city and signed up as a nurse's aide at the new military hospital on Spadina Avenue. It was her time in Toronto that inspired her to become a pilot — the city was a major centre for the Royal Flying Corps during the war.

Many nurses, however, would leave the safety of Toronto behind, volunteering to follow the men across the ocean to the killing fields of Europe.

One of them was Carola Josephine Douglas. She was born in Panama, but grew up with relatives in Toronto after both her parents died. She graduated from Harbord Collegiate before training to become a nurse. When the war broke out, she volunteered to head overseas — filling out enlistment forms that still assumed all new recruits were "he."

Soon, she found herself in the thick of the action in Europe, tending to the wounded at one of the most dangerous military hospitals in all of France. The town of Étaples was just a few kilometres from the front lines and it was full of hospitals, including several Canadian ones. By the end of the war, those hospitals had been bombed repeatedly. In just one of the attacks, the Germans killed and wounded more than eight hundred people — doctors, nurses, and patients alike. Three Canadian women died of the wounds they suffered that night, including one from Toronto: Nursing Sister Dorothy Baldwin would never return home to the Annex. She was just twenty-seven years old.

Douglas had been transferred by then, but things didn't get any easier. She served in the Somme and on the Macedonian Front. The threat of disease was even more dangerous than the bombings: Étaples was ground zero for the Spanish flu epidemic that would kill more people than the entire war; the hospital in Macedonia was a breeding ground for malaria and dysentery. After more than two years helping to stitch people back together near the front lines, Douglas became a patient herself: first for badly infected fingers, and then for exhaustion.

Not long after that, she was assigned to the *Llandovery Castle*. The hospital ship was supposed to provide the nurses and other personnel with something of a rest — a relatively easy assignment for those who had already seen more than their fair share of stressful duty. But now, on that black night in 1918, Douglas and the other nurses found themselves back in terrible danger.

The calm of the night was shattered by an explosion. The *Llandovery Castle* was under attack. The U-boat had launched a torpedo into the side of the hospital ship.

The lights on board went black. The wireless was knocked out, too; there would be no SOS. When the captain ordered the engines reversed, there was no reply: the engine room had been hit. The men inside were already dead or wounded. The ship continued to surge forward into the waves, filling with water as the prow plunged beneath the surface of the ocean. Within minutes, it was clear: the *Llandovery Castle* was doomed.

The order came to abandon ship. But the evacuation was dangerous work. As the decks pitched forward and the ship lurched through the waves, two lifeboats were swamped, broken, and swept away. Others had already been destroyed by the explosion. The crew kept at it, though;

they were calm, no one panicked. Within a few minutes, every single person who had survived the blast had been ushered into a lifeboat and lowered to the water below.

Douglas was among them. And she wasn't the only Toronto nurse in her lifeboat. Mary Agnes McKenzie — Nan, to her friends — had been born and raised in Toronto. She went to the Rose Avenue School in St. James Town as a young girl and then lived in the neighbourhood of Rathnelly (on Macpherson Avenue, near Dupont and Avenue Road). She was still just a teenager when she decided she wanted to become a nurse. She got a job at a hospital in Toronto and, in the years before the war broke out, gained some experience by working at the Military Hospital in Halifax.

When the war did come, McKenzie volunteered for duty. She was first posted to the Ontario Military Hospital in England, built by the provincial government, then found herself serving on the *Llandovery Castle*. While the ship had been docked in Halifax, she had hoped for a chance to head home to Toronto for a brief visit with her family. But all leave had been cancelled. She promised her mother she would try again the next time they were back in Canada.

Now, Douglas, McKenzie, and the ship's other dozen nurses found themselves in Lifeboat No. 5, being lowered over the side of the doomed vessel along with a few men from the crew.

But Lifeboat No. 5 was stuck. Even in the water, ropes still held it to the side of the sinking ship. As the small boat pitched in the waves, it kept smashing against the hull of the big steamer. One of the men — Sergeant Arthur Knight from London, Ontario — grabbed an axe and tried to cut the lifeboat free.

It was no use; the axe broke. So did the second one. After that, they tried to use the oars to brace themselves, to keep from being crushed. One by one, the oars broke, too. Until, finally, mercifully, the ropes snapped and they were free.

The lifeboat drifted away, but it still wasn't out of danger. They realized in horror that they were being drawn back toward the stern of the ship, caught in the suction as the *Llandovery Castle* sank. They were being dragged into a whirlpool and there was nothing they could do.

One of the nurses — Matron Margaret Fraser, daughter of the lieutenant governor of Nova Scotia — turned to Sergeant Knight as they drifted toward the swirling vacuum. "Sergeant," she asked, "do you think there is any hope for us?"

He later described those dreadful moments, stranded in a lifeboat with fourteen women who had spent much of the last few years up to their elbows in blood and guts, but whose entire gender was still dismissed by many Canadians as being too frail for that kind of work, too weak and emotional to be trusted with an equal say in the world:

> Unflinchingly and calmly, as steady and col-
> lected as if on parade, without a complaint
> or a single sign of emotion, our fourteen
> devoted nursing sisters faced the terrible

ordeal of certain death — only a matter of
minutes — as our lifeboat neared that mad
whirlpool of waters where all human power
was helpless.... In that whole time I did not
hear a complaint or murmur from one of the
sisters. There was not a cry for help or any
outward evidence of fear.

It took only ten minutes from the time of the explosion to the moment when the last of the *Llandovery
Castle* disappeared beneath the waves. And the ship
took Lifeboat No. 5 with it. Everyone on board was flung
into the churning water. The nurses were all wearing life
jackets, but most — if not all of them — were probably
drowned right away.

Sergeant Knight never saw any of them ever again.
He was saved only by a lucky explosion — maybe the
boilers exploding as the ship sank toward the ocean floor
— which propelled him back to the surface. If Douglas
or McKenzie or any of the other nurses did survive, they
found themselves stranded in the dark waters, clinging to
the wreckage as the night's final horrors began.

The U-boat wasn't finished yet.

The captain of the submarine had just committed a
war crime. It was illegal to attack a hospital ship. The red
crosses on the sides of the *Llandovery Castle* had been
brightly lit and easy to see. The Germans hadn't given any
warning or tried to board and search the ship first, which

would have been within their rights. Instead, they'd simply fired their torpedoes. That was against international law and against the standing orders of the Imperial German Navy. So now, it seems, Captain Helmut Patzig was anxious to cover his tracks.

At first, *U-86* seized one of the lifeboats and accused the Canadian crew of harbouring American flight officers or of shipping ammunition. But the crew denied both. And when it became clear they weren't getting anywhere, the Germans let that lifeboat go. As it rowed away into the darkness, Captain Patzig tried a new approach: the U-boat turned on the other survivors.

For the next two hours, while those in the water clung to the wreckage and cried out for help, *U-86* sailed between them, ramming the lifeboats that were still afloat, firing its deck gun at any that weren't completely destroyed.

Then, once all the Canadians had been forced into the water, the machine guns opened fire. They killed everyone they could find. If McKenzie or Douglas or any of the other nurses had managed to survive their initial plunge into the water, they didn't survive those guns.

There had been 258 people on board the *Llandovery Castle*. By the time the night was over, the only survivors were the twenty-four lucky enough to be on board the one lifeboat Captain Patzig couldn't find. They would spend the next thirty-six hours alone in the middle of the ocean, until they were finally rescued.

Later, the captain of a British ship sailed through the wreckage.

Suddenly we began going through corpses ...
we were sailing through floating bodies. We
were not allowed to stop — we just had to go
straight through. It was quite horrific, and my
reaction was to vomit over the edge. It was
something we could never have imagined ...
particularly the nurses: seeing these bodies
of women and nurses, floating in the ocean,
having been there some time. Huge aprons
and skirts in billows, which looked almost
like sails because they dried in the hot sun.

Nearly a century later, the sinking of the *Llandovery
Castle* is still considered one of the greatest atrocities of
the First World War. It immediately began to play an
inflammatory role in the cycle of hatred and violence
between the Allies and Germany that would keep the
world drenched in blood for decades to come.

In the days that followed the attack, Toronto's newspapers were filled with cries of outrage. The *Daily Star*
denounced "this latest exhibition of Hun devilry." The
Telegram went with "Hun savagery." Their words were
officially echoed by the Canadian government, which
decried the "savagery ... and the utter blackness and
dastardly character of the enemy." Whether or not any of
the nurses had survived long enough to be shot, Allied
propaganda posters showed them there in the water as
German submariners mowed them down.

For the remaining days of the war, the *Llandovery
Castle* became a rallying cry for Canadian troops. About

a month after the sinking of the ship, the Allies began their final major push — The Hundred Days Offensive — which drove the Germans back out of France and finally to their surrender. The Canadians played a leading role. At the Battle of Amiens, they used "Llandovery Castle" as a code word. One brigadier from Moose Jaw told his men "the battle cry ... should be 'Llandovery Castle,' and that cry should be the last to ring in the ears of the Hun as the bayonet was driven home." Some say the outrages of that night in the North Atlantic helped to inspire some Canadian soldiers to commit their own: choosing to kill surrendering German troops rather than take them prisoner.

In the wake of the war, the Allies insisted that the German officers responsible for the sinking of the *Llandovery Castle* face charges. The case became one of the Leipzig War Crimes Trials, held by the German government to prosecute their own troops. Captain Patzig fled the country, leaving two of his lieutenants behind to be tried and convicted to four years of hard labour. But they escaped on their way to prison and were later acquitted on the grounds that only their captain was ultimately responsible for their orders.

For many people living in Allied countries, the Leipzig Trials were seen as an example of the Germans being too lenient with their own war criminals. But many Germans saw the trials as yet another example of the unfair peace terms imposed upon them by the Treaty of Versailles. Some Allies had committed war crimes, too, but it was only the Germans who seemed to be forced to face the consequences. Those who stood trial in Leipzig were hailed as patriotic martyrs.

Many historians believe the anger over the peace terms — including the Leipzig Trials — eventually helped to propel Adolf Hitler into power. And when Hitler launched the Second World War, there was a familiar face on his payroll. Captain Patzig had been welcomed back into the German navy. This time, he was in charge of an entire flotilla, teaching a new generation of German submariners how to wage war.

22
THE GREAT BEYOND

The room was dimly lit, illuminated only by the weak, pink glow of a single lamp covered by a paper shade. Sometimes, there was music playing on a gramophone or the occasional chime of a bell. But most of the people gathered in the old house on Euclid Avenue were silent. They sat in a circle, all eyes on the man sitting at the centre of the group. His name was Louis Benjamin. And he could talk to the dead.

As the séance began, Benjamin took a long, deep breath and fell into a trance. His eyes were closed; his face relaxed. Across from him, his wife sat holding a Ouija board on her lap. Benjamin's fingers rested gently on the tripod pointer.

The house, just metres north of Queen Street, belonged to Dr. Albert Durrant Watson. He was Benjamin's mentor, a respected physician, scientist, and Methodist minister, with a professional interest in the occult. He was the one who usually asked the questions. And as he did Benjamin's hands began to move confidently and without hesitation, sliding the tripod across the board to point at one letter and then another,

gradually spelling out an answer: a message from the
spirits who spoke through him.

They said they were communicating from a place
called the Twentieth Plane. It was a world bathed in
eternal pink twilight, where the air was sweet with "the
distilled essence of astral flower perfume." The spirits
lived in groups of about twenty or so, sharing houses in
a landscape of mountains, valleys, and waterfalls. They
slept only four hours a night and ate only one daily meal
made of synthetic chemicals and liquid rice. There were
no doors in the afterlife: the spirits travelled by thought.
They communicated telepathically, too, and could even
control the weather with their minds. Their great purpose was to inspire and console those still living on the
earth plane. They brought a message of peace and of eternal life. Death, they insisted, was an illusion.

The spirits wanted that hopeful message spread far
and wide. Nearly all of those who spoke through Benjamin
were famous historical figures — the only exception was Dr. Watson's own dead mother. Shakespeare,
Mozart, Tennyson, Wagner, Hugo, Poe, Voltaire, Blake,
Wordsworth, even Jesus Christ himself all made appearances. Abraham Lincoln, Walt Whitman, and Ralph
Waldo Emerson were part of the Twentieth Plane's official
publication committee. They asked Dr. Watson to publish
a book of their communications — even insisted that he
include some of his own poems.

The timing could not have been more perfect: Toronto
was deep in mourning. According to Dr. Watson's account,
the spirits began speaking through Benjamin during the

final winter of the First World War. *The Twentieth Plane* hit the shelves just two months after the bloody conflict was finally brought to an end.

As the *Toronto Daily Star* splashed headlines about Benjamin's powers across the front page, the rest of the paper was filled with updates on the end of the war. Negotiations over the Treaty of Versailles were just beginning. German troops were marching back out of occupied territories. Ships were sailing across the Atlantic, bringing Canadian soldiers back to Canadian shores. Right beside the reports of the séances on Euclid Avenue, readers could find long lists of the Toronto soldiers who were disembarking at Halifax Harbour, and the times their trains were expected to arrive at Union Station, finally bringing them home after four dark years of slaughter.

But, of course, not everyone would be coming home. The spirits were well aware of that. "This work," the dead poet Samuel Taylor Coleridge explained in the introduction of the book, "is dedicated to the heroes of the war.... It is sent from the Twentieth Plane to be a light and a consolation to those left behind. In the name of manhood, womanhood, love and faith, we dedicate anew this truth of all time, *There is no death*."

Many people were longing to hear that message. Sixty thousand Canadians had died in the war; thousands of those were from Toronto. Interest in séances and the occult had been fading in the earliest years of the twentieth century, but now it soared again; people were desperate for some consolation, for some sign their loved ones weren't lost to them forever. A book like *The*

Twentieth Plane — written by an esteemed public thinker like Dr. Watson — gave them that hope.

Still, not everyone was convinced. Many doubted the book's extraordinary claims. One of them was Dr. James Mavor. He was a professor at the University of Toronto, the chair of the political science department and one of the most respected minds in the city. He was a co-founder of both the Royal Ontario Museum and the Art Gallery of Ontario. He was friends with Leo Tolstoy and the famous Russian anarchist Peter Kropotkin, having played a leading role in the resettlement of the pacifist Doukhobor refugees who had come to Canada to escape life under the tsar. Professor Mavor was a man of science; he even looked the part, with his long white beard and round glasses.

From the window of his house on campus, the professor had seen the war reach deep into the heart of Toronto. For four long years the city had been enveloped by the conflict — and the university along with it. Much of the campus had been taken over by the military. Entire buildings were turned over to the Royal Flying Corps. Biplanes soared through the air above the school. Troops marched with rifles across the Front Campus lawn. Tents were pitched on the grass behind University College. Classes ended early to allow young men to drill and young women to volunteer for the Red Cross. Hundreds of students left their studies behind to fight, and many of them would never return.

Professor Mavor didn't see Benjamin and Dr. Watson as visionaries offering hope to a suffering people; he saw them as charlatans preying on a grieving city. "A very deep moral responsibility," he wrote, "rests upon those who out of vanity or otherwise have embarked upon an exploitation of the grief of those who are sorrowing over the losses of the war."

Soon after *The Twentieth Plane* was published, the professor wrote a letter to the *Star*. He challenged Benjamin and Dr. Watson to a test: a pivotal séance to determine once and for all whether their messages were indeed from the great beyond.

The professor asked Benjamin to channel the spirit of a well-known friend who, before he died in the sinking of the *Titanic*, had promised to make contact from the other side if it were at all possible. If the séance could provide personal details that only Professor Mavor and his dead friend could know, it would prove Benjamin's powers were indeed real. If not, the fraud would be uncovered.

At first, Benjamin and Dr. Watson tried to avoid the professor's challenge, quibbling over the details and even going as far as to provide the *Star* with quotes from the spirits backing them up. But they eventually relented. On a winter's day in 1919, they headed to Professor Mavor's house near Convocation Hall. Benjamin fell into his usual trance and relayed messages from some of the most famous spirits who dwelled on the Twentieth Plane: Plato, Socrates, Coleridge, Shelley.... But the friend never made an appearance.

Benjamin had failed. The demonstration did nothing to convince the professor the spirits were real — quite the opposite. He told the *Star* that after seeing a séance for himself, he had no doubt the entire thing was a hoax. The communications, he declared, were "crude and clumsy concoctions chiefly from readily available books of reference such as the *Encyclopedia Britannica*…. The sources of inspiration … are to be found on the shelves of any library." Professor Mavor claimed victory.

But that was far from the end of the Twentieth Plane. Benjamin and Dr. Watson were undeterred. The losses of the war provided the pair with a receptive audience. Later that year, they began to hold séances in public halls on Sunday afternoons. Hundreds of people came to see the now-famous medium channel messages from the dead. The following year, Dr. Watson published a second book. He called the séances "by far the most important work of his life" and he claimed Benjamin's powers heralded the arrival of "a new religion, a great age, and a divine civilization."

Even some of the world's most respected intellectuals were curious to learn more about the strange happenings on Euclid Avenue. Sir Arthur Conan Doyle attended one of Benjamin's séances, and recorded details of the event in his extensive spiritualist studies. Lucy Maud Montgomery read *The Twentieth Plane*, but came away less than impressed. "I was much disappointed in it," she wrote in her journal. "It was absolute poppycock — utterly unconvincing. And I was so ready to be convinced."

Others, however, wouldn't give up on the hope of making contact with the dead — no matter how ridiculous Benjamin's claims might sound. In fact, one of them would soon be the most powerful person in Canada.

William Lyon Mackenzie King was the grandson of the old rebel mayor, William Lyon Mackenzie. As a student, he had studied under Professor Mavor at the University of Toronto and was deeply influenced by his ideas — though the two eventually fell out after King helped to organize a student strike. After graduation King entered politics; at the time *The Twentieth Plane* was published, he was the brand new leader of the federal Liberal Party — on his way to winning the next election. By the time he retired, King had spent a total of twenty-one years as prime minister. To this day, he's still the longest-serving prime minister in Canadian history.

And all the while, he was secretly consulting with the spirits of the dead.

Despite Mavor's influence, King had long been interested in the paranormal. He frequently saw supernatural messages in the patterns in his shaving cream, or the hands of a clock, or a seemingly random sequence of numbers and dates. He spent many hours consulting with psychics and read his own tea leaves — one particularly prophetic cup at the Royal York Hotel accurately predicted Liberal victory in an upcoming by-election.

In 1932 King finally attended his first séance. He was immediately hooked. "This is something too wonderful for words," he marvelled. In the following years, he would speak with many of his dearly departed loved ones — including his rebel grandfather — as well as other famous historical figures like Leonardo da Vinci and Sir Wilfrid Laurier. He sought political advice and predictions from the deceased on a variety of subjects, including foreign policy, a major constitutional crisis, and the abdication of King Edward VIII. When predictions proved false, King simply dismissed them as the work of evil spirits, refusing to allow his faith to be shaken.

The Liberals weren't in government when their leader spoke to the dead for the first time — King had lost the 1930 election. But within a few years, he was back in power as the clouds of war gathered on the horizon again. In Europe, the fatal pieces were falling into place. Fascism was on the rise. Hitler was now in power. Canada would soon find itself marching into a war even bloodier than the last. And as it did, the man leading the country wouldn't be relying on the advice of just his most trusted living advisers — but of a few dead ones, too.

23
THE MOST DANGEROUS
WOMAN IN THE WORLD

The Most Dangerous Woman in the World was playing a quiet game of cards. It was a snowy Toronto evening in the winter of 1940, that first terrible winter of the Second World War. She was staying with friends at their home on Vaughan Road, waiting for a meeting to begin. That's when she slumped over in her chair. It was a stroke. One of the greatest orators of the twentieth century couldn't speak a word.

This wasn't the end most people would have expected for Emma Goldman. For decades now, she'd been the most notorious anarchist on the planet. Her ideas made nations tremble: her thoughts about freedom and free speech and free love; about feminism and marriage and birth control; about violence and pacifism and war. She'd been thrown out of the United States for those ideas, forced to flee from Soviet Russia, driven out of Latvia, Sweden, Germany.... Canada was one of the very few places where she was still relatively welcome. She had spent decades in exile.

And everywhere she went, she refused to be intimidated: giving fiery speeches, sparking riots, inspiring assassins, and visiting war zones. Nothing could silence her. Not the years of exile, not prison, not threats of violence. Nothing, that is, until that quiet game of cards.

The first stroke didn't kill her. She still had a few weeks left to live, weakened and afraid, half-paralyzed, robbed of the powerful voice that had made her famous. But even on her deathbed she had one more fight to win. There was one last life to save.

His name was Attilio Bortolotti. Some people knew him as Art Bartell. He was a leader of the Toronto anarchists.

Bortolotti was born in Italy in the very early 1900s — which meant that he was still just a boy when the First World War swept into his hometown. He saw terrible things: death and destruction raining down from the sky; dead bodies dumped in ditches; drunken soldiers killing their own men. But he also saw an act of kindness that would change his life.

One day, during an air raid, his young nephew was in danger of being crushed by falling debris. Bortolotti watched in amazement as a German officer — the enemy — threw himself over the young boy and saved his life. It was a shock. This wasn't the image of the Germans that the Italian newspapers were painting: of the inhuman, savage "Hun."

"Young man," the German officer explained to the confused teenager, "I want you to listen to what I have to say to you. I am a professor; I was teaching at the University of Berlin when I was called to serve in the army. I don't feel that I have the right to kill you because you were born here; nor should you feel you can kill me because I was born in Berlin. I want you to remember three words: *Freiheit über alles*." Freedom above all.

"A revolution," Bortolotti later remembered, "began in my head."

Once the war was over, he left Italy for Canada where he wouldn't be forced into compulsory military service and could lead a more peaceful life. He was just sixteen when he sailed across the Atlantic, checking in at Ellis Island on his way north to join his brother in Windsor.

He spent the next few years working for a black-smith, on construction sites, and in auto factories — both in Windsor and just across the river in Detroit. But his new life wasn't entirely peaceful: the early 1900s were times of turmoil in North America, too — especially for the working class. These were the days of bloody union battles. Of police officers and soldiers killing striking workers in the streets. Of robber barons building private armies to crack down on dissent.

In Windsor, the young Bortolotti was exposed to new ideas. He spent hours reading in the public library, talked about politics with his fellow workers, went to meet-ings, marched in protests, and clashed with police. The more he learned, the more he saw, the more he became attracted to one idea in particular.

By then, anarchism was already an old idea: that government is inherently bad; that people should be completely free; that society should have no hierarchy at all. But in the last few decades, that old idea had been growing in popularity. Anarchists had played leading roles in some of the world's most important events. In France, they helped to establish the Paris Commune. In Russia, they fought alongside the Bolsheviks as they overthrew the tsar. In Canada and in the United States, they were on the front lines of the fight for labour rights: demanding reforms like an eight-hour workday.

They were also growing ever more notorious. While some anarchists didn't believe in violence at all, those who did were giving the philosophy a reputation for bomb-throwing and assassinations. All over the Western World, anarchists were answering the violence against workers by trying to kill those in power. They called it "propaganda of the deed."

They'd been doing it for decades. In Italy, King Umberto was shot three times in the chest as he climbed into his carriage. In Switzerland, Empress Elisabeth was stabbed to death with a file. In Spain, one prime minister was killed while relaxing at a spa and another while window-shopping at a bookstore in Madrid. In Kiev, the Russian prime minister was murdered during an opera. In Greece, King George was shot in the back while taking a walk. In the United States, President McKinley took two bullets to the stomach at point-blank range while visiting the Pan American Exposition in Buffalo. Bombs blew up weddings and carriages and crowds, all in the name of anarchy.

Governments responded with arrests, executions, and even more violence. Sometimes it didn't seem to matter whom they were putting to death — guilty or not — just as long as they were anarchists.

One of the most infamous examples was the case of Sacco and Vanzetti. After a deadly armed robbery in Massachusetts, two Italian immigrants were arrested. They were both anarchists, they were both found guilty, and they were both sentenced to death. But they were also both innocent. The evidence in the case was so flimsy that it sparked international outrage, with major protests held in cities all over the world. In the end, Sacco and Vanzetti were both electrocuted anyway. It wasn't until the 1980s that Massachusetts Governor Michael Dukakis finally cleared their names.

In Windsor, Attilio Bortolotti took up their cause. He organized meetings, raised money, and printed pamphlets. Even after the executions had been carried out, Bortolotti and his fellow anarchists continued to raise awareness of the case. Every year on the anniversary of the executions, you could find Bortolotti on the streets of Windsor and Detroit, handing out thousands of leaflets.

By that point, his politics were starting to get him into trouble. His tireless opposition to fascism — which plenty of Canadians and Americans still supported back then, even as Mussolini marched on Rome and seized power in Italy — had gotten him blacklisted from jobs in the auto industry. His support for Sacco and Vanzetti earned him a meeting with Windsor's chief of police, who told him he was no longer welcome in the city. He was ordered to leave town. At first, Bortolotti just moved across the river, but it quickly became clear that things were getting dangerous. He was arrested in Detroit for handing out pamphlets; the police, he said, beat him unconscious. When he made bail, he slipped back across the border into Windsor, and then kept right on running.

That's how Attilio Bortolotti ended up in Toronto.

He got off the train at Union Station in the fall of 1929 — just a few weeks before the stock market crashed. At first, he didn't know anyone in the city. But when he took his leaflets to an Italian neighbourhood on the anniversary of the Sacco and Vanzetti executions, he met a few Italian socialists and communists who introduced him to a fellow anarchist.

Before long they'd created their own Torontonian anarchist group: Il Gruppo Libertario. They published their own newspaper, organized meetings and events. They became familiar faces at the Labour Lyceum on Spadina Avenue: today, it's a dim sum restaurant in Chinatown (on the corner of St. Andrew Street), but back then it was the political hub for textile workers in the heart of Toronto's Jewish community. The Italians began to meet the city's other anarchists: mostly Jewish and Eastern European immigrants. The community grew. Bortolotti had finally found his home.

It was only a matter of time before he met another anarchist who had been staying in Toronto: the most infamous anarchist in the world.

Emma Goldman was born in Russia in the late 1800s, back in the days of the tsars. She grew up in what one of her biographers called "low-grade Tolstoyan unhappiness." Her father beat her, sometimes with a whip, and when she turned twelve, he forced her to leave school and go work in a factory instead. "All a Jewish girl need know," he told her, "is how to make gefilte fish, cut noodles fine, and give her husband babies."

Even as a child she was strong-willed and defiant. She had no patience for injustice. Decades before Bortolotti was shaped by the horrors of the First World War, Goldman was shaped by the horrors of tsarist Russia.

"I was born a rebel," she would later explain to the *Toronto Daily Star*, "but my first feeling of hatred for the present system came when I was six years old. At that time, I saw a Russian peasant flogged, and this sight of a human being degraded and tortured by his fiendish masters taught me that something was radically wrong somewhere. An indelible picture of the poor, suffering wretch has ever haunted my life."

When she turned sixteen, her father demanded that she get married, so Goldman left home instead. Just as Bortolotti did at that very same age many years later, she sailed across the Atlantic, checked in at Ellis Island, and then headed north. She settled in Rochester, on the American shore of Lake Ontario, where her sister lived.

There, she fell in love with America: with its people and its relative freedoms. But that didn't blind her to its flaws. Rochester was a city filled with sweatshops and slums. Workers toiled away over long hours in dangerous conditions for little pay. Goldman was still just a teenager, but she was bent over a sewing machine in a miserable factory for ten hours every day. It only got worse when her parents arrived from Russia. And when she did eventually get married, she discovered that her husband was impotent and depressed. She left him after only a few months.

Meanwhile, her political ideas were becoming ever more radical. It was the Haymarket affair that finally turned her into an anarchist. The case had a lot in common with the trial of Sacco and Vanzetti. After a deadly bombing during a labour march in Chicago, the police arrested eight anarchists. All of them were convicted. Four of them were hanged. A fifth committed suicide. But the trial was a farce: there was no real evidence, the jury was biased, and not even the prosecutor claimed that any of the suspects had actually thrown the bomb. People all over the world were appalled. Today, it's remembered as one of the darkest chapters in American labour history; it even served as the inspiration for International Workers Day, which is still celebrated on May Day every year.

Outraged, Goldman headed south to New York City to take up the cause. She arrived on a summer's day in 1889, just twenty years old, with nothing but five dollars and a sewing machine. It didn't take long for her to settle in, though. That very first afternoon, she headed straight for an anarchist café. That night, she went to see her first anarchist speech. Before long, she was giving her own speeches, earning a reputation as one of the most riveting lecturers in the country, passionately speaking about issues like labour rights, feminism, and political philosophy.

Today, many of her ideas seem pretty obvious — an eight-hour workday, legal birth control, gay rights — but in the late 1800s and early 1900s, even those ideas were deeply radical. She quickly attracted the attention not only of the press, but also of the police. Once she was arrested for giving a talk about methods of birth control. On another occasion, it was for inciting a riot. ("Ask for work," she told a crowd of the starving and unemployed. "If they don't give you work, ask for bread. If they do not give you work or bread, then take bread.") She got so used to spending time in prison that she started to carry a book with her wherever she went, just in case she suddenly found herself in a jail cell without anything to read.

By the end of the 1800s, Goldman had become one of the biggest celebrities in the country. She was a front-page staple. Red Emma, they called her. The Queen of Anarchism. The Most Dangerous Woman in the World.

And she *could* be dangerous. At least to some people. In those days, it felt like radical change could come at any moment. To many the revolution didn't just seem possible, it seemed inevitable. The young Goldman was willing to do whatever she could to help. If violence was necessary, that was okay with her. Even murder.

Just a few years after she arrived in New York, Goldman planned an assassination of her own. She and her lover, Alexander Berkman — whom she met at that anarchist café on her very first afternoon in the city — plotted to kill Henry Clay Frick, the chairman of the Carnegie Steel Corporation. He was responsible for a bloody crackdown on a strike at a steel mill in Pennsylvania, hiring hundreds of Pinkerton detectives — private mercenary soldiers — to attack the striking workers, killing nine of them. In retaliation, Berkman burst into Frick's office with a revolver, shot him twice, and then stabbed him with a steel file. But the attack failed: Frick survived and Berkman spent the next fourteen years in prison.

Goldman, though, walked free. No one knew she'd been involved. And in time her views on violence seemed to change. In later years, whenever asked, she would always distance herself from the use of force. "The only remedy for the people is anarchy ... the form of revolution I want is bloodless.... Anarchism does not believe in violence.... Ideas are the greatest of bombs."

Still, even then she wasn't willing to condemn those who *did* resort to violence. When President McKinley was shot, the assassin claimed that he was inspired to do it by Goldman's lectures. "Her words set me on fire," Leon Czolgosz said. Goldman was arrested and questioned, but she refused to denounce the killer. "I have never been an advocate of violence," she told the papers, but "I have always felt that when an individual resorts to violence it is the fault of the conditions above him that bring him to it."

It was a theme she often repeated. For her, the real blame for any assassination always lay with systemic oppression. "As an anarchist, I am opposed to violence. But if people want to do away with assassins, they must first do away with the conditions which produce murderers."

In the end, though, it wasn't Goldman's violence that got her kicked out of the United States. It was her pacifism.

When the First World War broke out, Goldman firmly opposed it. It was, she argued, a war to protect the interests of the rich: not a cause worth dying — or killing — for. For the first three years of the war, her opinion was widely shared in the United States. President Woodrow Wilson even won re-election on a promise to stay out of the fight. But once the Americans did join the war, speaking out against it was no longer allowed. Opinions that had been widely shared suddenly became illegal.

Goldman, as always, refused to back down, giving speeches denouncing the draft. That gave the American authorities the opportunity they'd been waiting for: an excuse to get rid of her.

She was rounded up with a bunch of other anarchists and deported — all loaded onto a ship and sent to Russia. If they believed in revolution, the government told them, then the brand new Soviet state was the perfect place for them.

Of course, it wasn't. At first, Goldman was actually pretty happy to be going back to Russia. As someone who had personally witnessed the horrors of life under the tsars, she had high hopes for the Russian Revolution. But when she saw it with her own eyes, she realized it had gone terribly wrong. A meeting with Lenin confirmed her fears. They had replaced one totalitarian system with another. She fled the country. Goldman would spend the rest of her life angrily denouncing the Communists.

After that she never really found another permanent home. She spent the rest of her life living out of her suitcase, forced out of one country after another. Finally, she arranged a marriage to a Welsh miner so that she could get a British passport. That gave her the right to live in Canada, where she would spend much of the rest of her life.

She would never again be allowed to live in her beloved United States, so she settled for the next best thing: she would stay in Toronto, just across the lake from Rochester, as close as she could get to her family and to the country she loved.

This was 1926. Toronto was still a deeply conservative city: a provincial town, deathly quiet on Sundays, staunchly British; not the kind of place you'd expect to find the world's most notorious anarchist. And not the kind of place the world's most notorious anarchist expected to find herself.

"I am so terribly cut off from intellectual contact," Goldman once wrote while she was staying in Toronto. "I grow so depressed and unhappy at times it seems I could not stand it another day."

When the old anarchist criticized the lack of modern books in the library, the librarian gave her a blunt reply: "We do not buy books we consider immoral."

Toronto was, Goldman complained, "deadly dull."

Still, it wasn't all bad. The authorities in Toronto were more tolerant of her ideas than those in the United States had been — even if they *did* still screen all her mail. And there was a small, dedicated community of anarchists, artists, and other progressive thinkers who were thrilled to have her in the city. They put her up in their homes, helped her to organize meetings and lectures, donated money to the causes she championed.

Plus, every time the *Toronto Daily Star* wrote about her — and they wrote about her a lot — it was in positively glowing terms. They called her "the world's greatest feminine apostle of free speech." "Brilliant." "A speaker of notable excellence." "You were impressed not only by her knowledge but also by her wisdom. She was a feminine Socrates conducting a brilliant dialogue on high and grave questions of human destiny and human conduct."

"No woman of her generation," the *Star* would remember after she died, "was more widely known or lived more fully than Emma Goldman. None clung more staunchly, through adversity, to her ideals."

Goldman became a familiar name in the local papers and in lecture halls across the city. She spoke at the Labour Lyceum on Spadina, the Heliconian Club in Yorkville, the Hygea Hall on Elm Street, the Oddfellows Temple on College — always after a stiff drink of whisky to calm her nerves. Crowds of hundreds came to see her talk about feminism, free love, politics, literature…. She thundered on about Sacco and Vanzetti, denounced Toronto schools for forcing all their boys to have military training, and railed against the dangers of Stalin with such passion that local Communists would attend her lectures just so they could shout her down. She warned of a coming war before Hitler had even taken power and gave speeches condemning him when many in Toronto still thought fascism was a perfectly acceptable idea.

She became a role model in a city starved for radical thought, inspiring those who were determined to make Toronto a more progressive place, and pressuring them to do better when she thought they were falling short. It was Emma Goldman who dared to speak about birth control back when it was still illegal, giving a lecture to a packed house at the Hygea Hall, earning a roar of applause when she declared contraception to be a right. (She was careful not to mention any specific methods — that would have been blatantly illegal and would surely have landed her in the clutches of the Toronto Police Morality Squad — but she did hand out cards directing women to doctors who might help.) And it was Emma Goldman who launched the movement to ban Toronto teachers from using physical violence as a method of disciplining their students.

She would never fully settle in Toronto; she kept living out of her suitcase, like she always did. She had three long stays in the city, but would spend long periods away from it: writing her autobiography in France, visiting the anarchists fighting the fascists in the Spanish Civil War, going on speaking tours across Canada — thanks to the support of Eleanor Roosevelt, she was even allowed to make one last trip to the United States.

But she always came back to Toronto. And that meant she was bound to run into Attilio Bortolotti eventually.

"I went to hear her," he said, "and was flabbergasted by the way she spoke, with her energy, with the beauty of her sentences." They were introduced after her speech, and eventually became close friends. Bortolotti volunteered as her unofficial chauffeur, happy to drive the old anarchist around the city as she gave lectures and attended meetings. Once, he even took her to Windsor so she could gaze longingly across the river at the country she adored. ("She looked at Belle Isle and Detroit," he said, "as though through the eyes of a lover. It was then that I understood how much America meant to her.")

But this was 1939. All of Goldman's dire warnings were about to come true: Hitler invaded Poland that September; the Second World War was underway.

That meant trouble for Toronto's anarchists. With tensions rising, Bortolotti found his fascist enemies even more dangerous than before. "I was threatened with being 'taken for a ride,'" he later remembered, "and for the only time in my life — I detest firearms and killing — I carried a pistol for a few months."

Meanwhile, the authorities were cracking down, too. As the paranoia of the war years set in, anyone with unusual ideas became a target for suspicion. Italians, even more than most; Mussolini didn't enter the war immediately, but he had long been one of Hitler's closest allies. It didn't matter that Bortolotti was one of the city's most ardent anti-fascists, or that he had been warning Canadians about the dangers of Hitler and Mussolini for years, or that Toronto's own Nazi supporters were trying to silence him. In fact, many have suggested that the police were working with the fascists, who gave them tips about the anarchists they both despised.

"We organized demonstrations and street meetings at which I ... spoke, and were attacked by mounted police," Bortolotti remembered. "The authorities kept me

under constant surveillance, and now they tried in earnest to deport me."

It was the war that finally gave them their chance.
When the country was at peace, the police had to respect
civil rights. But when war was declared, the War Measures
Act came into effect. Suddenly, the authorities had what
one historian has called "quasi-totalitarian powers." They
were, according to another, "the most serious restrictions
upon the civil liberties of Canadians since Confederation."
Habeas corpus was suspended. So was the right to a trial.
Political groups could be banned by the government. So
could entire religions. Eventually, William Lyon Mackenzie
King's government would use the War Measures Act to
round up Canadians of Japanese descent and imprison
them in internment camps — one of the most horrifying
abuses of power in the history of the country.

By the end of the first month of the war, the government
had expanded the Act to give itself the power to censor any
literature it didn't like — and to arrest anyone found with
this "dangerous" material. Hundreds of newspapers and
magazines were shut down. Bookstores were raided, their
owners arrested. Private homes were targeted, too. Word
began to spread among the Toronto anarchists: the police
were raiding their homes one by one. Some rushed to burn
their papers before it was too late.

The authorities came for Bortolotti just a few days
after the new rules went into effect. Before dawn one
morning in early October, police on horseback surrounded his home on Gladstone Avenue (at the very top
of the street, near Dupont). It was the Royal Canadian

Mounted Police and Toronto's notoriously brutal anti-Communist unit: the Red Squad. They burst into the house, grabbing all five anarchists who were staying there. "Get up," they told Bortolotti, "and put on your Sunday best. You won't be going to work for quite a while." They searched the house, finding two guns with the triggers removed (the anarchists used them as props in plays) and seized all of Bortolotti's books, magazines, and newspapers: a library of fifteen hundred volumes. The police would burn them all.

Bortolotti was arrested. He would spend months in the Don Jail while the government worked to deport him. The original charges were dropped, and most of the other anarchists were released. But Bortolotti wasn't a Canadian citizen and, having been threatened by Windsor's chief of police, he hadn't checked in at customs the last time he came across the border from Detroit. So the government was planning on sending him back to Italy anyway, where Mussolini's fascist government would be waiting for him. If he was lucky, he would be thrown into a fascist prison. Otherwise, he would simply be killed.

But not if Emma Goldman had anything to say about it. She was an old woman now, but still as defiant as ever. She leaped into action, asking her friends and allies to support Bortolotti's defence. She organized meetings, raised money, and hired a lawyer.

It wasn't easy. For the first few months, it was hard to find anyone to support the cause. The newspapers refused to cover the case. And even liberal Canadians were reluctant to challenge the government during a time of war.

"Unfortunately," Goldman complained, "there exists a conspiracy of silence among the daily journals.... More sad is the complete absence of individual animation of civic sense, disposed to defend civil rights from the invasion of authority ... no journal, no magazine socialist, liberal, unionist or other, in the US or Canada, said one word in defence of the arrested of Toronto."

Meanwhile, Bortolotti was falling ill, suffering in the cold, damp conditions of the Don Jail. He came down with bronchitis, lost twelve pounds, ran a fever of 103°F, and finally had to be transferred into the prison's hospital ward.

Goldman refused to give up, but the campaign was taking a toll. It was, she admitted, "the hardest thing I have done in many years.... [I am] frightfully weary of the struggle, and tired, tired beyond words."

That's when she suffered her first stroke.

Goldman was playing a quiet game of bridge with friends, passing the time on a snowy evening before yet another meeting about Bortolotti's case. "God damn it," she complained at the beginning of a new hand, "why did you lead with that?"

Then, the Most Dangerous Woman in the World slumped over sideways in her chair. At first, her friends thought she'd dropped a card and was bending over to pick it up. But she'd actually suffered a massive stroke.

Bortolotti was out on bail when he got the phone call. "I don't know how I drove without causing accidents," he remembered, "because I was out of my mind. And I arrived on Vaughan Road there, and saw Emma, moaning — she couldn't talk any more. Just to think that here was Emma, the greatest orator in America, unable to utter one word." She was half-paralyzed. There was fear in her eyes. Embarrassed that her bare knee was showing, she pulled her skirt down with one hand. Moments later, the ambulance arrived.

She spent the next six weeks at Toronto General Hospital, where they did what they could for her. She was in tears for much of that time. When she was finally well enough to go home, her speech still hadn't recovered; she struggled to say even a few words. Still, she kept working. She could understand conversations and read her letters, getting friends to write her replies.

Slowly but surely, her persistence had begun to pay off. People had started contributing to Bortolotti's defence. An Italian-American anarchist newspaper led the way. Then, a Yiddish-language paper in New York. There was a spaghetti dinner to raise money in Chicago. A play performed in Brooklyn. Another benefit in Massachusetts. Goldman had her letters to the editor published in *The Nation*, *The New Republic*, and *The Canadian Forum*. Eventually, some leading progressive Canadians — like the leader of the federal CCF party (the forerunner of the NDP) — were convinced to join the fight. More letters were written. There were meetings with MPs. The *Star* published an editorial asking the government to halt the deportation. The tide was finally turning.

Goldman lived long enough to hear the good news: Bortolotti was free to stay. They'd won. He would eventually get his Canadian citizenship, start his own successful business, and play a leading role in Toronto's anarchist community for decades to come. Thirty years later, the *Globe and Mail* would write about him fondly, calling him "the grand old man of Toronto anarchism."

A few months after Goldman's first stroke, she suffered a second. This time, she wouldn't recover at all. She died in the middle of May at the house on Vaughan Road.

A service was held at the Labour Lyceum, the same hall where Goldman's resounding voice had once filled the air. For three hours people shared their stories and remembered her. The crowd was so big there wasn't enough room inside the hall; the mourners spilled out onto Spadina. A full funeral in Chicago followed, where she was laid to rest next to the martyrs of the Haymarket affair who had inspired her to become an anarchist all those years ago.

She had gone down fighting, working hard for a cause she believed in right to the very end. It's all she ever wanted.

Once, years earlier, the *Star* asked her if she had any regrets. "Whatever will happen will happen," she said. "I hope to die on deck, true to my ideals with my eyes towards the east — the rising star."

That's exactly what she did.

24
I'LL NEVER SMILE AGAIN

I t was supposed to be routine surgery. But there's nothing
truly routine about cutting open a living human being.
There's always a chance something will go wrong. And for
Harold Cohen, it did. He was still in his twenties when
he went under the knife in 1939. During the operation,
his kidneys gave out. He never woke up. He left behind
a brand new wife; they'd only been married a few weeks.

Her name was Ruth Lowe. She was a piano player.
Born in Toronto, she dropped out of high school at sixteen
so she could support her family by working at the Song
Shoppe on Yonge Street. These were the years of the Great
Depression, when the people of the city scraped together
what little money they could and went dancing, forget-
ting their troubles for a few hours as they twirled across
the floor of jazz clubs like the Palais Royale or the Palace
Pier. Big bands were all the rage, and local orchestra leaders were constantly searching for new material, heading
down to the music stores on Yonge Street south of Queen
— "the Tin Pan Alley of Toronto." When they got there,
they would find young Ruth Lowe waiting for them at the

Song Shoppe, ready to play the piano for them so they could hear what the sheet music sounded like before they made their purchase. She had a reputation as one of the best sight-readers in the city, and soon she had her own group, too: The Shadows. But that was just the beginning.

Her big break came in the spring of 1935. That's when Ina Ray Hutton & Her Melodears came to town. They were one of the hottest acts around: a big band whose members were all women — the inspiration for the group in *Some Like It Hot*. That night, the Melodears had a big gig at Shea's Theatre (on Bay Street; it was eventually demolished to make way for Nathan Phillips Square), but their piano player was sick. When they asked around for a replacement, someone suggested Ruth Lowe.

She did such a good job they offered her a permanent position. And so, Lowe left the Song Shoppe and headed out on tour. She was now playing piano and writing the arrangements for one of the most popular bands on the continent.

That's how she met Harold Cohen, a music publicist from Chicago. They went on a blind date and fell madly in love; soon they were married. But they were able to spend only a few blissful weeks together before his ill-fated surgery.

When tragedy struck, Lowe was devastated. She was just twenty-three when she returned home to Toronto as a widow. She filled some of her lonely hours by working as an accompanist at the CBC, but she spent most of her time in mourning, holed up inside her mother's apartment overlooking Christie Pits, where she could watch as joyful couples strolled arm-in-arm through the park. That's when she sat down at the piano to write a new song. It was a slow, melancholy tune; full of longing for the love she'd lost.

> I'll never smile again
> Until I smile at you
> I'll never laugh again
> What good would it do?
> For tears would fill my eyes
> My heart would realize
> That our romance is through*

CBC listeners were the first to hear it. The famous Torontonian orchestra leader Percy Faith heard Lowe rehearsing the song at work one day and asked if he could perform it during his show on Canada's brand new public radio station. But he was just the first of many to cover the tune.

Lowe managed to get an acetate recording of that CBC performance and had an idea. One of the biggest of all the big bands was in town. Tommy Dorsey and His Orchestra were playing at the CNE, where a huge tent was pitched on the Exhibition Grounds — it had room for ten thousand on the dance floor. Lowe knew the guitarist in Dorsey's band, so she waited outside the tent until she ran into him — he promised to pass the record along to Dorsey himself.

---

* "I'll Never Smile Again." Words and music by Ruth Lowe. Copyright © 1939 UNIVERSAL MUSIC CORP. Copyright renewed. All Rights Reserved. Used by permission. *Reprinted with permission of Hal Leonard LLC.*

Dorsey loved it. And soon, he knew exactly who should perform it: an up-and-coming new singer he poached from another orchestra. He'd been searching for the perfect song to launch the young crooner's career. "I'll Never Smile Again" would prove to be exactly what Dorsey was looking for: the song that would make Frank Sinatra famous.

But it wasn't just the talent of Ol' Blue Eyes that would make the mournful tune one of the biggest hits of the big band era. The song came at just the right time. Sinatra's version of "I'll Never Smile Again" debuted in June of 1940. The Second World War was underway.

This war would be even more deadly than the last. By the time Sinatra's soulful tones began to fill the airwaves, the Nazis were already in Paris and German bombs were falling on British cities. Over the next few years, tens of millions of soldiers would leave their loved ones behind and head off to war: many of them would never come home.

Suddenly, Lowe's lyrics weren't just about the death of her own husband, but the death of millions. Her personal grief had become universal. The words she wrote at her mother's piano on Bloor Street were now speaking for an entire generation of mourners who felt they would never again be able to smile, or to laugh, or to love.

That same summer, for the first time ever, the editors of *Billboard* magazine published a chart of bestselling singles. When they did, "I'll Never Smile Again" was at the top of the list; it would stay there for the next twelve weeks. That little heartbroken tune from Toronto had become the defining soundtrack to the first dreadful summer of the Second World War.

25
JOURNEY'S END

For more than sixty years, they kept her note secret. It was found next to her body, lying on the bedside table along with an assortment of pill bottles. For decades, her family guarded the sad contents of that page, the painful final confession of one of the most beloved authors in Canadian history:

"I have lost my mind by spells and I do not dare think what I may do in those spells. May God forgive me and I hope everyone else will forgive me even if they cannot understand. My position is too awful to endure and nobody realizes it. What an end to a life in which I tried always to do my best."

Lucy Maud Montgomery had spent nearly forty years as one of the giants of the Canadian literary world. She was still in her early thirties when her first book was published, and *Anne of Green Gables* was an instant success. The story of the lovably precocious redheaded orphan Anne Shirley would sell tens of millions of copies, and spawn a series of sequels, movies, and eventually TV shows. By the end of the 1930s, the house that inspired Green Gables had already become such a popular tourist destination that the Canadian government turned it into a national park. No less an authority than Mark Twain once called Anne Shirley "the dearest and most moving and delightful child" since Lewis Carroll wrote *Alice's Adventures in Wonderland*.

It was Montgomery's stories about Prince Edward Island that made her famous. But it wasn't long after *Anne of Green Gables* that the author left the Maritimes for Ontario. Montgomery spent the last decade of her life living on the outskirts of Toronto in the suburban village of Swansea: the neighbourhood that stretches between High Park and the Humber. She moved into one of the stately old houses on Riverside Drive, standing high above the banks of the river. Knowing it was likely to be the last house she ever called home, Montgomery named it Journey's End.

Her first few years in Swansea were a vigorous whirl of activity. She was just one long streetcar ride away from downtown Toronto, the centre of the Canadian literary scene in the thirties. She gave speeches and readings, attended social teas, and lovingly answered her fan mail. She wrote several more novels, taking inspiration from the city around her, carrying a notebook with her wherever she went, scribbling down snippets of conversation she overheard on the TTC. All the while she acted as a passionate advocate for Canadian writers: giving advice, writing promotional blurbs, insisting that Canadian stories were worth telling and that Canadian voices were worth hearing.

But even as she wrote new books and championed up-and-coming young writers, Montgomery's own professional reputation was under attack. A new generation of male modernist critics dismissed her work as too "sugary" to be taken seriously. "Canadian fiction," as one influential detractor put it, "was to go no lower."

Montgomery's novels had once been read and adored by nearly everyone: from schoolchildren to the prime minister of Great Britain. Now, she was increasingly being pigeonholed as a children's author who wrote stories that could be enjoyed only by girls. Her lively accounts of Anne's adventures in PEI were derided as trivial compared to the stark, minimalist prose of writers like Ernest Hemingway (a one-time reporter for the *Star* who couldn't wait to leave Toronto). Montgomery's focus on local Canadian stories was branded as provincial regionalism — how could the stories of a schoolgirl in small-town Prince Edward Island have the same universal appeal as those of the famous drunk misogynists in Paris?

The battle to preserve her public reputation was exhausting. But it paled in comparison to her private struggles. Behind the scenes at Journey's End, all was not well. "There has never been any happiness in this house — there never will be," she confessed at the end of 1937.

Montgomery had long suffered from depression. And as she approached the end of her life, it deepened. She was plagued by mood swings and waves of crippling anxiety, haunted by nightmares and painful memories, beset by headaches, vomiting, shooting pains, and trembling hands. She had difficulty sleeping. At times, she couldn't concentrate well enough to write. The pills the doctors prescribed only made things worse, and before long she was hooked on them.

She found little comfort in her family life. She complained that her time at home was draining. Her husband, a retired minister, suffered from his own mental health issues, depressed and troubled to the point of hearing voices. Their eldest son was a constant concern: after years spent as a struggling law student, he graduated to become a struggling lawyer. Worse than his fragile financial situation, however, was his scandalous personal life — a source of constant concern for Montgomery. Privately, she was convinced he was a psychopath.

Her journal chronicled her despair. "I have lost every hope for things ever getting better," she admitted in one entry. "Everything I hoped and dreamed and planned for has gone with the wind. I am broken and defeated." In another she lamented, "The present is unbearable. The past is spoiled. There is no future."

And then came a new worry: the Second World War.

Montgomery had believed in the necessity of the First World War, calling it "a death-grapple between freedom and tyranny." She became the president of her local Red Cross Society, volunteering long hours in support of the war effort. She hoped it would indeed be the war to end all war, a necessary sacrifice in the pursuit of a better world. She looked forward to the stronger, more united Canada she expected to emerge in the wake of the conflict, along with a more distinctly Canadian literature.

The novel she wrote over the last two years of the First World War — another Anne sequel called *Rainbow Valley* — was an especially patriotic tome. She dedicated the novel to three Canadian soldiers she knew "who made the supreme sacrifice that the happy valleys of their home land might be kept sacred from the ravage of the invader."

Her next book, *Rilla of Ingleside*, would be filled with such vitriolic anti-German sentiment that her publisher censored parts of it after her death. In it, Anne's son Walter becomes a war hero. He writes a famous poem along the lines of "In Flanders Fields" and then dies fighting the Germans in France.

But the Second World War made it clear the First World War hadn't been the end of the carnage. This wasn't the new, more peaceful world Montgomery had imagined. And now she had sons of her own old enough to fight. She became obsessed by the idea that her "good" son, a medical student, would be called away to die on the front lines just as Anne's had.

You can see those dark thoughts reflected in her writing. Montgomery spent her final days working on one last book about Anne Shirley, the closing sequel to *Anne of Green Gables*. It's a collection of short stories and poems called *The Blythes Are Quoted* — most of the material previously published and repurposed for the book. The text is centred around the First World War and paints a much darker picture than Montgomery's earlier works. *The Blythes Are Quoted* is a far cry from the golden days of Anne's childhood. The stories in this last book are full of death and despair.

The manuscript arrived at her publisher's office on April 24, 1942. On that same day, the author's maid came into her room and found her lifeless body in bed.

It's possible that Lucy Maud Montgomery didn't kill herself. Some suggest she may have accidentally overdosed on the pills she was taking to combat her depression and her other ailments. But at her death-bed, her son and her doctor both assumed she'd taken her own life. The despairing tone of the words scribbled on the sheet of paper they found next to her certainly gave that impression (though the date on the page was from two days earlier). And so did some of the entries in her diary. "People talk about the bitterness of death," she wrote in one. "It is not to be compared to the bitterness of life. Bitterness like some gnawing incurable disease." And in another: "death would be so welcome."

Her family kept the true circumstances of Montgomery's passing a secret for six decades. It wasn't until 2008 — the one hundredth anniversary of the publication of *Anne of Green Gables* — that Montgomery's granddaughter went public with the story on behalf of the family. "I have come to feel very strongly," she wrote in the *Globe and Mail* as she revealed the apparent suicide, "that the stigma surrounding mental illness will be forever upon us as a society until we sweep away the misconception that depression happens to other people, not us — and most certainly not to our heroes and icons."

It took even longer for the secrets of *The Blythes Are Quoted* to be revealed. Montgomery's last manuscript was filed away in the archives, forgotten, for years. An incomplete version was published in the 1970s, but the full version didn't hit the shelves until 2009. That's the first time we got to read Anne Shirley's final words.

The book ends with a conversation between Anne and her eldest son. She's an old woman now. She, like Montgomery, has lived long enough to see the Second World War bring death and destruction back to the globe. She, too, is deeply shaken by it, her faith in the bloody cause shattered.

The last words Anne Shirley ever speaks are heartbreaking: now, she admits, she is glad her second son died in the First World War. "He could never have lived with his memories," she says, "and if he had seen the futility of the sacrifice they made then mirrored in this ghastly holocaust ..."

She trails off and says nothing more. Anne and her creator fall silent.

26
HOW TOPPY TOPHAM DIED

The morning of March 24, 1945 witnessed the biggest airborne operation in the history of anything ever. It was called Operation Varsity. Thousands upon thousands of planes and gliders took off in England and soared across the skies of Europe. They stretched out for more than three hundred kilometres — the distance from London to Paris — and took two and a half hours to pass. They were on their way to Germany.

The Second World War was nearly over. It had already been nine months since the Allies landed in Normandy. The 1st Canadian Parachute Battalion had been there, students and shopkeepers and dentists from places like Calgary and Saskatoon and Toronto leaping out of planes into the air above France, dropping behind German lines to secure bridges and roads. Hundreds of them had died doing it. The following winter, the battalion had patrolled the freezing snows of the Ardennes Forest, resisting the brutal German counterattack at the Battle of the Bulge.

Now, the Allies had pushed all the way across Western Europe into Germany itself, but hundreds of thousands of people were still dying. The Allies had one more mammoth task ahead before they could fan out across the country and overrun it: they needed to cross the Rhine River. What was left of Hitler's army was waiting for them on the other side. And so they launched Operation Varsity.

When they reached the Rhine, tens of thousands of men leaped out of the planes, white parachutes bursting open in the morning light. They were easy targets for the bullets and anti-aircraft shells that rose to meet them. Many men died before they hit the ground. Hundreds of planes fell burning from the sky.

But that's not how Toppy Topham died.

Frederick George Topham had been born in Toronto during the First World War, had gone to school at Runnymede Collegiate on Jane Street, and spent some time working as a miner at Kirkland Lake. He'd come to Europe as a medic with the 1st Canadian Parachute Battalion, stitching up men on the front lines. Now, he was among those floating down out of the sky — and, unlike so many others, he was lucky enough to survive the drop.

That was good news for the men below. They needed him that bloody morning. Many had been shot on their way down. So Topham got to work, rushing from one injured paratrooper to the next: performing first aid, tending to wounds, saving lives.

It was about eleven o'clock — an hour after his jump — when Topham heard another cry for help. An injured soldier was lying out in the open, bullets whizzing around him. A medical orderly ran over, knelt down at the man's side, and was shot dead. A second

medic died the same way. Topham saw it all happen —
and then he rushed out to help.

They say the air was laced with machine gun and
sniper fire, but he made it all the way through to the
wounded soldier, and began tending to his patient among
the dead bodies. That's how Toppy Topham got shot. In
the face.

But that's not how Toppy Topham died.

Fighting the pain, blood pouring from his mangled
nose and cheek, he stood his ground, gave the soldier first aid and then picked him up and carried him
through the hail of bullets into the woods to safety. Then
he turned around and headed right back out again to
help more of the wounded men. For the next two hours,
he refused to stop working, refused to let anyone take
care of his bloodied face until the entire area had been
cleared of casualties.

And his day wasn't over yet. On his way back to
join his company, Topham came across an armoured
machine gun carrier that had been hit by a shell. Men
were trapped inside as it burned. Mortars were still landing all around it. An officer warned everyone to stand
back. Topham rushed in.

Flames leaped from the carrier and explosions burst all
around him, but that's not how Toppy Topham died, either.

He found three men inside the vehicle and carried
each of them to safety. One died of his wounds, but the
other two survived. They wouldn't be the last lives he
saved that day. The Torontonian medic kept working for
hours on end.

It would take the Allies a day and a half to win that battle. More than sixty Canadians died; nearly two hundred were wounded. Then, they pressed on deeper into Germany until they finally ran into the Soviet army coming the other way. The war in Europe was over.

The 1st Canadian Parachute Battalion was the very first unit sent home to Canada. They arrived in Halifax having completed every mission they'd ever been given, and having never given up an objective they'd won.

Back home in Toronto, the city had been waiting to celebrate their new hero. They threw Topham a parade along Bay Street to Old City Hall with a hundred members of his battalion serving as an honour guard. He was asked to lay the cornerstone for the new Sunnybrook Memorial Hospital for veterans of the war. Soon, an entire new neighbourhood on St. Clair East would bear his name: Topham Park. King George V would award him the Victoria Cross — the highest military honour in the Commonwealth. Nearly sixty years later, when the medal went up for auction in 2004, the members of his old battalion raised hundreds of thousands of dollars to keep it in Canada. They gave it to the Canadian War Museum in Ottawa.

Topham remained modest even as he was hailed as a hero. "I don't believe that one boy in the outfit wouldn't have done the same," he told the *Star*. With the war over, he settled down to a quiet life in Etobicoke. He briefly worked for the Toronto police until he realized they wanted to use him for public relations rather than to patrol a beat. Then he went to work for Toronto Hydro instead.

It was on a spring day in 1968 that Topham climbed high up a hydro pole to check a power line in the Junction. It was an ordinary part of his job, nowhere near as risky as that death-defying day on the banks of the Rhine. But something went terribly wrong. Four thousand volts of electricity were suddenly sent coursing through his body. He lost his grip and fell twenty-five feet onto the ground below.

But that's not how Toppy Topham died, either. He was rushed to Toronto General Hospital and survived the shock and the fall.

No, it was years later that Toppy Topham died. He'd survived the horrors of the Second World War, a bullet to the face, a burning machine gun carrier, a terrible electrical accident, and a dangerous fall, but in the end it was the most mundane of causes that ended his life.

Toppy Topham died of a simple heart attack in 1974.

27
TORONTO HEARTS STALINGRAD

Things were looking good for Hitler. It was the summer of 1942: the Nazis had already swept across Europe; now they were pushing on into Russia, marching toward Stalingrad. The Russians were in deep trouble. In the first year of fighting, the Red Army had lost half of their men. And Stalin — a bloodthirsty lunatic of a dictator at the best of times — was starting to get a little bit desperate.

Stalingrad was a city teeming with people. It was a major metropolis before the war began; since then, refugees had doubled the population. But as the Germans prepared to attack, Stalin refused to organize an evacuation. While food and supplies were shipped away to safety, the human beings were left behind. His soldiers, he figured, would fight more passionately to defend a city full of innocent civilians. And in case that wasn't enough to guarantee victory, he ordered that any officer found retreating should be put on trial or shot on the spot — "Not one step back!" — and that anyone who could carry a rifle should fight. Men, women, *and* children would all be part of one of the bloodiest battles in history.

People in Toronto and all over the world watched as two of the most powerful empires on Earth brought their military fury down upon the city. Stalingrad was turned into a living hell. The planes of the German Luftwaffe began by dropping more than a thousand tons of bombs, reducing most of the city to a burning pile of rubble. The fighting on the ground that followed was brutal, even by the horrifying standards of the Second World War.

"The entire city became an inferno," the *Toronto Daily Star* reported, "but it put up the fiercest fight in modern warfare. The fight for each building lasted for days, even weeks, at a time. Each room, each floor, constituted a separate front within a front. Every structure became a fortress."

Civilians who tried to flee by foot or by ferry were bombed, massacred by the hundreds. Corpses piled up in the streets.

Meanwhile, thousands of orphaned children were left on their own in the middle of the destruction; they lived in the rubble for months on end, starving and freezing to death, terrified, and easy targets for snipers. "Under constant bombardment, life went on;" the *Star* wrote, "the people clung to the ruins of the city, children were fed in the shadows of broken buildings, put to bed in dugouts, nursed in cellars when sick."

The bloodbath raged on for five straight months, through the autumn and on into the harsh Russian winter. At times, it seemed as if the Nazis were on the verge of winning, but they could never quite kill the last few Soviet soldiers.

By February, the tide had turned. The Red Army retook the city and in doing so they helped to shift the momentum of the entire war. Hitler's army was deeply wounded. The Nazis would never again win an important battle on the Eastern Front. The following year, the Allies would land at Normandy. The year after that, the war would finally be over.

But victory at Stalingrad in 1943 came at a terrible price. Nearly two million people had been killed or wounded in that one battle. *Two million.* And the suffering wasn't over yet. The city was a smouldering ruin. It would take years to rebuild. "Stalingrad, city of heroes, still shivers in the icy Russian winter," the *Star* told its readers in Toronto, half a world away. There were orphans who needed help, the newspaper reported. "Many of them had been living for months during the siege in holes in the ground, and when they were found they were swollen with hunger and their limbs were frozen." Some estimates say fifteen million Russian children lost their parents during the war.

Toronto had plenty of its own dead to mourn. More than four thousand men and women from the city would lose their lives during the Second World War. But the staggering death toll in Stalingrad struck a chord with Torontonians worried about their own loved ones who were fighting and dying on the other side of the ocean.

So Toronto decided to help.

A few months after the end of the Battle of Stalingrad, Toronto City Council declared "Friendship With Russia

Week" and then "Stalingrad Day." They followed that up by officially "adopting" Stalingrad. The next two winters in Toronto produced a massive outpouring of support for the Russians living in their ruined city more than eight thousand kilometres away.

The City of Toronto Stalingrad Committee was created. And a Stalingrad Fund, too. The mayor was made honorary chairman. "Citizens of Toronto could not support a more worthy cause than the noble people of Stalingrad," he declared. "These people have shown us the way to be real heroes. We must give thanks to the Soviet armies and the brave Russian people who gave us those armies. I sincerely hope that all Toronto will get behind this great cause in the name of humanity."

And they did. Millions of dollars were raised in donations. More than 150 organizations came together to organize an ambitious clothing drive, going door to door asking for whatever spare clothing and knitted goods they could find. They collected thirty tons of it, which was stored at a depot on Yonge Street and then shipped off to the USSR.

Many of the most powerful people in Canada worked hard to improve the relationship with "our gallant allies" in Russia. A National Council for Canadian-Soviet Friendship was formed, with the active support of wealthy businessmen, premiers, lieutenant governors, and justices of the Supreme Court. Prime Minister King served as chair.

In 1943, thanks in part to the Eaton family and the heir to the Maple Leaf Foods fortune, there was a three-day Congress of Canadian-Soviet Friendship at the swanky Royal York Hotel. In 1944, there was a second. The event ended with a rally at Maple Leaf Gardens: seventeen thousand people showed up. The Congress was billed as an exchange of information. Torontonians had the chance to learn all about Soviet advances in agriculture, science, education, and art. Delegates urged every university in Canada to start its own Russian Department. The free flow and exchange of ideas with the Communists was hailed as a vital part of Canada's future.

At Maple Leaf Gardens, a representative from the Soviet embassy in Ottawa thanked Torontonians for their support of Stalingrad. "Your gifts are cementing the post-war relations of Canada and Russia," she said.

Of course, that's not exactly how things turned out.

In fact, some of the seeds of the Cold War could already be found at that rally. For one thing, there was still plenty of anti-communist suspicion in Canada. Being a member of the Canadian Communist Party was illegal. It had been for most of the twentieth century. Back in the 1920s, R.B. Bennett's Conservative government had arrested the Communist leader; some believe they tried to assassinate him while they had him in jail. Even now, while Mackenzie King was heading up the Friendship Committee, his government was keeping tabs. The RCMP kept a close eye on the Friendship Congress and the rally at Maple Leaf Gardens, including a detailed assessment in their Monthly Intelligence Report, taking care to note that 80 percent of the audience was "of foreign extraction."

But they did have some legitimate reasons to be suspicious — reasons like Colonel Nikolai Zabotin. He worked at the Soviet embassy in Ottawa and was one of the Russian representatives who attended the Congress. He was also a spy. He had been sent to Canada to collect secrets about the Allied attempts to build a nuclear bomb. And he was getting them. He used his position at the embassy to gain access to the Canadian government, charming officials into spilling the beans. One naive army officer even took him in a canoe up the Ottawa River, where Zabotin snapped photos of the construction of the Chalk River nuclear facility. Most important, he had an operative inside the British scientific team trying to build a bomb in Canada, who also slipped him secrets about the Manhattan Project in the United States.

It was only a month after the Americans dropped their bombs on Hiroshima and Nagasaki that Zabotin's spy ring was uncovered. With the war over, one of his cipher clerks at the Soviet embassy defected, bringing Mackenzie King's government proof of the espionage. At first, the Canadians were reluctant to listen; it would risk damaging their relationship with the Communists. But after they whisked the defector away to be interviewed at Camp X — the secret base just outside Toronto (on the border between Whitby and Oshawa) — they began to believe the things he was telling them. When the information finally became public, people were shocked. Those old anti-Communist feelings were stirred up once again. Many historians consider the Zabotin episode to be "the spark that ignited the Cold War."

That spark caught fire quickly. Soon, the Communists were testing their own bomb and, with Hitler defeated, people were remembering the true brutality of Stalin's regime: the purges, the gulags, the Soviet famine. At Stalingrad, the Russians took 110,000 German prisoners; only six thousand survived Stalin's camps.

In North America, the attitude toward Russia suddenly swung hard the other way. The hatred wasn't reserved just for Stalin and the Soviet leadership, but for every Communist or Communist sympathizer or supposed Communist sympathizer anywhere in the world. After the war, some of the same experts who had been asked to speak at the Friendship Congress were denounced as radicals and investigated as traitors. At least one of them would be dragged in front of Joseph McCarthy's infamous House Committee on Un-American Activities. Just a few years earlier, Canadian leaders were hailing the people of Stalingrad as the saviours of democracy and the entire free world. Now, those very same leaders were demonizing those very same people as the gravest threat to democracy the world had ever known.

And in Toronto, the city whose citizens had once held the dead of Stalingrad dear in their hearts, the fact that it had ever happened at all was quickly and conveniently forgotten.

THE MODERN CITY

28
DISASTER!

It was late. The ship was quiet. The *Noronic* was docked at the foot of Yonge Street, gently rocking in the dark waves. Almost everyone on board was asleep. It was 2:30 in the morning; most of those who had enjoyed a night out in the city had already come back to their cabins and gone to bed. Hundreds of passengers were tucked beneath their sheets.

Don Church was still up, though, heading back to his room from the lounge. He worked as an appraiser for a fire insurance company, so he knew what it meant when he found a strange haze in one of the corridors. He followed it back to its source: smoke billowed out from under the closed door of a linen closet. The most deadly fire in Toronto's history had begun.

The *Noronic* first set sail back in 1913: in the glory days of the Great Lakes cruise ships. In the late 1800s and early 1900s, the Great Lakes were filled with luxury liners. The ships carried hundreds of passengers from ports on both sides of the border, steaming around the lakes in style. It was a major industry for nearly a century. As a member of the Toronto Marine Historical

Society once put it: "At one time there were more people asleep on boats on the Great Lakes than on any ocean in the world."

SS *Noronic* was one of the biggest and most decadent of them all. They called the ship "The Queen of the Lakes." It had a ballroom, a dining hall, a barber shop and a beauty salon, music rooms and writing rooms, a library, a playroom for children, even its own newspaper printed on board for the passengers.

But, as fancy as it all was, taking a cruise was also risky. The *Noronic* was christened just a year after the unsinkable *Titanic* sank. And even on the Great Lakes, where there weren't any icebergs lurking in the dark, there was still plenty of danger.

The *Noronic*'s maiden voyage had almost been a disaster. The ship was scheduled to set sail for the first time in November of 1913, just as the biggest storm in the recorded history of the Great Lakes rolled into the region. For three straight days, the tempest lashed the lakes with hurricane-force winds, waves fifteen metres high, and torrents of rain and snow. The *Noronic* was lucky: the ship stayed in port where it was safe. But more than two hundred and fifty people died in the storm. So many ships were destroyed there's an entire *Wikipedia* page dedicated to listing them.

And storms were far from the only danger. Ships capsized or collided. They sank. Many — like one of the *Noronic*'s own sister ships, the *Hamonic* — burst into flame. In the early days of the industry, there were essentially no meaningful, enforced safety regulations at all.

Even when the first new laws were introduced, there were loopholes for existing ships. The *Noronic* was shockingly unprepared for an emergency. But no one seemed to think that was a major concern: for thirty-six years, the ship sailed without incident.

Right up until 1949. That September, the *Noronic* left Detroit for a week-long trip to the Thousand Islands. The cruise brought the ship to Toronto on a cool Friday night, docked at Pier 9 (near where the ferry terminal is today). The passengers and crew streamed ashore to enjoy the city. And when they came back at the end of their night out, all was quiet and calm. For a while.

By the time Don Church discovered the source of the smoke, it was already too late. And when he finally found a bellboy to help him, the bellboy didn't pull the fire alarm; instead, he got the keys to open the closet door. That was a mistake: a hellish backdraft burst out of the closet and into the corridor. When Church and the bellboy tried to use a fire hose, the fire hose didn't work. Neither did any of the others.

The flames were spreading quickly. The ship's hallways were lined with wood panelling: for decades, the wood had been carefully polished with lemon oil, the perfect fuel for the flames. Stairwells acted like chimneys, sucking oxygen into the blaze.

Eight minutes later, the ship's whistle jammed while issuing a distress signal and let loose one endless, piercing shriek. By then, half the ship was on fire. In a few minutes, the rest would be, too. Survivors later said the whole vessel went up like the head of a match.

On board, there was chaos and panic. The safety equipment didn't work. There weren't enough emergency exits. Only a few crew members were on duty and they had no training for an emergency like this one. Most of them fled the ship, leaving the sleeping passengers behind.

People were burned alive in their beds. They were suffocated in their rooms. They rushed along the decks and hallways in flames. A few were trampled to death. Some smashed through windows in a bid to escape, leaving blood pouring down their faces. The most desperate jumped over the sides of the ship, the lucky ones hitting the water where rescuers — police, firemen, and passersby — were pulling people from the lake. One person drowned. Another hit the pier and died from the impact. Other jumpers didn't make it clear of the ship; they smashed into the decks below, making them slippery with their blood. When the first ladder was finally hoisted up against the burning hull, passengers pushed forward in such a rush that the ladder snapped, tossing people into the water.

They say the screams of the victims were even louder than the sirens and the ship's piercing whistle. It was one of the most horrifying scenes ever witnessed in the city of Toronto.

About five in the morning, just as the first light began to appear on the horizon, the blaze finally died out. Two hours later, the *Noronic* had cooled off enough for people to begin the grisly search through the wreckage. Bodies were everywhere: skeletons found embracing in the hallways, others still in bed, some turned entirely to ash by a heat so intense it could incinerate bone.

At first, the dead were pulled from the wreckage and piled up on the pier, but there were so many that eventually the Horticultural Building at the CNE was turned into a makeshift morgue. (Today, that same building is home to the Muzik nightclub.)

For the next few weeks, the authorities struggled to identify the bodies. It was nearly impossible. No one even knew how many people had been on board the ship. Some of them were unregistered: guests from Toronto visiting friends. Some had registered under fake names to hide the fact they were taking a romantic cruise with someone who wasn't their spouse. Most of the passengers were from the United States, so their families would have to make the grim journey across the border to see if they could identify any of the charred remains. Even then, many of the bodies were burned so badly they were unrecognizable. Entirely new techniques of x-ray identification had to be developed. It was one of the first times dental records were used for forensic purposes.

Eventually, the death toll was recorded at 119 lives. To this day, no one is entirely sure that number is accurate. But if it's anywhere close, it's the most people ever killed by a single disaster in the history of the city.

In the wake of the fire, Canada Steamship Lines paid more than $2 million to the victims and their families. And it didn't take long for safety laws to be overhauled. For the first time, all ships sailing on the Great Lakes would have to meet real, enforced safety regulations. But it wouldn't be cheap. It cost a lot to run a big ship that *wasn't* a death trap; it was expensive to keep a luxury liner afloat if it wasn't allowed to burst into flames every once in a while. In the wake of the tragedy in Toronto, the industry collapsed. The golden age of cruising on the Great Lakes in style had come to a bloody end.

It rained and rained and rained. Day after day it rained, barely ever stopping — a thoroughly grey and soggy week in October of 1954. And as that week finally came to an end, it was raining even harder than before. By the time Toronto's soaking commuters headed home on Friday evening — packed into damp streetcars and Toronto's brand new subway line — the steady shower had grown into a torrential downpour.

Everyone knew the storm was coming. Scientists had been tracking it for ten days now — ever since a plane full of hurricane hunters first spotted it off the coast of South America. All week long, they'd been watching as Hazel made its way north, devastating every community in its path. On Tuesday night, the hurricane tore through Haiti, killing hundreds. On Wednesday afternoon, it hit the Bahamas and killed six more. On Friday morning, as people in Toronto settled in at work, Hazel was crashing into the coast of the southern United States. Dozens of Americans died over the course of the day. The storm cut a vicious swath through the Carolinas and up into Virginia. By dinnertime, Hazel was raging through the streets of Washington, D.C.

But Toronto was protected: the Allegheny mountain range stood in the way. Meteorologists assumed the mountains would do what they usually did: push the hurricane to the east, away from the Great Lakes, or break it up as it passed over them. The last official weather report came out at 9:30 that night: Toronto would see high winds and maybe even record-breaking rainfall, but nothing like the destruction Hazel had unleashed farther south. The storm was losing steam.

By the time of that report, though, the flooding had already started. Hazel had made it past the mountains. The storm was now centred on Buffalo and still heading north. The rain kept hammering away at the city. The winds were picking up. Rivers and creeks — already swollen from the week of rain — were steadily rising.

On Raymore Drive in Etobicoke, a few locals began to walk up and down the street, warning residents they should head for higher ground. The quiet, residential road curved along the heights above the Humber River, down a hill, and onto the floodplain. A whole block was sitting at the bottom of the valley, just metres away from the angry river as it slowly but surely rose.

A few did head up the hill, taking refuge at the nearby Army & Navy Club. But many others stayed. Some had been living on the street for fifty years. They were used to a bit of flooding; it was inconvenient but nothing too serious. They weren't worried, not even when the power went out. They went to sleep that night in their own beds, just as they always did.

Outside, in the dark, Hazel raged. The hurricane *had* slowed down on its way over the Alleghenies, but then it ran into a front of cold, Canadian air. As it reached the

northern shore of Lake Ontario, the storm stalled —
pausing above Toronto as the rain fell harder and harder,
drenching the city below.

That night, 150 billion litres of water fell into the
Humber River's watershed — hundreds of tons of rain —
and the earth, already soaked to the point of saturation,
couldn't absorb any more. Almost all of it was being fun-
nelled into the river. And so the river kept getting higher.

It only took a few minutes for the neighbourhood to
flood. Raymore Drive was suddenly squarely in the middle
of the Humber. The river roared like a freight train — the
force of the water made even more powerful by tons of
dirt and debris swept along in the current. Some witnesses
remembered waves nearly two storeys high.

Homes were being pummelled. The nearby pedes-
trian bridge across the river was torn from its foundations
and hurled into the street like a battering ram. Entire
houses were knocked off their foundations. Walls were
ripped clean off, living rooms and kitchens suddenly
open to the air. Families scrambled in the dark, clutching flashlights, climbing up onto the roofs of their homes,
clinging to TV antennas, screaming for help.

Some houses were carried away by the river. Others
just disintegrated. Flashlights winked out as the buildings disappeared.

It was a fury unlike any the city had ever seen. All over
Toronto, waterways were bursting their banks — the Don,
the Rouge, Etobicoke Creek, Mimico Creek, Highland
Creek — sending raging torrents of water flooding through
residential neighbourhoods. Even Garrison Creek — buried

in a sewer for nearly a hundred years — was brought rushing back to the surface. In Trinity Bellwoods Park, people watched in astonishment as manhole covers went flying and geysers burst high into the air. Roads were destroyed, bridges washed away, homes flattened. Cars were plucked from the streets and hurled downstream. Trees snapped like matchsticks, smashing into houses. Downed hydro wires hissed and sparked in the dark.

People were dying. Drowning. Still more found themselves stranded in the midst of angry, churning torrents. Some would spend the whole night desperately clinging to trees, soaked by the ice-cold water, suffering from exposure. Firefighters, police officers, and volunteers leaped into action — but many of them got stranded, too, or were swept away by a rush of water. A warning went out over the police radio: the currents were so strong that even big rescue boats were too dangerous to use.

Brian Mitchell, a volunteer firefighter who would eventually become the Etobicoke fire chief, was on Raymore Drive that night. "All hell broke loose," he remembered years later. "People were screaming, 'Save us.… Save us.' We could get spotlights on them. We could see them … but they were just so far out you couldn't throw ropes."

The rescuers did all they could, wading out into the wild river, but they were forced to turn back: the rushing water came all the way up to their chins.

"I felt so helpless," Mitchell told the *Toronto Star*. "It was like something out of a Cecil B. DeMille movie. The incredible roar of the water, like the roar of Niagara Falls.

It was a gigantic flood with smashed houses and uprooted trees bobbing like corks, everything going down the river so fast. Houses crashing into the sides of other houses, people everywhere screaming. And then you couldn't even hear the screams anymore."

John Neil came home to Raymore Drive late that night to find his whole street gone. Assuming his wife and three children had been evacuated, he joined the rescue efforts — it wasn't until the next day that he learned they'd all been killed. His wife's brother and family shared their duplex; all five of them were dead, too.

Tom McGarvey came home to find his family trapped in their house in the middle of the swirling river; he was so desperate to save them that a friend had to tie him to a tree to keep him from rushing out into the thundering white water. He watched, helpless, as his house was carried away — with his wife and two of his children inside.

Downriver, near Dundas Street, the Humber swamped a fire truck responding to a call — five firefighters drowned. At the Old Mill, the bridge was washed out — cars were driving straight into the river. At the mouth of Etobicoke Creek, a trailer park was swept into the lake. It was a night filled with horrors.

As dawn finally broke the next morning, survivors found an entire block of Raymore Drive had been wiped off the map. Sixteen houses were gone. In their place were tons of mud, boulders, and wreckage. Just a day earlier, Raymore had been a lovely residential road; now, it looked like the bottom of a riverbed. It would become known as "The Street That Never Was."

The hurricane killed more than thirty people on Raymore Drive that night — dozens more across the rest of Toronto and the surrounding area. Neighbourhoods all over the region were in ruins, leaving thousands of people homeless, transformed into refugees overnight. The recovery effort would be massive: helicopters buzzed up and down the Humber valley; the military moved in with flamethrowers to burn the wreckage. Boy Scouts helped to search the valley for the missing, wandering through a surreal landscape of flooded streets and broken homes, passing dead cows and pigs stuck in trees. Schools, churches, and fire halls were turned into makeshift morgues. Bodies were being found for days. Rebuilding would take much longer than that; it was months before all the roads and bridges were repaired.

In the wake of the disaster, the city developed a groundbreaking new plan for flood control. They built dams and reservoirs and retaining walls, installed concrete channels, and redirected streams. Thousands upon thousands of acres of land were expropriated in order to turn Toronto's floodplains into parkland. The city didn't want anyone living there when the next big storm hit.

And so that's what happened to Raymore Drive. Those houses were never rebuilt: the block that was once underwater is now home to Raymore Park, where children play on swings and race each other along the running trail. But not all the signs of Hazel have been completely erased. There on the banks of the river, you'll still find the ruins of the original footbridge, battered and destroyed by the storm — a chilling concrete reminder of the horror that swept through Toronto on that terrible October night.

It was around six o'clock in the evening when they first noticed the smoke. A dozen construction workers were toiling away, more than ten metres beneath the snowy earth of Hogg's Hollow near Yonge and York Mills. They were putting in a new water main. It would be the last thing some of them ever did.

Much of Toronto has quite literally been built by immigrants. For more than two hundred years, new arrivals to the city have been hired to build its bridges, pave its streets, and dig its sewers. British hands raised the timbers of Fort York. Germans carved Yonge Street out of the forest. The country's railways were connected to the West by thousands of Chinese workers. As one decade has turned into the next, labourers have streamed into Toronto from Ireland, Ukraine, Poland, the Caribbean ... countless countries from all over the world. And in return, those new Canadians have generally been treated very poorly. Many of them have died building the city.

It was no different in 1960. With the war over, Toronto was booming. New towers were being added to the skyline. The subway was being expanded. Brand new suburban neighbourhoods were sprawling out in every direction; new houses and apartment buildings demanded new roads, sewers, and other infrastructure.

Meanwhile, the city was welcoming an influx of immigration from Italy. Young families left the bombed-out towns where they'd grown up and headed across the Atlantic in the hope of finding a better life in Canada. In the first two decades after the end of the Second World War, more than a hundred thousand new Canadians streamed into Toronto from Italy. A full third of the men who found jobs in the city found those jobs in the construction industry. A full third of all of the builders in Toronto were Italian.

The working conditions were terrible. Competition between subcontractors led to poor wages and corruption. They forced their employees to work long hours for little pay. Some refused to hire a worker unless that worker was willing to give them a cut of their wages. Some employers disappeared without paying wages at all. Unions, already facing hard times, looked down on the new arrivals as unskilled labour, and were reluctant to represent them.

Many employers refused to follow safety regulations. All over Toronto, men were falling to their deaths, or being impaled, or cut by broken glass, or weakened by exposure. "It was like our life was so cheap," one Italian bricklayer remembered, "not worth anything. Like we could hear a builder saying, 'Some Italians died today, got injured, Oh well, send us another load.'"

The men putting in the water main at Hogg's Hollow that night were no exception. They were working in wildly dangerous conditions, unprotected by any meaningfully enforced safety regulations. There were no fire extinguishers. No flashlights. The equipment was inadequate. The support beams were weak. There was no way to communicate with the outside world. Supervisors who complained about the dangers were let go.

When the fire started and the men first noticed the smoke, half of them were able to escape quickly to safety. But six men were trapped below as the flames spread. The heat was intense. The smoke was toxic. And the tunnel was filling with water.

"I tore my shirt off, soaked it in water and covered my face with it," one of the workers, Walter Andruschuk, later remembered. (From Belgium, he was the only non-Italian in the group.) "The other five ... started screaming 'Mamma Mia.' They got down on their knees and started to pray.... The smoke was awful and then the water hit us. It came up to our knees. I was scared but I knew they would come and get us out."

On the surface, though, rescue workers were in disarray. Their equipment wasn't working. There was no backup plan, and no one could get to the men; the fire was just too hot. The valve to clear the tunnel of smoke was stuck, and there was a risk the whole thing would collapse. A couple of rescuers who did crawl in only made it far enough to hear the moaning voices before they were forced to turn back. The trapped men were on their own.

"There was a glimmer of hope," Andruschuk remembered, "I could see a light from the shaft.... The other five wouldn't come with me. They were screaming and down on their knees praying."

But he refused to let them all die without a fight. "I grabbed Pasquale Allegrezza by the shirt and started dragging him along the pipe. There was no room to carry him and I couldn't fight the smoke any longer. I had to let go of Pasquale. Another few feet and I had to put my face down on the pipe. I was sleepy. And then I guess I passed out. Just before I passed out I was afraid for the first time that I would not get out."

It would be more than an hour before anyone else could enter the tunnel. By then, Pasquale Allegrezza, Giovanni Fusillo, Giovanni Correglio, Alessandro Mantella, and Guido Mantella were all dead. Andruschuk was the only survivor, miraculously dragged to safety, disoriented but alive, hours after the fire had started.

The city's Italian community was devastated — and outraged. In the wake of the disaster, a fund was created to help the victims' families. There was a benefit concert at Massey Hall. Italian construction workers organized strikes: thousands walked off the job demanding stronger safety regulations and enforcement. The big unions eventually backed them, too, organizing their own sym- pathy strikes. The *Toronto Telegram* newspaper ran one front-page story after another in support, with headlines like "SLAVE IMMIGRANTS." The provincial govern- ment finally ordered a royal commission to investigate. In the end, stricter safety and labour laws were passed.

Of course, for those five dead workers, the new rules came too late. It's a pattern Toronto has repeated many times over the last two hundred years: new public health regulations introduced after cholera devastated the city in 1832, new sewer system improvements after typhoid outbreaks in the late 1800s and early 1900s, new building codes after the Great Fire of 1849 and then again after the

Great Fire of 1904, new safety laws after the burning of the
Noronic, flood plain protection after Hazel. Over and over
again: it takes death and disaster for things to change.

29
NEIL YOUNG'S HEARSE AND A DEAD MAN'S NAME

It all started with the coffeehouses. For decades, Toronto had had a reputation as a notoriously boring city. More than a century after the end of the Family Compact, it was still a very conservative place: very British and very reserved. But by the end of the 1950s, that was finally beginning to change. Toronto was becoming multicultural. In the wake of the war, European immigrants were moving to the city in bigger numbers than ever before. Many of them ended up in Yorkville — attracted by the low rents of the rundown Victorian homes — and they brought their European-style cafés with them.

It was the beginning of a revolution. Suddenly, there was somewhere cool where you could hang out and get buzzed on caffeine and nicotine: you could drink fancy coffee, smoke cigarettes, and talk about ideas. Some of the cafés even had patios — something Toronto had never really seen before.

Those first few coffeehouses helped turn Yorkville into a magnet for young artists and intellectuals. By the beginning of the 1960s, the first Beatniks had arrived. Over the course of the next few years, the quiet, residential neighbourhood was transformed into a bustling scene of sex, drugs, and rock & roll.

Young people came from all over the continent, streaming into those few blocks near Yonge and Bloor. There were hippies, greasers, and weekenders. Bohemian runaways from the suburbs. Hitchhikers from the Prairies. Draft-dodgers from the United States. There were bikers, potheads, and acid freaks. Writers like Margaret Atwood and William Gibson. Poets like Gwendolyn MacEwen and Dennis Lee.

Everywhere you went, there was music. It spilled out onto the sidewalks from almost every doorway. The coffeehouses hired folk musicians; some turned into rock & roll clubs. At the height of the scene, those few blocks were home to as many as thirty or forty music venues. Inside, you would find some of the greatest musicians Canada has ever produced: Gordon Lightfoot at the Riverboat; Ian and Sylvia at the Village Corner; Murray McLaughlin and David Clayton-Thomas and visitors from out of town like Leonard Cohen and Buffy Sainte-Marie.

Right in the middle of it all — on the corner of Yorkville Avenue and Hazelton — you would find a club called the Mynah Bird; it was famous for its topless go-go dancers and a naked chef. Inside, as you peered through the haze of cigarette smoke, you would find a band called the Mynah Birds on stage. The group's manager was the owner of the club; he also owned a pet store where he sold real, live mynah birds. He used the band as something of a sales gimmick. He even convinced them to dress up in mynah bird-inspired outfits: black leather jackets and pants with yellow turtlenecks and boots. He got the band to sing tunes like "The Mynah Bird Hop" and "The Mynah Bird Song."

But behind all of the cheesy gimmicks, the Mynah Birds were one of the most promising young bands in Yorkville. The group was full of future stars — members of the Mynah Birds would go on to play in some of the defining bands of the 1960s. Two are still household names: one of them a folk singer from Winnipeg who loved hearses, the other a black R&B singer with a dead man's name.

The R&B singer's real name was James Johnson. He grew up in Buffalo, raised by a mother who ran numbers for the mob. His was a rough childhood. By the time he was a teenager, he was already hooked on heroin, falling in with gangs, committing burglaries, and spending time in juvenile detention. But that wasn't his biggest worry — these were the years of the Vietnam War. Scared of the draft, he joined the Navy Reserve so he would get exempted — but he was more interested in singing doo-wop and playing drums for jazz bands than in actually showing up for duty. One morning, after a night sitting in with Thelonious Monk, he got a letter: he was being called into active service and sent off to war. Haunted by dreams of bombs and bayonets, he bought a one-way bus ticket to Toronto and fled across the border.

"If you get to Canada," his mentor, a priest, had once told him, "head straight for Yorkville. It's where the crazy artists hang out. You'll feel right at home."

So that's what he did. He was still in his uniform when he arrived in Yorkville, his navy bag slung over his shoulder.

It wouldn't take him long to find his place in the scene, but at first it must have seemed like a terrible mistake. He was quickly spotted by some American soldiers who guessed he was AWOL. Drunk and aggressively racist, they threatened to beat him to a pulp.

Thankfully, when the scrap started, three locals jumped in to defend him. They were no strangers to a fight: two of them played in a hard-nosed rock band on the rough-and-tumble Yonge Street Strip, where brawling was all part of the job. Their names were Levon Helm and Garth Hudson. Their band was called the Hawks back then, but a year later, when Bob Dylan hired them to play as his backing group on his first electric tour, they would become known simply as the Band.

Having won their fight against the American thugs, they showed their new friend around the neighbourhood. Yorkville was a dream come true. Growing up, Johnson had stolen money from his mother's purse every few weeks so he could run away to New York City, risking a whipping for the sake of a few hours hanging out in the music clubs of Harlem and Greenwich Village. Now, still just sixteen years old, he was going to be part of that bohemian lifestyle. Yorkville, he said, was "the hippest college in the world."

By the end of that first night, he was stoned and getting up on stage at a coffeehouse on Yorkville Avenue, convinced he was a better singer than the frontman of that night's band. And he was right. Impressed, the group's bassist — a future member of Steppenwolf, just like the keyboardist — came up to him after the gig and offered him a job as their regular vocalist. Soon, they were calling themselves The Sailor Boys, repurposing bits and pieces from his navy uniform for their stage costumes. In time, they would morph into the Mynah Birds.

After just a few hours in Yorkville, Johnson already had a new band. And now, he would get a new name, too. One of his newfound friends offered to let him crash at his apartment. And when he got there, the guy's girlfriend asked for Johnson's name.

"If you AWOL," she said, "you best change your name.... We'll call you Rick — Ricky James Mathews. That's my cousin's name. He's dead, so he won't mind."

A couple of years later, when Ricky James Mathews found himself recording at the Motown studios in Detroit, a sixteen-year-old Stevie Wonder told him his new name was too long. "Ricky James more like it." Ricky got shortened to Rick. And so James Johnson was calling himself Rick James when he became famous — the funk star behind the 1980s smash hit "Super Freak." He would go on to sell millions of albums under that dead man's name.

Neil Young got off to a much slower start in Yorkville.

Young grew up in Toronto and Pickering, but he

moved away to Winnipeg after his parents got divorced. There, he started a high school band and found some success with local gigs before heading off to spend a few months playing in Thunder Bay. But in the summer of 1965, he was drawn back to Toronto: a shaggy, long-haired teenager with dreams of making it big.

"The Yorkville scene," he later remembered, "I'd never seen anything like it. Music was everywhere.... It was like this big deal. Toronto in '65."

A couple of his bandmates followed him there. They spent long hours rehearsing in the lobby of the Poor Alex Theatre in the Annex, popping amyl nitrates to keep their energy up. But no matter how hard they worked, they couldn't catch a break. "It was a tough time," Young remembered in his autobiography. "We were small fish in a big pond.... We were out of our league." The band never played a single show in Toronto.

Frustrated, Young left the group and went solo, playing his strange folk songs to the coffeehouse crowds. But he didn't get the response he was looking for. The first time he played "Oh Lonesome Me" — a song that would eventually find its way onto his bestselling *After the Gold Rush* album — the audience laughed at him. They thought his performance was a parody.

"Toronto was a very humbling experience for me," Young admitted. "I just couldn't get anything going." After a brief stay at his father's house in Rosedale, he bounced around from one apartment to another, crashing on friends' floors, trying new drugs, staying up all night to write new songs. For a while, he worked in the stockroom of a bookstore on Yonge Street to make ends meet, but got fired after just a few weeks. He was having health problems. His career was sputtering. Some friends were beginning to worry.

But thanks to the Mynah Birds, everything was about to change.

Rick James was feeling inspired. He'd just made a trip down to New York City, checking out the Greenwich Village scene. One night, he got high on coke and headed to see a new band play at The Night Owl Café. The guitarist was another old veteran of the Yorkville scene: Zal Yanovsky.

Yanovsky grew up in the Toronto suburb of Downsview before heading downtown to try his hand at folk music. To get by, he worked as a waiter at the Purple Onion coffeehouse (where Buffy Sainte-Marie wrote "Universal Soldier"); he stole milk bottles off front porches and spent his nights sleeping wherever he could. He met his future wife — the actor Jackie Burroughs, who would eventually play Aunt Hetty in *Road to Avonlea* — while he was sleeping in a dryer in a laundromat at Dupont and St. George.

It didn't take long for Yanovsky's career to pick up steam. Once it did, he moved to New York City with his Yorkville bandmate, Denny Doherty. In Greenwich Village, they started a new band with an up-and-coming young folk singer called Mama Cass. And while she and Doherty eventually dropped acid with some friends, threw a dart at a map, and moved to the Virgin Islands where they became the Mamas & the Papas, Yanovsky stayed behind and started the Lovin' Spoonful instead.

The Spoonful's upbeat pop songs — like "Do You Believe in Magic?" and "Summer in the City" — mixed folk and blues with rock & roll. When James saw them play that night in Greenwich Village, he was deeply impressed. "It felt fresh," he later explained. "After their first set, we hung out for a long time and exchanged ideas. I dug the Spoonful so much that I went to see them two more times before [I] flew back to Canada."

When he returned to Yorkville, James shared those fresh ideas with the Mynah Birds' new bassist, Bruce Palmer. Palmer knew exactly which guitar player they should get to complement their new, folk-influenced sound. His name was Neil Young. He was living with Joni Mitchell, crashing at her apartment above the Purple Onion.

Mitchell and James were already close friends. She'd come to Yorkville from Saskatoon. During the days, she worked as a server at the Penny Farthing coffeehouse — right next door to the Mynah Bird, it was known for its rooftop pool and bikini-clad wait staff. At night, she would head downstairs to play her ornate folk tunes to the caffeinated crowd. She and James would sometimes stay up all night, playing each other jazz albums and classical music.

"Joni had killer taste," James remembered, "so if she recommended a musician — the way she and Bruce were recommending Neil Young — that was all the assurance I needed."

And he was right to listen. Young was exactly what the Mynah Birds were looking for.

"Neil was cool," James remembered. "He had a quirky sense of humour and a quick mind. Like most of the other white musicians in Toronto, he was into black music. His singing was a little strange, but his facility on the guitar was crazy.... Neil helped reshape the Mynah Birds into the band I'd been hearing inside my head.... Neil bridged folk, blues, and rock in a format that didn't sound artificial. It sounded real. He was the missing ingredient."

The Mynah Birds were now on the cutting edge. In just a few years, nearly everyone would be doing what they were doing now; that drug-fuelled blend of folk, blues, and rock became one of the defining sounds of the hippie era. With Rick James on vocals and Neil Young on guitar, the Mynah Birds were the sound of the future.

Success came quickly. Just a few weeks after Young joined the band, they were heading down Highway 401 to Detroit to launch their recording career with Motown Records.

By then, the Mynah Birds were doing things their own way. They'd fired their old manager and burned their gimmicky clothes. Now, they had a new benefactor to pay their bills: John Craig Eaton II, great-grandson of Timothy Eaton, the Toronto department store mogul. He seemed to get a kick out of being involved with a rock & roll band. He was more than happy to use the Eaton family fortune to buy anything the Mynah Birds wanted.

Armed with thousands of dollars' worth of new equipment, and with Young now teaming up with James to write their songs, the Mynah Birds had come into their own. They signed a six-year contract with Motown and immediately got to work recording songs at one of the most famous record studios in the world, working with the same producer who co-wrote classics like "Dancing In the Street" and "Devil with a Blue Dress On." Just a few months earlier, Neil Young's band couldn't get a gig in Toronto. Now, his band was hanging out with legends like Marvin Gaye and Stevie Wonder.

But it didn't last long. Just a few days after they started, everything went terribly wrong. They hadn't seen any of their Motown money yet; they suspected their manager was using it to subsidize his heroin addiction. James, high on speed, confronted him. And then, he beat him up.

That was a mistake. Most of the band had no clue James was AWOL. But the manager did. He ratted James out to the FBI. Suddenly, Motown didn't want to work with the Mynah Birds anymore. They pulled the contract. And the band wouldn't be able to sign with any other major American label, either. Just when it seemed everything was finally coming together, it was suddenly over. The Mynah Birds were done.

James was out of options. Tired of running, he decided to turn himself in. He headed back to Buffalo to spend one last night of freedom with his mother; she bought them tickets to see Miles Davis.

The next morning, the FBI came to take Rick James away in handcuffs. His Yorkville dream was dead. While his bandmates were headed for near-instant stardom, it would be years before James got his career back on track.

* * *

Neil Young was done with Yorkville, too. Things just weren't working out. One night, while he and Bruce Palmer were hanging out at a coffeehouse on Avenue Road, he suggested a new plan. He'd seen an ad for a hearse in the newspaper. They could buy the used funeral coach and head off to California to try their luck there.

This wasn't Young's first hearse. Back in Winnipeg, he'd bought a big old 1948 Buick Roadmaster. He called it Mort. It was perfect for a young musician. It had lots of space for equipment, and the rollers that had once been used to move coffins in and out of the back of the velvet-lined interior could just as easily be used to move amplifiers, drum kits, and guitars.

Mort had taken Young from Winnipeg to Thunder Bay, and he hoped to drive it all the way south to Toronto. But the Roadmaster didn't make it. Mort died on the side of the Trans-Canada Highway. Young made up a whole story about giving Mort a proper sendoff by pushing it over a cliff, but the truth is he just left it there, abandoned in a hotel parking lot somewhere between Sault Ste. Marie and Sudbury. He hitchhiked the rest of the way to Toronto. One day he would write a song about that car: "Long May You Run" — fifty years later he played it as the flame was extinguished at the Vancouver Winter Olympics.

Mort II was a 1953 Pontiac Hearse — not quite as stylish as its predecessor but with many of the same morbid features that made it a great fit for a travelling band.

To buy the hearse, Young sold all of the Mynah Birds' equipment — never mind that the gear really belonged to John Craig Eaton II.

Young spent one last night at a friend's apartment on Avenue Road, jamming with Jon Kay — the frontman of the Sparrows, a band that featured a couple of former Mynah Birds and would soon move to California and become Steppenwolf. The next morning, Young parked Mort II on a corner of Avenue Road and asked if anyone wanted to go to Los Angeles. Friends piled in.

"We were just an old funeral coach full of stoned hippies heading southwest to Hollywood, California, where the music scene was vibrant and the West Coast Sound was on fire."

One week later, Young and Palmer had a brand new band: Buffalo Springfield. By the end of the month, they were on tour opening for the Byrds. Just days after leaving Yorkville behind, Neil Young was already well on his way to becoming one of the most famous rock stars in the world.

Young and James were far from the only future stars who left Yorkville behind. By the end of the decade, many of the big names had already left. There just wasn't enough support for the local music scene in Toronto — or anywhere else in Canada. There weren't enough recording studios. There weren't enough record labels. The airwaves were dominated by big American companies that wanted to sell American music to Canadians, not the other way around. If you were a Canadian musician who wanted to make it big in the 1960s, it helped to leave Canada behind.

And that wasn't the only reason the Yorkville scene was doomed. For many young Canadians, Yorkville was the most exciting neighbourhood in the country. But there were lots of people in Toronto who were perfectly happy to live in a safe, conservative city with a reputation for being boring. To them, the idea of a horde of young people taking over an entire neighbourhood so they could smoke pot, play music, and get laid was a deeply frightening one. Newspapers were filled with scaremongering stories about "ruined" young women, worried parents, and a wildly exaggerated hepatitis outbreak. Some of the stories did have some truth to them: as the 1970s approached, the scene did begin to fall into harder drugs like amphetamines and the influence of the Vagabonds biker gang grew ever more powerful. But the neighbourhood was never the rancid pit of depravity many Torontonians imagined it to be.

One Conservative politician — Hockey Hall of Famer Syl Apps — went so far as to call Yorkville "a festering sore in the middle of the city" that had to be "eradicated." He wasn't alone. Some people said all the hippies in Yorkville should be rounded up and sent off to work camps. There were crackdowns by police. City Hall consciously tried to kill the scene with new bylaws and regulations.

In the end, it worked. As the sixties concluded and the seventies began, developers moved in with bulldozers; wrecking balls tore through one coffeehouse after another. Today, only a few of those old Victorian buildings survive — and most of those that haven't been turned into rubble have been turned into upscale fashion boutiques. The neighbourhood that once served as a giant crash pad for Canadian youth is now a shopping district for some of Toronto's wealthiest residents and tourists.

Still, while the hippies of Yorkville might have lost the battle for their neighbourhood, they won the war. Yorkville's musicians, writers, and artists spread out across the city; they turned up in Kensington Market and on Queen Street West and just down Bloor Street at Rochdale College for a while. They started new record labels and publishing houses; they kept writing books and poems and songs. In time, they filled Toronto with dozens of new art galleries, bookstores, and grungy music clubs that have fostered countless new music scenes since the days of Neil Young and Rick James. There's now a coffeehouse on nearly every corner.

Toronto might have killed Yorkville. But before it did, Yorkville changed Toronto forever.

30
SHOESHINE BOY

By the summer of 1977 more than two million people called Toronto home; new arrivals were pouring in from every corner of the globe. The days when people could claim the big city felt like a small town were rapidly coming to an end. And for many, that made it an uneasy time. The city had managed to eradicate the Yorkville scene, but that did little to stem the tide of change. In recent years, the indignation of the city's more conservative citizens had been centred on the seedy Yonge Street Strip, which was lined with strip clubs, body-rub parlours, and porno theatres. Now, worries about the Strip were joined by a new concern: punk rock.

As the summer of '77 began, Queen Street West was becoming the centre of the city's new punk scene: art students and working-class kids in leather jackets roamed the sidewalks, some looking so strange they brought traffic to a halt. The songs they liked were short, fast, loud, and furious. Their shows became notorious for displays of theatrical violence: the most infamous band in the city was the Viletones, whose frontman, Steven

Leckie, called himself "Nazi Dog" and sliced his veins
open with broken glass on stage. The scene was raw and
wild. That summer, those in the know started talking
about Toronto as being home to some of the greatest
punk bands on the planet.

The burgeoning scene was centred on the Crash 'N'
Burn, an artist-run punk club in the basement of a small
office building on Duncan Street (just a few blocks south
of Queen). On a Friday or Saturday night, when most of
downtown Toronto was dead quiet, the Crash 'N' Burn
was a roar of distortion. It was packed with sweaty kids
and bathtubs full of beer. The crowd bounced and danced
and hurled themselves at the stage. Every decent punk
band in the city was invited to play in that basement
during that whirlwind of a summer.

One of those bands was called The Curse. Mickey
Skin, Trixie Danger, Dr. Bourque, and Patsy Poison were
the first women on the continent to form their own punk
band. That spring, they spent three weeks teaching themselves how to play their instruments and write songs,
then they leaped right into the fire, making their debut
by opening for the Viletones at the Crash 'N' Burn.

"Mostly," the *Toronto Sun* reported, "they perform as
if they'd never seen their instruments before." But that
was part of the fun.

"They *couldn't* play," one fan admitted. "But they had
an energy and a presence that was so strong and so powerful that their ability to play really well didn't matter; it
became part of their performance and their charm and
their energy and why we went to see them."

That first night, the band threw a birthday cake at the audience; an audience member threw a garbage can back at the band. But The Curse weren't about to be intimidated. On one of their live recordings, you can hear a man in the audience shout "Take it off!"; the band shouts back, "You take it off first!" Their lyrics were deeply confrontational: sexual, political, feminist. They sang songs like "If It Tastes So Great, Swallow It Yourself." Dr. Bourque and a friend once sent used tampons to the finance minister to protest the tax on feminine hygiene products. Mickey Skin turned some other tampons into a bra to wear on stage. In a music scene that valued provocation, The Curse quickly became one of the most popular bands.

But they would soon be known well beyond the confines of the Crash 'N' Burn.

Just a few weeks after The Curse debuted, Toronto was rocked by one of the most brutal and shocking murders the city had ever seen. Emanuel Jaques was just twelve years old when he was killed — a shoeshine boy who worked on the Yonge Street Strip, polishing shoes in the neon glow of the strip clubs and porno theatres. One day, near the end of July, as he was shining shoes on the corner of Yonge and Dundas, he was approached by a stranger who bought him a hamburger and offered him a job moving some photography equipment. It was the last time anyone saw Jaques alive.

His body was found four days later, wrapped in a green garbage bag on the roof of a massage parlour just across the street from the Eaton Centre. He'd been raped repeatedly, injected with needles, and finally drowned in a sink.

The city was horrified. So were the punks. Many of them were only a few years older than Jaques was when he died; some even spent time hanging out next door to the building where his body was found, where their friends in the art collective General Idea had a studio.

The Curse were so upset they wrote a song about the murder. "Shoeshine Boy" was an angry screed against those who let Jaques work alone on the Strip. The lyrics were graphic and upsetting. "They'll beat you / Mistreat you / Find you wrapped in a plastic bag." The band financed a recording of the song with money they'd recently won by suing a bus company after getting into a fight with some other young passengers over a bottle of Southern Comfort. At the launch party, they served tampons soaked in Purple Jesus punch.

When the public caught wind of the song, it caused an uproar. Toronto, already suspicious of the punk scene and charged with emotion over the murder and the subsequent trial, turned on the band. The Curse were accused of exploiting the tragedy for their own personal gain. A ranting letter to the editor of the *Hamilton Spectator* proudly described throwing the record on a fire and watching it melt. "How can we as parents and citizens of the upcoming generation permit our children to have their minds brainwashed by this drivel in the name of music?"

"We got death threats," Poison later remembered, "big time."

And that was only one of the challenges the scene was facing. A city that had shut down the Yorkville coffee-houses just a few years earlier certainly wasn't comfortable with punks taking the place of hippies. Bands had a hard time finding anywhere to play. The Crash 'N' Burn lasted only a few raucous months. The Liberal Party of Ontario had an office upstairs; by the end of the summer, their complaints about the noise and rowdiness forced the club to shut down. The heart of the scene moved into the Horseshoe Tavern, but the owners soon told the punks they weren't welcome there anymore, either. The final concert, "The Last Pogo," descended into a riot when police tried to shut it down.

On Yonge Street, things got even uglier. In the wake of the murder, City Hall cracked down on the Strip. Mayor David Crombie called it "a yawning cesspool" and demanded immediate action. Police launched a wave of raids. Within two weeks, more than a dozen businesses had already closed. More would follow. And when the boy's murderers were revealed to be gay men, a wave of homophobia swept the city — even the judge presiding over the trial suggested the murder should cast doubt on the entire idea of gay rights.

The "cleanup" of Yonge Street never did drive the sex industry completely off the Strip; it's still home to strip clubs and sex shops today. And the punks didn't go anywhere, either; forty years later, you can still find punk bands playing the bars of Queen West. In the battle over the future of Toronto — between those who wanted to pretend it was still a small, sheltered town and those who recognized it had become a major cosmopolitan metropolis — there was never any question which side would win. For better and for worse, Toronto really was a big city.

31
NO SAD SONGS

"I am going to die. I am going to be young when I die." Jim Black was thirty-seven years old when he said those words. And he was right. He wouldn't live to see his next birthday. He'd been diagnosed earlier that year — one of the first people in Canada to be told he had AIDS.

This was 1985. It had only been four years since doctors began to notice the first signs of the outbreak in the United States. Since then, it had spread across the continent with terrifying speed.

Now, AIDS had arrived in Toronto. By the spring of '85, fifty-four people in the city had been diagnosed. More than twenty of them were already dead. The number of cases was growing quickly. By fall, the number had nearly doubled. On average, a new case was being diagnosed somewhere in Canada every thirty-six hours.

As thousands of people across the continent fell ill, they were met with fear and prejudice. Some doctors and nurses refused to take blood samples from AIDS patients. Some funeral homes refused to bury the dead.

Schools denied admission to infected students. Families abandoned sick relatives.

More than one columnist at the *Toronto Sun* argued that AIDS patients should be quarantined. When a teacher at Jarvis Collegiate died of the disease, parents demanded the same. Even the Canadian Bar Association was divided on the issue.

Not all of those infected were gay men, but the disease was widely labelled as a "gay plague." The famous American televangelist Jerry Falwell declared "AIDS is not just God's punishment for homosexuals; it is God's punishment for the society that tolerates homosexuals."

Even in an increasingly liberal metropolis like Toronto, homophobia intensified the paranoia — the disease arrived in the city just two years after police unleashed one of their most notorious crackdowns on the gay community, arresting hundreds in the "Operation Soap" bathhouse raids. As one local advocate put it, AIDS was "a bigot's dream."

In those early years, silence was a powerful and frightening enemy. As 1985 dawned, U.S. President Ronald Reagan had yet to even say the word *AIDS*, refusing to publicly name the plague as thousands of his citizens died. Many patients were understandably worried about going public with their story, scared of the discrimination they would face if they did. Fear and prejudice filled the vacuum. Misinformation was everywhere.

In cities all over the continent, community organizations were being formed to fight the disease and the ignorance that came with it. The AIDS Committee of Toronto was founded just a year after the first case was discovered in Canada. Staff and volunteers worked together, not only to organize care and support for those who were in desperate need of it, but also to educate the community and the public about the disease.

As part of those efforts, they decided to produce a documentary film. There had been movies made about the medical issues related to the disease, but *No Sad Songs* would be the first to focus on the human impact. Directed by Nik Sheehan, it would use interviews and artistic performances to explore the emotional toll AIDS was taking.

Jim Black would be at the centre of the film. He became one of the very first Canadian AIDS patients to go public with his case.

That decision cost him dearly: his father and his sister both disowned him when they found out. He'd grown up in the small town of Simcoe, Ontario, as a self-described "closet case." He was in his early thirties before he finally moved to Toronto and began to more fully explore his sexuality, living in a small apartment on Jarvis Avenue. By then, he'd already attempted suicide four times.

It started just a year after his move: he fell seriously ill, collapsed, and was taken to hospital. The doctors hoped it was malaria, but six months later Black was diagnosed with AIDS. Within a week, he'd turned up at the offices of the AIDS Committee, offering to share his story.

In *No Sad Songs*, he speaks with candour and humour about his symptoms and his impending death, determined to make his final days count.

"I'm going to go," he explains in the film, "but I'm going kicking and screaming.... I want to make my life, what I have left of it, worthwhile.... We have to remove the fear, and the only way to remove the fear is through knowledge. You've got to go and more or less kick the public in the teeth and say, 'Look at me: I am a flesh and blood person. I have a disease you don't want to talk about, but you'd better.'"

By then, Black was already losing weight at a dramatic rate. He looked thin in *No Sad Songs*; he admitted his clothes didn't fit him anymore. His spleen, his liver, his throat, and his stomach were all infected. He had hepatitis. His legs were beginning to go numb. "I'm finding I don't have the strength and the ability to walk great distances," he confessed. "I could walk from here down to Harbourfront and it never used to bother me; now I walk from here to Yonge Street — which is only two blocks — and I have to stop because I'm winded."

But even as his strength ebbed away, Black made the most of the time he had left. He shared his story not only in the film, but also by speaking in public and giving interviews to the media, quick to crack a joke about blowjobs or share a candid anecdote about having anonymous sex in Allan Gardens. "I'm not going to sit in a corner and die," he told an audience at U of T.

Progress was slow, but things were gradually changing. By the end of that year, the AIDS Committee of Toronto had organized the city's first AIDS vigil and the first Canadian Conference on AIDS had been held in Montreal. The year after that, the City of Toronto introduced an official AIDS strategy. And while Black was one of the first, in the years to come more and more AIDS patients would go public with their stories, following in the footsteps of those first few pioneers.

Toronto activists, filmmakers, writers, musicians, artists, and actors would all produce work about the disease, helping to change public perception. The Torontonian art collective General Idea would lose two of three members to AIDS: but first they took Robert Indiana's famous *LOVE* logo and swapped L-O-V-E out for A-I-D-S, creating stickers and posters that would be plastered all over cities on both sides of the Atlantic. While the struggle against AIDS continues to this day, the silence was finally broken.

Jim Black didn't live to see that progress. He died at his mother's house in Simcoe just sixteen months after he was diagnosed. "This is my one contribution to life," he told a reporter during that final, extraordinary summer. "And I have to die to make it."

32
THE FALLING LAWYER

Garry Hoy died in 1993. By then, Toronto was the biggest city in Canada. Asphalt highways now twisted through neighbourhoods where First Nations trails used to run. Passenger jets roared through the same skies once darkened by the flight of passenger pigeons. Skyscrapers rose along the same shoreline where the Simcoes lived in a tent. The SkyDome sat like an egg on the waterfront, home to a baseball team that made good on the promise of Cannonball Crane: they had just won their first World Series and were about to win again. They played their games on a futuristic Astroturf field in the shadow of the tallest tower civilization had ever built. Toronto was well on its way to taking its place as one of the great cities of the world.

But the circumstances that led to Garry Hoy's death didn't begin with the modern metropolis; you can trace the tangled roots of his demise all the way back to the days when Toronto was still a muddy colonial outpost on the edge of the British Empire.

You can follow one of those roots all the way back to 1855 — exactly one hundred years before Garry Hoy was born. The city was small back then: only forty thousand people called it home. But the boom had already begun.

Just two years earlier, Toronto had opened its first railway and built its first locomotive. They called it the *Toronto*: the great iron beast spent nearly a week crawling through the streets of the city, inched forward by crowbars along temporary tracks until it finally took its place on the rails. The new wonder of the industrial age would serve the very same function as the ancient Toronto Carrying Place trail: the city's first railway would run north, connecting Lake Ontario to the Upper Great Lakes.

Now, goods could be shipped more quickly, easily, and efficiently than ever before. And that would become increasingly important as vast forests of timber were felled in northern Ontario, nuggets of gold were dug out of the Canadian Shield, and settlers pushed even farther west — the Prairies would soon be turned into the breadbasket of the British Empire. An endless stream of the country's bounty would be sent back east, much of it being shipped across the Great Lakes and then down the new railway and through Toronto. As the city built even more railways, it would become an ever more important economic hub, sitting between the new growth out West and the old cities of Quebec and the United States.

And so, if you were a Toronto entrepreneur who made your living off grain, the new railway and the promise of future profit made 1855 the perfect time to charter a new bank.

They called it the Bank of Toronto. They opened their first branch on Church Street near Adelaide (the building is still there today, number 80, right across the road from St. James Cathedral). They began with three employees, but as Canadian agriculture boomed, so did the bank. Soon, they were opening new branches across the province; they expanded into Montreal just a few years later. At first, their customers were almost all farmers and grain merchants, although the bank's clientele also included the millers, brewers, and distillers who relied on grain to make their products. And in time, they would branch out into other sectors of the growing Canadian economy.

They weren't alone. The city's first bank was the Bank of Upper Canada, founded all the way back in 1821 and controlled by the Family Compact. But now, more and more banks were being chartered in Toronto.

The Dominion Bank would prove to be one of the most successful. It was founded by another group of Toronto investors — this one led by James Austin. He was an Irish Protestant who had come to the city as a teenager. He got his start serving as a printing apprentice under William Lyon Mackenzie; he'd been forced to flee after the rebellion and spent a few years living in the United States. But when he returned he opened a grocery with another Irish immigrant — a rare partnership between a Protestant and a Catholic — which went so well he was soon able to expand into other businesses. By the end of the 1860s, he was rich enough to buy the old Baldwin estate at Spadina. He tore down their home and built his own: the Spadina House you'll find there today.

Over the next hundred years, both of the banks flourished, growing in step with the Canadian economy.

Before long, they were opening branches all over the country — and then, the world. Each built lavish new headquarters in what became Toronto's financial district. The Bank of Toronto Building stood at the corner of King and Bay: a majestic Beaux-Arts masterpiece designed by the same architects as the New York Public Library. The Dominion Bank was at King and Yonge; it's still there today, serving as the base to the modern, fin-shaped tower of One King West. With the opulent magnificence of its banking hall and an impregnable vault in the basement, it's one of the great surviving jewels from Toronto's Edwardian age.

But soon, a new architectural style would come to define Toronto's bank buildings — and the city's skyline with them.

In the years when those new bank offices in Toronto were still being planned and built, another root of Garry Hoy's death was beginning to take shape far on the other side of the Atlantic. You can trace it back all the way to Berlin, to the studio of the one of the world's most important designers. Peter Behrens used to run one of the legendary Arts and Crafts schools and became the first person to design an entire corporate brand. He was also an architect, and hired students and assistants to help him with his work. Three in particular would go on to take their place among the most important architects of the twentieth century: Le Corbusier, Walter Gropius, and Ludwig Mies van der Rohe.

By the time the 1920s rolled around, that trio had already begun to change architecture forever. The giant bloody horrifying mess of the First World War had convinced plenty of artists that traditional aesthetics — like traditional politics — had failed. The architects embraced the new. They stripped their designs down to the essentials and built them out of modern materials: steel, concrete, and glass. They would become associated with slogans like "Form follows function," "Ornament is a crime," "Truth to materials," and "Less is more." Their stark rectangles and straight lines would change the face of the world. Le Corbusier would become the most famous architect on Earth. Gropius would open the influential Bauhaus art school. And he would eventually get Mies to run it.

But times were changing again. The 1930s were going to be dark days for German artists. The Nazis hated modernism. They wanted a return to traditional aesthetics. Before the Second World War had even started, the Nazis rounded up every piece of modernist artwork they could find in the entire country. Modernists were fired from their teaching positions and were forbidden to sell their work. Some fled the country. Some committed suicide. The Bauhaus school was closed. Gropius fled to England. Mies escaped to the United States.

He ended up in Chicago, where he launched an entire "Second Chicago School" of architecture, based on the modernist principles he brought with him from Europe. Soon, slick, grid-based skyscrapers of steel and glass were towering over downtown Chicago. And Mies started getting commissions to design other important buildings across the United States.

The most famous of them all actually came from some Canadians.

Samuel Bronfman had been born in Russia in the late 1800s, back when it was still run by the tsars. Those were the days of the pogroms: mobs of anti-Semitic rioters beat and killed and set fire to the homes of their Jewish neighbours. The Bronfmans, who were Jewish them-selves, escaped to Canada, moving from Saskatchewan to Manitoba, from tobacco farming to railway labour to sawmill work to selling firewood and fish before finally settling in Montreal, where they got into the business of making booze. Their timing was perfect: the United States was entering the days of prohibition. The Bronfmans made a fortune. Before long, they had enough money to buy out one of Canada's big liquor companies: Seagram's. It was under the Seagram brand that they would become world-famous.

Things went so well that in 1954 they began to build brand new headquarters in New York City. An iconic new skyscraper. Black. Steel. Walls of glass. The most expensive ever built. And the man they hired to design it was, of course, Ludwig Mies van der Rohe.

With the Seagram Building, Mies helped to set the standard for skyscraper construction in New York City for decades to come. And soon, he would turn his atten-tion to Toronto.

* * *

Garry Hoy was still just a child when construction began. It was the 1960s. Canada was ready to make a splash on the international stage. The centennial year was coming up. Montreal was about to host Expo '67. And at the corner of Queen and Bay in Toronto, an entire neighbourhood was being bulldozed: the shacks of the Ward were being levelled to make way for Nathan Phillips Square and Viljo Revell's iconic new modernist city hall.

In the century since they were chartered, the Bank of Toronto and the Dominion Bank had continued to grow. They came out of the Second World War stronger than ever. But with the world's economy evolving, they decided they needed to take another big step: in the mid-fifties, while Mies was building the new Seagram offices, the two big Toronto banks negotiated a merger. The Toronto-Dominion Bank was born.

A new company called for new headquarters. And the optimism of the new age called for a bold, ambitious design by one of the world's great modernist architects. The bank teamed up with the Bronfmans to hire Ludwig Mies van der Rohe.

The Toronto-Dominion Centre would be deeply informed by the Seagram Building: simple, sleek, and elegant — what Mies called "skin and bones architecture." The gorgeous old Bank of Toronto Building was demolished to make way for two new black bank towers. They would rise far above every other skyscraper in town. For decades, the Bank of Commerce Building had been the city's tallest at thirty-six storeys; the TD Centre would have fifty-six and become the tallest in Canada. It would dominate the skyline for years to come: two imposing black monoliths towering over Toronto.

But, as big as they would be, much of their charm would be found in the smallest of touches. "God is in the details," Mies once said — and he would put that philosophy to use in his new Toronto complex. Every detail was meticulously planned: from the Barcelona chairs in the lobby to yellow daisies sitting in round vases on the tellers' counter. Five decades later, you can still find those endearing flourishes being used today.

At the foot of the towers, Mies left room for open spaces: the buildings were set back from the road to allow room for a granite square and a lush green lawn — a fresh idea in a world filled with skyscraper canyons lining downtown streets. Eventually, Joe Fafard's *The Pasture* would find a home on the lawn: seven bronze cows graze in the heart of the city's financial district, bringing a whimsical touch of the countryside to the middle of the country's biggest city. And, right on the corner of King and Bay, Mies designed a banking pavilion: inside the box of steel and glass is a soaring open space uncluttered by any interior columns.

In the ground beneath the towers, the basement of the Toronto-Dominion Centre would become home to the first section of the city's new subterranean labyrinth of a shopping mall. Mies designed the inaugural section of the PATH with the same attention to detail as the rest of the complex. Even the font on the signs of the stores was designed by the architect and standardized across the board.

In the years since, the measured perfection of Mies's original vision has been gradually diluted. Three more towers were added to the complex — built, for the most part, according to the specifications he established with the first two. But this time, when the old Toronto Stock Exchange had to be torn down, the facade was preserved and incorporated into one of the sleek black towers — a strange mix of old and new that defied the Miesian philosophy. Almost all of the stores in the PATH have abandoned the elegant font Mies designed for them. And more recently, the bank itself chose to compromise the integrity of Mies's design, sticking their bright green logo on two of the facades.

Today, it's easy to lose sight of those pioneering black towers in the jumble of the city's skyline. Since they first opened, many other modern bank towers have followed: from the red granite of Scotia Plaza to the golden glass of Royal Bank Plaza. Now, countless condo towers are joining them as the Toronto skyline grows thick with steel and glass. But the Toronto-Dominion Centre will always be the graceful original. As the *Globe*'s architecture critic, Alex Bozikovic, puts it, "TD Centre still retains the purity of a temple ... the most distinguished set of buildings in Canada."

It's no surprise that fifty years after they were built, Mies's sleek black towers still attract some of the most powerful and affluent tenants in the city: from tech giants to multinational investment groups to the Consulate General of Japan ... and more than a few law firms, too.

* * *

Garry Hoy was a lawyer. He worked on the twenty-fourth floor. He was a partner at Holden Day Wilson LLP, one of the oldest law firms in Canada, founded all the way back in the early 1900s. Over the course of the century it had grown into one of the more successful firms in the city. Ninety lawyers and two hundred employees were on the payroll. Its office could be found in the most prestigious skyscraper in Toronto: the first and tallest of Mies's black towers.

Hoy was clearly impressed by the workmanship that had gone into the construction of the sleek skyscraper — and he was quick to demonstrate that fact to anyone who came into the office. He was known to throw himself against the windows, showing just how much confidence he had in the strength of the Toronto-Dominion Centre's glass.

And that glass never did break.

The firm was hosting a reception on a Friday afternoon in July, a chance to impress young articling students as they began their lives in the law. Hoy tried his old trick: gave himself a running start and launched his body against the glass.

It held.

Then he did it again. Up to that point, he'd been lucky. Skyscraper windows simply aren't built to stand up to the kind of force Hoy was throwing against them. "I don't know any building code in the world," a structural engineer would later tell the *Toronto Star*, "that would allow a 160-pound man to run up against a glass and withstand it."

This time, while the glass didn't break, the window did pop out of the frame. It went sailing out into the void toward the concrete below. Hoy went with it. A hubristic case of accidental autodefenestration.

It must have taken Garry Hoy about fifteen seconds to fall those twenty-four floors. For fifteen seconds, he was flying alone in the chaos of the Toronto skyline, a fragile being of flesh and bone spending its final few moments surrounded by towers of steel and glass, plummeting toward an earth made of concrete and granite where once there was a forest floor.

And then he hit the ground.

CONCLUSION

THE WORK OF REMEMBERING

For the better part of fifty years, they sat in the basement of the Royal Ontario Museum: three hundred boxes filled with bones. They were the dead of Ossossané, the Wendat village where the Feast of the Dead was held in 1636. They were the very same bones Jean de Brébeuf had seen buried nearly four centuries ago.

The exact location of the famous ossuary had been tracked down on the shores of Georgian Bay by an amateur archaeologist. When he found the spot in the 1940s, he contacted the ROM to let them know. The museum sent a team of archaeologists to the site and for six weeks in the summer of 1947, they dug into the communal grave; then again in the summer of '48. By the end of their excavations, they had unearthed the bones of more than six hundred people.

Most of the dead were taken to the ROM. They were stored away in cardboard boxes while artifacts from the grave were put on public display. Some of the bones were loaned out to researchers: teams from the University of Toronto and Temple University in Philadelphia studied the remains.

No one bothered to ask permission. The Wendat nation was never consulted in any way during the excavation. Their ancestors were dug up out of the ground and hauled off to a museum without their consent.

It was a profound desecration. As Wendat historian Georges E. Sioui points out, "The Wendats had strict moral precepts about the disposal of human remains." One of the French missionaries who attended a Feast of the Dead in the early 1600s was clear about that in his own writing. "Nothing could give them greater offence than to ransack and remove anything in the tombs of their relatives," the missionary explained, "and if anyone is found doing so he cannot look for anything short of a most cruel and painful death." When a fire broke out in a Wendat village, he said, they would rush to protect the bodies of their dead relatives before saving even their own homes.

The ROM was far from alone. For many, many years, archaeologists and trophy hunters all over the continent thought nothing of digging up the graves of Indigenous people. Human remains were lifted out of their resting places and sent off to join museum collections. While the graveyards of settlers and their descendants were held to be sacred, Indigenous graveyards were seen to be fair game for research and plunder — treated as if they were the curious remains of long-extinct civilizations.

Even more history has been wiped out by impatient developers. While the burial mound of Tabor Hill was saved, we'll never know how many other graves and precious historical sites have been destroyed over the last two hundred years as Toronto has risen from the shoreline. Over and over again, the histories of Indigenous people and the city's own settlers have been bulldozed in the name of progress. In the early 1900s, when city workers found ancient footprints on the bottom of Toronto Harbour — thought to have been made eleven thousand years ago; one of the most remarkable pieces of history ever discovered in this part of the world — they simply poured over them with concrete and kept going. There was work to be done: a city to be built.

Through it all, of course, the First Nations have never left Toronto. The apocalyptic mission of Brébeuf and his priests — taken up by generations of colonial authorities in the centuries since — has failed. Even after Denonville's scorched-earth campaign, the Toronto Purchase swindle, the betrayal at the end of the War of 1812, generations of residential schools, and countless other forms of genocide, there are tens of thousands of Indigenous people still living on this land today.

Many of the descendants of the Wendat villagers who performed the Feast of the Dead now live on the Wendake reserve in Quebec. They never gave up on the souls of Ossossané.

In the late 1990s, they contacted the ROM to begin the process of reclaiming their dead. First, the museum returned ownership of the land to the Wendat nation. And then, on a summer day in 1999, the souls of the dead made their journey out of downtown Toronto and back to the land where they had first been buried four hundred years ago.

On that sunny August day at the end of the millennium, a modern version of the Feast of the Dead was held on the shores of Georgian Bay. Centuries after Brébeuf stood on that same spot and prayed for the end of the sacred tradition, it was being performed once again.

Francis Gros Louis was one of the members of the Wendat nation who took part in the ceremony. "My eyes blurred from the salty tears running down my cheeks," he later remembered, "My hands trembled in anticipation of what I was about to do and my heart pounded as the realization of what I was about to participate in overwhelmed me." As a Wendat funeral chant filled the air, he helped to lay the bones of his ancestors back to rest in their centuries-old grave.

In the years since that ceremony, there have been other repatriations of the dead; Canadian institutions have gradually begun to realize their obligations. In 2015, the final report of the Truth and Reconciliation Commission called on museums and archives to ensure they're complying with the United Nations Declaration on the Rights of Indigenous Peoples. It specifically states, "Indigenous peoples have ... the right to the repatriation of their human remains."

The City of Toronto, too, is hoping to take better care of the history held in the ground beneath it: of the First Nations and their ancestors, and of the settlers who have made this place their home over the last two hundred years. In 2002, the city began to develop an Archaeological Master Plan to help ensure the physical traces of those who have lived and died here won't be so carelessly wiped out in the future.

When they published an interim report on their progress, they asked William Woodworth Raweno:kwas, a Mohawk professor and architect, to provide the foreword. "All land is sacred," he wrote. "Held in the land are ... the remains of all that has come before us. This endowment deserves our respect.... In order to heal our relationships with one another, with the Mother Earth, and indeed with Creation itself, we must begin in earnest the work of remembering."

The dead are all around us. We live in *their* city: the Toronto they built. We sleep in their homes. We drive on their roads. They founded our institutions and our traditions, building on patterns of life and death that stretch back for thousands upon thousands of years in this place. They haunt us and guide us even as we forget they are there. Some rest in the ground below our city to this very day, their bones collected in Victorian cemeteries and ancient burial mounds. Their flesh turned to dust, they have become the land beneath our feet.

ACKNOWLEDGEMENTS

This book was written on and about the traditional territories of the Anishinabek, Haudenosaunee, and Wendat peoples, most recently the Mississaugas of the New Credit First Nation.

I'd very much like to thank everyone at Dundurn Press for all they've done to make *The Toronto Book of the Dead* a reality. I'd especially like to thank my editor, Dominic Farrell. And I'd like also to thank my publicist, Kendra Martin, as well as Margaret Bryant and Carrie Gleason, who first invited me into the office to ask me whether I might have an idea for a book and then encouraged me when I gave them a rather morbid answer.

I owe a deep debt of gratitude to *Spacing* magazine, which gave an early home to several of the stories that appear in this book, and to Shawn Micallef and Matthew Blackett in particular. I'm also grateful to everyone else who has given me the opportunity to publish my writing in their publications, helping me to develop some of the ideas that eventually evolved into chapters. I'd like to thank Andrew Hunter at the Art Gallery of Ontario for inviting my dreams into the gallery. And Kevin Seymour at the Royal Ontario Museum for helping me to understand the origins of the Don Valley's giant beaver tooth.

I also owe an enormous, heartfelt thank-you to all the librarians and archivists whose work makes books like this possible.

I've been very lucky to be writing about the history of Toronto at a time when there are so many exciting people and projects exploring stories about our city. This book would not exist if it weren't for the Historicist crew at *Torontoist* and the inspiration they've provided since the very early days of the Toronto Dreams Project: Jamie Bradburn, David Wencer, Kevin Plummer, and Kaitlin Wainwright. It has been a pleasure to follow and be inspired by the work of many others, too: by Chris Bateman's writing, by Lindsay Zier-Vogel's love letters to the city, by Alden Cudanin and Summer Leigh's photographic mashups, by Daniel Rotsztain's drawings, and by those who work at the city's museums, especially Adrianna Prossner and Kristine Williamson at the City of Toronto Historic Sites and Kat Akerfeldt at Toronto's First Post Office.

As a Canadian travelling alone though the English countryside, I was warmly welcomed by Michael Downes at the Fairlynch Museum, and by Ioan and Alice Thomas at the Oundle Museum, who fed me, guided me, and helped me trace the story of the Simcoes on the other side of the ocean, sharing their enthusiasm for the history of Toronto in small towns three thousand kilometres away.

Over the last few years, as the history of the city has become an ever deepening and unhealthy obsession, there have been an unfortunate number of people who have spent hours on end patiently listening to me ramble on about it. I owe an especially big thank you to Laurie McGregor, Christina Ivanowich, and Melissa Hughes, who have lent not only their unending patience, but also their editing help to my work. Matthew Ivanowich, Cody McGraw, Carmen Cheung, Nicholas Van Exan, and George Van Cheung have all spent more than their fair share of time humouring me and keeping me sane. I've been exploring Toronto's nooks and crannies with Tim Spurr and Karen Clipsham since our high school days. Kathleen Keenan, Carmela Quirino, Alex Snider, and Val Adriaanse have all provided invaluable advice. I'm deeply excited to have found kindred storytellers in *Canadiana*'s Ashley Brook, Kyle Cucco, and Josef Beeby. And I couldn't possibly forget to thank Chris Stevenson, Scott Mckean, and everyone who worked with us at *SoundProof Magazine*.

To my family: Mum and Dad, Megan, Mary, Becky, Martin, Matthew, their partners, their children, and everyone who has spent snowy Christmas Eves talking long into the night — it is by listening to your stories that I learned how to tell my own. Thank you.

And finally, thank you to Irene and Old Tom, whose wonderful tales of growing up in Toronto in a time long before I was born — about fires and snowstorms, dance halls and dates — laid the *very* early foundations for this book and will be with me until the day I join them as the land beneath our feet.

SELECTED BIBLIOGRAPHY AND FURTHER READING

1. THE FEAST OF THE DEAD

Brébeuf, Jean de. "Of The Solemn Feast of the Dead." In *The Jesuit Relations and Allied Documents: Travels and Explorations of the Jesuit Missionaries in New France 1610–1791*. Edited by Reuben Gold Thwaites. Cleveland: Burrows Brothers, 1898. Accessed January 7, 2017. http://moses.creighton.edu/kripke/jesuitrelations/relations_10.html.

Hamilton, Michelle A. "Native American Repatriation at 20." *History News Network*. Accessed January 7, 2017. http://historynewsnetwork.org/article/134757.

Heidenreich, C.E. "Huron-Wendat." *Canadian Encyclopedia*. January 4, 2011. Last modified July 23, 2015. www.thecanadianencyclopedia.ca/en/article/huron.

Labelle, Kathryn Magee. *Dispersed but Not Destroyed: A History of the Seventeenth-Century Wendat People*. Vancouver: UBC Press, 2013.

———. "'Faire le Chaudière': The Wendat Feast of Souls, 1636." In *French and Indians in the Heart of North America, 1630–1815*, edited by Robert Englebert and Guillaume Teasdale. Winnipeg: University of Manitoba Press, 2013.

Munson, Marit K. *Before Ontario: The Archaeology of a Province*. Montreal: McGill-Queen's University Press, 2013.

Nierop, Claire van. "Scarborough's Mound of Bones: The Taber Hill Ossuary." *Toronto in Time*. Accessed January 7, 2017. http://citiesintime.ca/toronto/story/TaborHill.

Seeman, Erik R. *The Huron-Wendat Feast of the Dead: Indian-European Encounters in Early North America*. Baltimore: Johns Hopkins University Press, 2011.

Sioui, Georges E. *Huron-Wendat: The Heritage of the Circle*. Vancouver: UBC Press, 1999.

Warrick, Gary. *A Population History of the Huron-Petun, A.D. 500–1650*. New York: Cambridge University Press, 2008.

Wencer, David. "Historicist: The Tabor Hill Ossuary." *Torontoist*, February 28, 2015. Accessed January 7, 2017. http://torontoist.com/2015/02/historicist-the-tabor-hill-ossuary.

Williamson, Ronald F. "The Archaeological History of the Wendat to A.D. 1651: An Overview." *Ontario Archaeology* 94 (2014). Accessed January 7, 2017. http://asiheritage.ca/wp-content/uploads/2016/01/The_Archaeological_History_of_the_Wendat.pdf.

2. THE BEAVER WARS

Eccles, W.J. "Brisay de Denonville, Jacques-René de, Marquis de Denonville." *Dictionary of Canadian Biography*. Accessed December 15, 2015. www.biographi.ca/en/bio/brisay_de_denonville_jacques_rene_de_2E.html.

"Mammals of Toronto: A Guide to Their Remarkable World." In *The City of Toronto Biodiversity Series*. Accessed December 31, 2016. www1.toronto.ca/City%20Of%20Toronto/City%20Planning/Zoning%20&%20Environment/Files/pdf/B/Biodiversity_MammalsToronto_Tagged_Final.pdf.

Marsh, James H. "Toronto Feature: Teiaiagon Seneca Village." *Canadian Encyclopedia*, February 4, 2013. Last modified

July 2, 2015. www.thecanadianencyclopedia.ca/en/article/
   toronto-feature-teiaiagon-seneca-village.

McLeod, Susanna. "Denonville's Deception." *Kingston
   Whig-Standard*, December 2, 2009. Accessed
   December 15, 2015. www.thewhig.com/2009/12/02/
   denonvilles-deception.

O'Callaghan, E.B. *The Documentary History of the State
   of New-York; Arranged Under Direction of the Hon.
   Christopher Morgan, Secretary of State.* Vol. 1. Albany:
   Weed, Parsons, 1849.

Wencer, David. "Historicist: The Village of Teiaiagon." *Torontoist*,
   June 20, 2015. Accessed December 15, 2015. http://
   torontoist.com/2015/06/historicist-the-village-of-teiaiagon.

3. ELIZABETH SIMCOE'S NIGHTMARE

Cruikshank, E.A., ed. *The Correspondence of Lieut. Governor
   John Graves Simcoe, with Allied Documents Relating to
   His Administration of the Government of Upper Canada.*
   Toronto: The Society, 1924.

Esdaile, Charles. *The Peninsular War: A New History.* Toronto:
   Allen Lane, 2002.

Firth, Edith G. "Gwillim, Elizabeth Posthuma (Simcoe)."
   Dictionary of Canadian Biography. Accessed January
   2014. www.biographi.ca/en/bio/gwillim_elizabeth_
   posthuma_7E.html.

Fletcher, Ian. *Badajoz 1812: Wellington's Bloodiest Siege.*
   Oxford: Osprey, 1999.

Fryer, Mary Beacock. *Elizabeth Postuma Simcoe, 1762–1850:
   A Biography.* Toronto: Dundurn, 1989.

———. *Our Young Soldier: Lieutenant Francis Simcoe, 6 June
   1791–6 April 1812.* Toronto: Dundurn, 1996.

Fryer, Mary Beacock, and Christopher Dracott. *John Graves
   Simcoe, 1752–1806: A Biography.* Toronto: Dundurn, 1998.

MacIntosh, Robert M. *Earliest Toronto*. Renfrew, ON: General Store, 2006

McLaughlin, Florence. *First Lady of Upper Canada*. Toronto: Burns & MacEachern, 1968.

Mealing, S.M. "Simcoe, John Graves." *Dictionary of Canadian Biography*. Accessed January 2014. www.biographi.ca/en/bio/simcoe_john_graves_5E.html.

Scadding, Henry. *The Story of Castle Frank, Toronto*. Toronto: Hunter, Rose, 1895.

Simcoe, Elizabeth. *Mrs. Simcoe's Diary*. Edited by Mary Quayle Innis. Toronto: Macmillan, 1965.

Simcoe, John Graves. *Letter to Sir Joseph Banks, (President of the Royal Society of Great Britain) Written by Lieut.-Governor Simcoe, in 1791, Prior to His Departure from England for the Purpose of Organizing the New Province of Upper Canada; to Which Is Added Five Official Speeches Delivered by Him at the Opening or Closing of Parliament in the Same Province*. Edited by Henry Scadding. Toronto: Copp, Clark, 1890.

Wesley, Bathsheba Susannah. "Finding the Sublime: Assessing Elizabeth Simcoe's Fires as an Art Practice." Master's thesis, Concordia University, 2008. http://spectrum.library.concordia.ca/976091/1/MR45353.pdf.

4. THE MURDER OF CHIEF WABAKININE

Benn, Carl. *Historic Fort York, 1793–1993*. Toronto: Dundurn, 1993.

Craig, Gerald M. *Upper Canada: The Formative Years, 1784–1841*. Don Mills: Oxford, 1963.

Edwards, Peter. "Shrugs Greet Historic $145 Million Toronto Land Claim Settlement." *Toronto Star*, June 8, 2010.

Freeman, Victoria Jane. "Toronto Has No History!: Indigeneity, Settler Colonialism and Historical Memory in Canada's Largest City." Ph.D. diss., University of Toronto, 2010.

SELECTED BIBLIOGRAPHY AND FURTHER READING 385

Graymont, Barbara. "Thayendanegea." *Dictionary of Canadian Biography*. Accessed July 31, 2016. www.biographi.ca/en/bio/thayendanegea_5E.html.

Hall, Anthony J. "Royal Proclamation of 1763." *Canadian Encyclopedia*, February 7, 2006. Last modified July 23, 2015. www.thecanadianencyclopedia.ca/en/article/royal-proclamation-of-1763.

Hayes, Derek. *Historical Atlas of Toronto*. Vancouver: Douglas & McIntyre, 2008.

Indian Claims Commission. "Mississaugas of the New Credit First Nation Inquiry: Toronto Purchase Claim." *Aaron and Aaron Barristers and Solicitors*. Accessed January 3, 2017. www.aaron.ca/columns/Mississauga_English.pdf.

LeBlanc, Deanne Aline Marie. "Identifying the Settler Denizen Within Settler Colonialism." Master's thesis, University of Victoria, 2014.

Levin, Allan. *Toronto: Biography of a City*. Vancouver: Douglas & McIntyre, 2014.

MacIntosh, Robert M. *Earliest Toronto*. Renfrew, ON: General Store, 2006.

Mississaugas of the New Credit First Nation. "Toronto Purchase Specific Claim: Arriving at an Agreement." Accessed January 3, 2017. www.newcreditfirstnation.com/uploads/1/8/1/4/18145011/torontopurchasebkltsm.pdf.

"Mississaugas of the New Credit First Nation Inquiry: Toronto Purchase Claim." *Aaron and Aaron Barristers and Solicitors*. Accessed January 3, 2017. www.aaron.ca/columns/Mississauga_English.pdf.

Murton Stoehr, Catherine. "Salvation from Empire: The Roots of Anishinabe Christianity in Upper Canada, 1650–1840." Ph.D. diss., Queen's University, 2008.

Plummer, Kevin. "Historicist: The Murder of Wabakinine." *Torontoist*, May 30, 2015. Accessed July 26, 2016. http://torontoist.com/2015/05/historicist-the-murder-of-wabakinine.

Russell, Peter. *The Correspondence of the Honourable Peter Russell: With Allied Documents Relating to His Administration of the Government of Upper Canada during the Official Term of Lieut.-Governor J.G. Simcoe While on Leave of Absence.* Vols. 1–4. Edited by E.A. Cruikshank and Andrew F. Hunter. Toronto: Ontario Historical Society, 1932.

Smith, Donald B. "The Dispossession of the Mississauga Indians: A Missing Chapter in the Early History of Upper Canada." In *Historical Essays on Upper Canada: New Perspectives*, edited by J.K. Johnson and Bruce G. Wilson. Ottawa: Carleton University Press, 1989.

———.*Sacred Feathers: The Reverend Peter Jones (Kahkewaquonaby) and the Mississauga Indians.* Toronto: University of Toronto Press, 2013.

———."Wabakinine (Wabacoming. Wabicanine, Waipyakanine)." *Dictionary of Canadian Biography.* Accessed July 26, 2016. www.biographi.ca/en/bio/wabakinine_4E.html.

Taylor, Alan. *The Divided Ground: Indians, Settlers, and the Northern Borderland of the American Revolution.* Toronto: Random House, 2006.

Weld, Isaac. *Travels Through the States of North America, and the Provinces of Upper and Lower Canada, During the Years 1795, 1796, and 1797.* London: John Stockdale, 1800.

5. THE TOWN'S FIRST HANGING AND HOW IT WENT WRONG

Alamenciak, Tim. "The End of the Rope: The Story of Canada's Last Executions." *Toronto Star*, December 10, 2012. Accessed May 26, 2016. www.thestar.com/news/gta/2012/12/10/the_end_of_the_rope_the_story_of_canadas_last_executions.html.

Bateman, Chris. "The Story of the First Public Hanging in Toronto." *blogTO*, October 11, 2015. Accessed May 26, 2016. www.blogto.com/city/2015/10/the_story_of_the_first_public_hanging_in_toronto.

Boyle, Terry. *Hidden Ontario: Secrets from Ontario's Past.* Toronto: Dundurn, 2011.

Vronsky, Peter. "Crime & Punishment in York Town (Toronto): 1790–1834 (With a Note on Slavery)." *Crime and Punishment in Canada*. Accessed May 26, 2016. www.russianbooks.org/crime/cph2.htm.

6. WHATEVER HAPPENED TO PEGGY POMPADOUR?

Arthur, Eric. *Toronto, No Mean City*. Toronto: University of Toronto Press, 1986.

"Black Enslavement." *Canadian Encyclopedia*, June 13, 2016. Last modified June 15, 2016. www.thecanadianencyclopedia.ca/en/article/black-enslavement.

"Chloe Cooley and the Act to Limit Slavery in Upper Canada." *Canadian Encyclopedia*, October 30, 2013. Last modified January 5, 2016. www.thecanadianencyclopedia.ca/en/article/chloe-cooley-and-the-act-to-limit-slavery-in-upper-canada.

Craig, Gerald M. *Upper Canada: The Formative Years, 1784–1841*. Don Mills: Oxford, 1963.

Firth, Edith G. "Russell, Peter." *Dictionary of Canadian Biography*. Accessed August 6, 2016. www.biographi.ca/en/bio/russell_peter_5E.html.

Hamilton, James Cleland. *Osgoode Hall — Reminiscences of the Bench and Bar*. Toronto: Carswell, 1904.

Henry, Natasha L. *Talking About Freedom: Celebrating Emancipation Day in Canada*. Toronto: Dundurn, 2012.

Levine, Allan. *Toronto: Biography of a City*. Vancouver: Douglas & MacIntyre, 2014.

MacIntosh, Robert M. *Earliest Toronto*. Renfrew, ON: General
    Store, 2006.
"Petersfield." *Lost Rivers*, accessed August 6, 2016. http://
    lostrivers.ca/content/points/Petersfield.html.
Read, David Breakenridge. *The Lieutenant-Governors of Upper
    Canada 1792–1899*. Toronto: William Briggs, 1900.
Riddell, William Renwick. "The Slave in Upper Canada."
    Journal of Law and Criminology 14, no. 2 (1923).
———. "Upper Canada — Early Period." *Journal of Negro
    History* 5, no. 3 (1920). Accessed August 6, 2016. www.
    jstor.org/stable/2713625.
Robertson, John Ross. *Robertson's Landmarks of Toronto*.
    Toronto: John Ross Robertson, 1908.
Scadding, Henry. *Toronto of Old*. Toronto: Adam, Stevenson, 1873.
Shadd, Adrienne. *The Journey from Tollgate to Parkway:
    African Canadians in Hamilton*. Toronto: Dundurn, 2010.
Shadd, Adrienne, Afua Cooper, and Karolyn Smardz Frost.
    The Underground Railroad: Next Stop, Toronto! Toronto:
    Natural Heritage Books, 2002.
Taylor, Alan. *The Divided Ground: Indians, Settlers, and the
    Northern Borderland of the American Revolution*. Toronto:
    Random House, 2006.
Winks, Robin W. *The Blacks in Canada: A History*. Montreal:
    McGill-Queen's University Press, 1997.

7. THE BATTLE OF YORK

Berton, Pierre. *Flames Across the Border: 1813–1814*. Toronto:
    Anchor, 1981.
Collins, Gilbert. *Guidebook to the Historic Sites of the War of
    1812*. Toronto: Dundurn, 2006.
Craig, G.M. "Strachan, John." *Dictionary of Canadian
    Biography*. Accessed December 10, 2016. www.biographi.
    ca/en/bio/strachan_john_9E.html.

Finan, P. *Journal of a Voyage to Quebec in the Year 1825: With Recollections of Canada During the Late American War, in the Years 1812-13*. Newry: Alexander Peacock, 1828.

Grogan, Mick, dir. *Explosion 1812*. Toronto: Yap Films, 2012.

Humphries, Charles. "The Capture of York." In *The Defended Border*, edited by Morris Zaslow. Toronto: Macmillan, 1964.

Malcomson, Robert. *Capital in Flames: The American Attack on York, 1813*. Montreal: Robin Brass, 2008.

———. "Ka-Boom!!! The Explosion of the Grand Magazine." *Fife and Drum* 12, no. 2 (2008).

Mayers, Adam. "Blood-Stained Floor Told the Tale." *Toronto Star*, May 3, 2007. Accessed December 10, 2016. www.thestar.com/news/2007/05/03/bloodstained_floor_told_the_tale.html.

Myer, Jesse S. *Life and Letters of Dr. William Beaumont, Including Hitherto Unpublished Data Concerning the Case of Alexis St. Martin*. St. Louis: C.V. Mosby, 1912.

Proceedings of the Massachusetts Historical Society. Vol. 11. Massachusetts: The Society, 1871.

Robertson, John Ross. *Landmarks of Toronto*. Vol 1. Toronto: J. Ross Robertson, 1894.

Stanley, George F.G. *The War of 1812: Land Operations*. Toronto: Macmillan, 1983.

Sylvester, Erin. "Now and Then: James Givins." *Torontoist*, March 31, 2016. Accessed December 10, 2016. http://torontoist.com/2016/03/now-and-then-james-givins.

Taylor, Alan. *The Civil War of 1812: American Citizens, British Subjects, Irish Rebels, & Indian Allies*. New York: Vintage, 2010.

Watson, Robert P. *America's First Crisis: The War of 1812*. Albany: SUNY Press, 2014.

"Who Started the War of 1812?" *Ideas*. Toronto: CBC Radio, June 18, 2012.

"York In Flames." *Ideas*. Toronto: CBC Radio, April 26, 2013.
Zuehlke, Mark. *For Honour's Sake: The War of 1812 and the Brokering of an Uneasy Peace*. Toronto: Knopf, 2006.

8. THE BLOODY BURLINGTON RACES

Dudley, William S., ed. *The Naval War of 1812: A Documentary History*. Vol. 2. Washington: Naval Historical Center, 1992.

Gardner, Robert. *The Naval War of 1812*. London: Caxton Editions, 2001.

Gough, Barry. "War on the Lakes in the War of 1812." *War of 1812*. Accessed March 30, 2015. www.eighteentwelve. ca/?q=eng/Topic/28&img=11.

Malcomson, Robert. *Lords of the Lake*. Toronto: R. Brass Studio, 1998.

———. "U.S. Commodore Chauncey at Burlington Bay." *The War of 1812 Website*. Accessed March 30, 2015. www.warof1812. ca/chauncey.htm.

Marsh, James. "Ships of the War of 1812." *War of 1812*. Accessed March 30, 2015. www.eighteentwelve.ca/?q=eng/Topic/27.

Parr, Pepper. "Hard, Dogged Work by a Local History Buff Results in Plaque to Mark a Major War of 1812–14 Event Played Out on Burlington's Waterfront." *Burlington Gazette*, September 26, 2013. Accessed March 30, 2015. http:// burlingtongazette.ca/ata/2013/09/hard-dogged-work-by-a-local-history-buff-results-in-plaque-to-mark-a-major-war-of-1812-14-war-event-played-out-on-burlingtons-waterfront.

Smith, Daphne. "Burlington Connections to the War of 1812." Museum of Burlington, April 2008. Accessed March 30, 2015. https://museumsofburlington.ca/system/documents/ documents/69/original/war_of_1812_paper.pdf?1331327111.

Williamson, Robert J. "The Burlington Races Revisited: A Revised Analysis of an 1813 Naval Battle for Supremacy on Lake Ontario." *Canadian Military History* 8, no. 4 (2012).

9. THE TRUE STORY OF TORONTO'S ISLAND GHOST

Bateman, Chris. "Remembering Gibraltar Point's Grisly Past." *blogTO*, August 11, 2012. Accessed April 29, 2015. www.blogto.com/city/2012/08/remembering_gibraltar_points_grisly_past.

Butts, Edward. *Murder: Twelve True Stories of Homicide in Canada*. Toronto: Dundurn, 2011.

"Gibraltar Point Lighthouse — The Legend Exposed! (A OCPRS Toronto, Canada, Investigation)." *OCPRS Toronto*, July 27, 2011. Accessed April 29, 2015. https://ocprstoronto.wordpress.com/2011/07/27/gibraltar-point-lighthouse-%E2%80%93-the-legend-exposed.

Kohane, Jack. "Unsolved Mystery: Toronto's Gibraltar Point Lighthouse." *Lighthouse Digest* (January 2002).

Martinz, Jacqueline. "Toronto Haunts." *Torontoist*, October 30, 2009. Accessed April 29, 2015. http://torontoist.com/2009/10/toronto_haunts.

Miedema, Gary. "Casting Light on Toronto Island History." *Spacing*, June 27, 2008. Accessed April 29, 2015. http://spacing.ca/toronto/2008/06/27/casting-light-on-toronto-island-history.

"No Ghost for Island Control Board Edict 'Just A Myth' — Brand." *Toronto Star*, December 6, 1957.

O'Keefe, Eamon. "New Light on Toronto's Oldest Cold Case." *Fife and Drum* 19, no. 5 (2015).

Robertson, John Ross. *Robertson's Landmarks of Toronto: Fifth Series*. Toronto: John Ross Robertson, 1908.

Taylor, Bill. "Manuel's Labour." *Toronto Star*, May 8, 2008. Accessed April 29, 2015. www.thestar.com/news/2008/05/08/manuels_labour.html.

10. THE DEADLY DUEL

Allen, Robert S. "Mr. Secretary Jarvis: William Jarvis of
    Connecticut and York." In *Eleven Exiles: Accounts of
    Loyalists of the American Revolution*, edited by Phyllis R.
    Blakeley and John Grant. Toronto: Dundurn, 1982.

Armstrong, Frederick H. "Small, James Edward." *Dictionary
    of Canadian Biography*. Accessed August 17, 2016. www.
    biographi.ca/en/bio/small_james_edward_9E.html.

Armstrong, Frederick H., and Ronald J. Stagg. "Mackenzie,
    William Lyon." *Dictionary of Canadian Biography*.
    Accessed August 17, 2016. www.biographi.ca/en/bio.
    php?BioId=38684.

Bassler, Gerhard P. "German Canadians." *Canadian
    Encyclopedia*, July 30, 2013. Last modified March 4,
    2015. www.thecanadianencyclopedia.ca/en/article/
    german-canadians.

Bendici, Ray. *Speaking Ill of the Dead: Jerks in Connecticut
    History*. Guilford, CT: Globe Pequot, 2012.

Burns, Robert J. "Jarvis, William." *Dictionary of Canadian
    Biography*. Accessed August 17, 2016. www.biographi.ca/
    en/bio/jarvis_william_5E.html.

———. "Ridout, Thomas." *Dictionary of Canadian Biography*.
    Accessed August 17, 2016. www.biographi.ca/en/bio/
    ridout_thomas_6E.html.

Craig, Gerald M. *Upper Canada: The Formative Years, 1784–
    1841*. Don Mills, ON: Oxford University Press, 1963.

Davidson, Stephen. "My Calamitous Situation: The Life
    of Polly Jarvis Dibblee." *United Empire Loyalists'
    Association of Canada*. Accessed July 29, 2014.
    www.uelac.org/Loyalist-Info/extras/Dibblee-Fyler/
    Dibblee-Polly-Jarvis-biography.pdf.

Davis-Fisch, Heather. "Lawless Lawyers: Indigeneity,
    Civility, and Violence." *TRIC/RTAC* 35, no. 1 (2014):
    31–48.

Jarvis, Stephen. "Manuscript of Colonel Jarvis — Born in
    1756." *Journal of American History* 1, no. 3 (1907).
    Accessed July 29, 2014. http://lib.jrshelby.com/jarvis.htm.

Leighton, Douglas, and Robert J. Burns. "Jarvis, Samuel
    Peters." *Dictionary of Canadian Biography.* Accessed
    August 17, 2016. www.biographi.ca/en/bio/jarvis_
    samuel_peters_8E.html.

Raible, Chris. *Muddy York Mud: Scandal & Scurrility in Upper
    Canada.* Creemore, ON: Curiosity House, 1992.

Riddell, William Renwick. "The Duel in Early Upper Canada."
    Journal of Criminal Law and Criminology 6, no. 2 (1915):
    165–176.

Robertson, John Ross. *Robertson's Landmarks of Toronto.*
    Toronto: John Ross Robertson, 1908.

Scadding, Henry. *Toronto of Old.* Toronto: Adam, Stevenson,
    1873.

Senior, Hereward, and Elinor Senior. "Boulton, Henry John."
    Dictionary of Canadian Biography. Accessed August 17,
    2016. www.biographi.ca/en/bio/boulton_henry_john_9E.
    html.

Symonds, Thomas S.B. "Ridout, George." *Dictionary of
    Canadian Biography.* Accessed August 17, 2016. www.
    biographi.ca/en/bio/ridout_george_10E.html.

11. THE BLUE DEATH

Atkinson, Logan. "The Impact of Cholera on the Design and
    Implementation of Toronto's First Municipal Bylaws,
    1834." *Urban History Review* 30, no. 2 (2002): 3–15.

Bethune, N.A. *Memoir of the Right Reverend John Strachan:
    First Bishop of Toronto.* Toronto: Roswell, 1870.

Bradburn, Jamie. "Toronto Is Born." *Torontoist,* March 6, 2014.
    Accessed August 26, 2016. http://torontoist.com/2014/03/
    toronto-is-born.

"Cholera." *World Health Organization*. Accessed August 26, 2016. www.who.int/mediacentre/factsheets/fs107/en.

Firth, Edith G., ed. *The Town of York: 1815–1834: A Further Collection of Documents of Early Toronto*. Toronto: University of Toronto Press, 1966.

Fraser, Robert L. "Baldwin, William Warren." *Dictionary of Canadian Biography*. Accessed August 26, 2016. www.biographi.ca/en/bio/baldwin_william_warren_7E.html.

Godfrey, Charles M. *The Cholera Epidemics in Upper Canada, 1832–1866*. Toronto: Seccombe House, 1968.

"History of Toronto Paramedic Services." *Toronto Paramedic Services*. Accessed August 24, 2016. http://torontoparamedic services.ca/history-of-toronto-paramedic-services.

Jackson, Paul S.B. "From Liability to Profitability: How Disease, Fear, and Medical Science Cleaned Up the Marshes of Ashbridge's Bay." In *Reshaping Toronto's Waterfront*, edited by Gene Desfor and Jennefer Laidley. Toronto: University of Toronto Press, 2011.

Javed, Noor. "Toronto Forged Its Identity Amid Cholera Outbreak." *Toronto Star*, March 7, 2009. Accessed August 26, 2016. www.thestar.com/life/health_wellness/2009/03/07/toronto_forged_its_identity_Amid_cholera_outbreak.html.

Kilbourn, William. *The Firebrand: William Lyon Mackenzie and the Rebellion in Upper Canada*. Toronto: Dundurn, 1956.

Levy, Sharon. "Cholera's Life Aquatic." *Bioscience* 55, no. 9 (2005): 728–732.

Lindsey, Charles. *The Life and Times of Wm. Lyon Mackenzie: With an Account of the Canadian Rebellion of 1837, and the Subsequent Border Disturbances, Chiefly from Unpublished Documents*. Vol. 1. Toronto: P.R. Randall, 1862.

Patterson, Marian A. "The Cholera Epidemic of 1832 in York, Upper Canada." *Bulletin of the Medical Library Association* 46, no. 2 (1958): 165–184.

Wilton, Carol. *Popular Politics and Political Culture in Upper Canada, 1800–1850*. Montreal: McGill-Queen's Press, 2000.

12. REVOLUTION! ISH!

Armstrong, Frederick H. *Toronto The Place of Meeting*. Toronto: Ontario Historical Society and Windsor Publications, 1983.

Armstrong, Frederick H., and Ronald J. Stragg. "Mackenzie, William Lyon." *Dictionary of Canadian Biography*. Accessed December 18, 2016. www.biographi.ca/en/bio/mackenzie_william_lyon_9E.html.

Charles, Ashok, and Randall White. "Lount and Matthews Commemoration Salon." *Active History*. Accessed December 17, 2016. http://activehistory.ca/2013/04/lount-and-matthews-commemoration-salon.

Craig, Gerald M. *Upper Canada: The Formative Years, 1784–1841*. Don Mills: Oxford University Press, 1963.

Dent, John Charles. *The Story of the Upper Canadian Rebellion*. Toronto: C. Blackett Robinson, 1885. www.gutenberg.ca/ebooks/dent-uppercanadian2/dent-uppercanadian2-00-h-dir/dent-uppercanadian2-00-h.html.

Head, Sir Francis Bond. *A Narrative*. London: J. Murray, 1839.

Kilbourn, William. *The Firebrand: William Lyon Mackenzie and the Rebellion in Upper Canada*. Toronto: Dundurn, 2008.

Mackenzie, William Lyon. *Mackenzie's Own Narrative of the Late Rebellion*. Edited by Charles Fothergill. Toronto: Palladium, 1838.

McKenzie, Ruth. "FitzGibbon, James." *Dictionary of Canadian Biography*. Accessed December 18, 2016. www.biographi.ca/en/bio.php?BioId=38548.

Mulvany, Charles Pelham. *History of Toronto and County of York, Ontario: Containing an Outline of the History of the Dominion of Canada; A History of the City of Toronto and the County of York, with the Townships, Towns,*

Villages, Churches, Schools, General and Local Statistics;
Biographical Sketches, etc., etc. Vol. 1. Toronto: C. Blackett
Robinson, 1885.

Read, Colin. *The Rebellion of 1837 in Upper Canada.*
Montreal: McGill-Queen's University Press, 1985.

Ryerson, Egerton. *The Story of My Life.* Toronto: W. Briggs, 1883.

Sewell, John. *Mackenzie: A Political Biography of William Lyon
Mackenzie.* Toronto: James Lorimer, 2002.

Stamp, Richard. "Chapter 5: Tories and Reformers." *Early
Days in Richmond Hill: A History of the Community
to 1930.* Accessed October 8, 2016. http://edrh.rhpl.
richmondhill.on.ca/default.asp?ID=s5.6.

Wilson, William R. "Francis Bond Head, Part 1" *Historical
Narratives of Early Canada.* Accessed December 18, 2016.
www.uppercanadahistory.ca/tt/tt2.html.

———. "Road To Rebellion." *Historical Narratives of Early
Canada.* Accessed December 18, 2016. www.upper
canadahistory.ca/pp/pp6.html.

———. "Upper Canada's Lieutenant-Governors and the Colonial
Office." *Historical Narratives of Early Canada.* Accessed
December 18, 2016. www.uppercanadahistory.ca/pp/pp5.
html.

Wise, S.F. "Head, Sir Francis Bond." *Dictionary of Canadian
Biography.* Accessed December 18, 2016. www.biographi.
ca/en/bio/head_francis_bond_10E.html.

13. THE GRISLY GRAVE OF ROBERT BALDWIN

Cross, Michael S. *The Morning Star of Memory: A Biography of
Robert Baldwin.* Don Mills: Oxford University Press, 2012.

Cross, Michael S., and Robert Lochiel Fraser. "Baldwin,
Robert." *Dictionary of Canadian Biography.* Accessed
December 26, 2016. www.biographi.ca/en/bio/baldwin_
robert_8E.html.

Dent, John Charles, ed. *The Canadian Portrait Gallery.* Vol. 1.
    Toronto: J.B. Magurn, 1880.

Fraser, Robert L. "Baldwin, William Warren." *Dictionary
    of Canadian Biography.* Accessed December 26, 2016.
    www.biographi.ca/en/bio/baldwin_william_warren_7E.
    html.

Lucas, Sir C.P., ed. *Lord Durham's Report on the Affairs of
    British North America.* Toronto: Henry Frowde, 1912.

Saul, John Ralston. *Louis-Hippolyte LaFontaine and Robert
    Baldwin.* Toronto: Penguin, 2010.

14. BLACK '47 IN THE ORANGE CITY

"Blighted Nation." *The History Show.* Dublin, RTÉ Radio,
    January 2013.

Bradburn, Jamie. "Toronto Feature: Irish Potato Famine
    Refugees." *Canadian Encyclopedia*, February 4, 2013. Last
    modified July 2, 2015. www.thecanadianencyclopedia.ca/
    en/article/toronto-feature-irish-potato-famine-refugees.

Choquette, Robert. "Power, Michael." *Dictionary of Canadian
    Biography.* Accessed January 2, 2017. www.biographi.ca/
    en/bio/power_michael_7E.html.

"History of the Cathedral." *St. Michael's Cathedral.* Accessed
    January 2, 2017. www.stmichaelscathedral.com/
    history-of-the-cathedral.

Magan, Ruan, dir. *Death or Canada.* Dublin: Title Films,
    2008.

McGowan, Mark. *Death or Canada: The Irish Famine
    Migration to Toronto, 1847.* Toronto: Novalis, 2009.

———. *Michael Power: The Struggle to Build the Catholic Church
    on the Canadian Frontier.* Montreal: McGill-Queen's
    University Press, 2005.

McGowan, Mark G., and Michael Chard. "Great Famine History."
    Ireland Park Foundation. Accessed January 2, 2017. http://

irelandparkfoundation.com/famine-memorial/great-
famine-history.
Smyth, William J. *Toronto, the Belfast of Canada: The Orange
Order and the Shaping of Municipal Culture*. Toronto:
University of Toronto Press, 2015.

15. ABRAHAM LINCOLN'S SHAWL

Abbott, A.R. "Some Recollections of Lincoln's Assassination."
Anglo-American Magazine 5 (1901).
Beatty, Roxanne and Jill L. Newmark. "A Day That Changed
American History." *Circulating Now, U.S. National Library
of Medicine*, April 14, 2015. Accessed June 26, 2016. https://
circulatingnow.nlm.nih.gov/2015/04/14/a-day-that-
changed-american-history.
Cobb, W. Montague. "A Short History of the Freedmen's
Hospital." *Journal of the National Medical Association* 54,
no. 3 (1962).
Coddington, Ronald S. *African American Faces of the Civil War:
An Album*. Baltimore: Johns Hopkins University Press, 2012.
Craughwell, Thomas J. *Stealing Lincoln's Body*. Cambridge,
MA: Belknap, 2009.
Edwards, William C. and Edward Steers. *The Lincoln
Assassination: The Evidence*. Champaign, IL: University of
Illinois Press, 2010.
Goodman, Barak, director. *The Assassination of Abraham
Lincoln*. Toronto: Ark Media, 2009.
Hendrick, George and Willene Hendrick. *Black Refugees in
Canada: Accounts of Escape During the Era of Slavery*.
Jefferson, NC: McFarland, 2010.
Henry, Natasha L. *Talking About Freedom: Emancipation Day
in Canada*. Toronto: Dundurn, 2012.
Hill, Daniel G. *The Freedom-Seekers: Blacks in Early Canada*.
Toronto: Book Society of Canada, 1981.

Mansch, Larry D. *Abraham Lincoln, President-Elect*. Baltimore: McFarland, 2005.

Newby, M. Dalyce. *Anderson Ruffin Abbott: First Afro-Canadian Doctor*. Markham, ON: Fitzhenry & Whiteside, 1998.

Newmark, Jill L. "Contraband Hospital, 1862–1863: Health Care For the First Freedpeople." *Online Encyclopedia of Significant People and Places in African American History*. Accessed June 26, 2016. www.blackpast.org/perspectives/contraband-hospital-1862-1863-heath-care-first-freedpeople.

———. "Lincoln's Last Hours." *Circulating Now, U.S. National Library of Medicine*, April 15, 2015. Accessed June 26, 2016. https://circulatingnow.nlm.nih.gov/2015/04/15/lincolns-last-hours.

Newmark, Jill L., and Roxanne Beatty. "The Lincoln Autopsy." *Circulating Now, U.S. National Library of Medicine*, April 16, 2015. Accessed June 26, 2016. https://circulatingnow.nlm.nih.gov/2015/04/16/the-lincoln-autopsy.

Prince, Bryan. *My Brother's Keeper: African Canadians and the American Civil War*. Toronto: Dundurn, 2015.

Reid, Richard M. *African Canadians in Union Blue: Enlisting for the Cause in the Civil War*. Vancouver: UBC Press, 2014.

Slaney, Catherine. *Family Secrets: Crossing the Colour Line*. Toronto: Dundurn, 2003.

Steers Jr., Edward. "The Assassination." In *Abraham Lincoln: Great American Historians on Our Sixteenth President*, edited by Brian Lamb, Susan Swain, and C-SPAN. New York City: PublicAffairs, 2008.

Stolp-Smith, Michael. "Freedmen's Hospital/Howard University Hospital (1862–)." *BlackPast.org*. Accessed June 26, 2016. www.blackpast.org/aah/freedmen-s-hospital-howard-university-hospital-1862.

Thomas, Owen. "Abbott, Anderson Ruffin." *Dictionary of Canadian Biography*. Accessed June 24, 2016. www.biographi.ca/en/bio/abbott_anderson_ruffin_14E.html.

Winks, Robert W. "Abbot, Wilson Ruffin." *Dictionary of Canadian Biography*. Accessed June 24, 2016. http://www. biographi.ca/en/bio.php?id_nbr=4787.

―――. *The Blacks in Canada: A History*. Montreal: McGill-Queen's University Press, 1997.

16. CANNONBALL

Amernic, Jerry. "Grand Old Game's Glory Days." *Toronto Star*, November 6, 2002.

Bateman, Chris. "That Time Toronto Won the 1887 Baseball Pennant." *blogTO*, April 12, 2015. Accessed October 13, 2015. www.blogto.com/city/2015/04/that_time_toronto_won_the_1887_baseball_pennant.

Cauz, Louis. *Baseball's Back in Town: From the Don to the Blue Jays, a History of Baseball in Toronto*. Toronto: CMC, 1977.

"Crane Was Easy: Toronto Baseball Team Overwhelms Springfield." *Globe*, July 1, 1896.

"Ed Crane." *Baseball Reference*. Accessed October 13, 2015. www.baseball-reference.com/players/c/craneed01.shtml.

Hagey, Lamont J. "Old Time Citizen Turns Back Pages On Baseball Here." *Globe*, April 14, 1936.

Lamster, Mark. *Spalding's World Tour: The Epic Adventure that Took Baseball Around the Globe*. New York: PublicAffairs, 2007.

McKenna, Brian. "Ed Crane." *Society for American Baseball Research*. Accessed October 13, 2015. http://sabr.org/bioproj/person/fcc93495.

"Ned Crane a Suicide." *Evening Star*, September 21, 1896.

"Ned Crane Is No More." *Globe*, September 21, 1896.

"Players Wanted: The Toronto Baseball Team Must Be Strengthened." *Evening Star*, May 3, 1895.

Ryan, Allan. "Where Baseball Found Its Home." *Toronto Star*, September 17, 1999.

"Two Famous Ball Games Recalled." *Toronto Daily Star,*
January 4, 1902.

"When Baseball Went Global: 'Spalding's World Tour.'" *Talk of
the Nation,* NPR, April 4, 2006.

17. A BRIEF HISTORY OF THE PIGEONS OF TORONTO

Godfrey, W. Earl. "Passenger Pigeon." *Canadian Encyclopedia,*
February 7, 2006. Last modified May 21, 2014. www.
thecanadianencyclopedia.com/en/article/passenger-pigeon.

"The Great Passenger Pigeon Comeback." *Long Now Foundation.*
Accessed January 9, 2017. http://reviverestore.org/projects/
the-great-passenger-pigeon-comeback.

Haag-Wackernagel, Daniel. "The Feral Pigeon." *Institute
of Anatomy, Department of Biomedicine, University of
Basel.* Accessed June 10, 2013. https://anatomie.unibas.
ch/IntegrativeBiology/haag/Culture-History-Pigeon/
feral-pigeon-haag.html.

Hall, Joseph. "How to De-Extinct the Passenger Pigeon."
Toronto Star, February 2, 2014. Accessed January 9, 2017.
www.thestar.com/news/insight/2014/02/02/how_to_
deextinct_the_passenger_pigeon.html.

Humphries, Courtney. *Superdove: How the Pigeon Took
Manhattan ... And the World.* Toronto: HarperCollins,
2009.

Mitchell, Margaret H. *The Passenger Pigeon in Ontario.* Toronto:
University of Toronto Press, 1935.

"Rock Pigeon." *Cornell Lab of Ornithology.* Accessed June 10,
2013. https://www.allaboutbirds.org/guide/rock_pigeon/
lifehistory.

Simcoe, Elizabeth. *Mrs. Simcoe's Diary.* Edited by Mary Quayle
Innis. Toronto: Macmillan, 1965.

18. THE TOOTH

"Brick Works Quarry — North Wall." *Lost Rivers.* Accessed
    January 9, 2017. www.lostrivers.ca/content/points/
    BrickworksNorthwall.html.

Coleman, Arthur Philemon. *The Last Million Years: A History
    of the Pleistocene in North America.* New York: AMS
    Press, 1941.

Prehistoric. "New York." Silver Spring, MD: Discovery Channel,
    2010.

Remiz, Frank. "Toronto's Geology." *Toronto Field Naturalists.*
    Accessed January 9, 2017. www.torontofieldnaturalists.
    org/documents/TorontoGeology-2012Jan24_web.pdf.

Sellers, Daniel. "Prehistoric Toronto: The Paleozoic Era."
    Torontoist, March 7, 2012. Accessed January 8, 2017. http://
    torontoist.com/2012/03/prehistoric-toronto-the-paleozoic-
    era.

19. THE CROOKED KNIGHT OF CASA LOMA

Bradburn, Jamie. "Historicist: How Do You Solve a Problem
    Like Casa Loma?" *Torontoist,* May 29, 2011. December 5,
    2012. http://torontoist.com/2011/05/historicst_how_do_
    you_solve_a_problem_like_casa_loma.

Canada. Royal Commission on Life Insurance. *Report.* Ottawa:
    S.E. Dawson, 1907. http://epe.lac-bac.gc.ca/100/200/301/
    pco-bcp/commissions-ef/mactavish1907-eng/mactavish
    1907-eng.htm.

"The Early Days." *Casa Loma.* Accessed December 5, 2012.
    www.casaloma.org/about.history.gk.

Fleming, R.B. *The Railway King of Canada: Sir William
    MacKenzie, 1849–1923.* Vancouver: UBC Press, 1991.

Freeman, Bill. *Casa Loma: Canada's Fairy-Tale Castle and Its
    Owner, Sir Henry Pellatt.* Toronto: Lorimer, 1999.

Mouriopoulus, Nikolas A.E. "'A Serious Piece of Business': Sir

Henry Pellatt, The Queen's Own Rifles of Canada, and the 'English Trip' of 1910." *The Queen's Own Rifles of Canada Regimental Museum and Archives*, September 20, 2014. Accessed December 5, 2012. https://qormuseum.org/2014/09/20/a-serious-piece-of-business-part-iv.

Oreskovich, Carlie. *Sir Henry Pellatt, the King of Casa Loma.* Whitby, ON: McGraw-Hill Ryerson, 1982.

Plummer, Kevin. "Historicist: The Forgotten Urban Squalor of The Ward." *Torontoist*, October 11, 2008. Accessed December 5, 2012. http://torontoist.com/2008/10/historicist_forgotten_urban_squalor_1.

Storzt, Gerald J. "Archbishop Lynch and the Toronto Savings Bank." *CCHA Study Sessions* 45 (1978).

20. THE GROUP OF SEVEN ON THE WESTERN FRONT

Barker Fairley. "Canadian War Pictures." *Canadian Magazine*, November 31, 1919. Reproduced in *Great Unsolved Mysteries in Canadian History*. Accessed November 10, 2013. www.canadianmysteries.ca/sites/thomson/artistsworld/artistsatwar/5168en.html.

Brandon, Laura. "Shattered Landscape: The Great War and the Art of the Group of Seven." *Canadian Military History* 10, no. 1 (2001).

"Death on a Painted Lake: The Tom Thomson Tragedy." *Great Unsolved Mysteries in Canadian History*. Accessed November 10, 2013. www.canadianmysteries.ca/sites/thomson/home/indexen.html.

Jackson, A.Y. *A Painter's Country: The Autobiography of A.Y. Jackson.* Toronto: Clarke, Irwin, 1976.

Klages, Gregory. *The Many Deaths of Tom Thomson: Separating Fact from Fiction.* Toronto: Dundurn, 2016.

Larsen, Wayne. *A.Y. Jackson: The Life of a Landscape Painter.* Toronto: Dundurn, 2009.

"Lord Beaverbrook." *Canadian War Museum.* Accessed
    November 10, 2013. www.warmuseum.ca/firstworldwar/
    history/after-the-war/history/lord-beaverbrook.
MacCallum, J.M. "Tom Thomson: Painter of the North."
    Canadian Magazine, March 31, 1918. Reproduced in
    Great Unsolved Mysteries in Canadian History. Accessed
    November 10, 2013. www.canadianmysteries.ca/sites/
    thomson/artistsworld/artistspatrons/5226en.html.
Morse, Jennifer. "Frederick Horsman Varley." *Legion Magazine*,
    January 1, 2000. Accessed on October 7, 2016. https://
    legionmagazine.com/en/2000/01/frederick-horsman-varley.

21. THE NIGHT OF THE DROWNING NURSES

Crowe, David M. *Crimes of State Past and Present: Government-
    Sponsored Atrocities and International Legal Responses.*
    Oxford: Routledge, 2013.
"Dorothy Mary Yarwood Baldwin." *Great War Centenary
    Association.* Accessed January 8, 2017. www.doingourbit.
    ca/profile/dorothy-baldwin.
Fowler, T. Robert. "The Canadian Nursing Service and the
    British War Office: The Debate Over Awarding the Military
    Cross, 1918." *Canadian Military History* 14 (2005).
"Hospital Ship Attack Hideous in Ferocity." *Toronto Daily Star*,
    July 2, 1918.
"In Memory of Nursing Sister Carola Josephine Douglas
    June 27, 1918." *Canadian Virtual War Memorial, Veterans
    Affairs Canada.* Accessed November 10, 2014. www.veterans.
    gc.ca/eng/remembrance/memorials/canadian-virtual-war-
    memorial/detail/4021495?Carola%20Josephine%20
    Douglas.
"In Memory of Nursing Sister Dorothy Mary Yarwood Baldwin
    May 30, 1918." *Canadian Virtual War Memorial, Veterans
    Affairs Canada.* Accessed January 8, 2017. www.veterans.gc.

ca/eng/remembrance/memorials/canadian-virtual-war-memorial/Detail/56954.

"In Memory of Nursing Sister Mary Agnes McKenzie June 27, 1918." *Canadian Virtual War Memorial, Veterans Affairs Canada.* Accessed November 10, 2014. www.veterans.gc.ca/eng/remembrance/memorials/canadian-virtual-war-memorial/Detail/4021637.

MacLellan, Stephanie. "World War 1 Encyclopedia: Earhart, Amelia." *Toronto Star*, August 1, 2014. Accessed January 8, 2017. www.thestar.com/news/world/ww1/2014/08/01/world_war_1_encyclopedia_earhart_amelia.html.

Marshall, Debbie. "Carola Douglas Revisited." *Finding the Forty-Seven: Canadian Sisters of the First World War*, July 31, 2012. Accessed November 10, 2014. http://rememberingfirstworldwarnurses.blogspot.ca/2012/07/carola-douglas-revisited.html.

———. "Nursing Sister Dorothy Baldwin Remembered." *Finding the Forty-Seven: Canadian Sisters of the First World War*, October 24, 2011. Accessed January 8, 2017. http://rememberingfirstworldwarnurses.blogspot.ca/2011/10/nursing-sister-dorothy-baldwin.html.

———. "Nursing Sister Mary Agnes McKenzie." *Finding the Forty-Seven: Canadian Sisters of the First World War*, April 5, 2011. Accessed November 10, 2014. http://rememberingfirstworldwarnurses.blogspot.ca/2010/04/nursing-sister-mary-agnes-mckenzie.html.

———. "Remembering Carola Douglas and Anna Stamers." *Finding the Forty-Seven: Canadian Sisters of the First World War*, October 11, 2011. Accessed November 10, 2014. http://rememberingfirstworldwarnurses.blogspot.ca/2010/10/remembering-carola-douglas-and-anna.html

Nicholson, G.W.L., and Mark Osborne Humphries. *Canadian Expeditionary Force, 1914–1919: Official History of the Canadian Army in the First World War*. Montreal: McGill-Queen's Press, 2015.

"Nurse 'Nan' M'Kenzie Is Believed To Be Lost." *Toronto Daily Star*, July 3, 1918.

"Nursing Sister Mary Agnes McKenzie, Died: June 27, 1918." *Canadian Great War Project*. Accessed November 10, 2014. www.canadiangreatwarproject.com/searches/soldierDetail.asp?ID=66076.

"The Sinking of the Canadian Hospital Ship." *Canadian Great War Project*. Accessed November 10, 2014. www.canadiangreatwarproject.com/writing/llandoveryCastle.asp.

Sivénas, Nikifóros. "The Nos 4 and 5 Canadian Military Hospitals in Salonika." *Little Stories of Big History*. Accessed January 8, 2017. https://sivenas.wordpress.com/2016/04/02/the-nos-4-and-5-canadian-general-hospitals-in-salonika.

"We Were There." *Library and Archives Canada*. Accessed January 8, 2017. www.collectionscanada.gc.ca/firstworldwar/025005-2500-e.html.

"Women in World War I." *For King and Country: A Project to Transcribe the War Memorials in Toronto Schools*. Accessed November 10, 2014. http://torontofamilyhistory.org/kingandcountry/archives/677.

22. THE GREAT BEYOND

Barr, Debra, and Walter Meyer zu Erpen. "Watson, Albert Durrant." *Dictionary of Canadian Biography Online*. Accessed November 29, 2016. www.biographi.ca/en/bio/watson_albert_durrant_15E.html.

"Benjamin Discusses His 'Psychic Powers.'" *Toronto Daily Star*, January 8, 1919.

"Bringing 'Spiritualism' into the Open." *Toronto Daily Star*, January 18, 1919.

Brown, Craig. *Arts and Science at Toronto: A History, 1827–1990*. Toronto: University of Toronto Press, 2013.

Bullock, Allison Christine. "William Lyon Mackenzie King;

A Very Double Life?" Master's thesis, Queen's University, 2009.

Colombo, John Robert. *Haunted Toronto*. Toronto: Dundurn, 1996.

"Criticize Mavor, But Declines His Test." *Toronto Daily Star*, January 20, 1919.

Ferns, Henry, and Bernard Ostry. *The Age of Mackenzie King*. Toronto: Lorimer, 1976.

Levine, Allan. *King: William Lyon Mackeznie King, A Life Guided by the Hand of Destiny*. Vancouver: Douglas & McIntyre, 2011.

Mavor, James. *My Windows on the Street of the World*. Vol. 1. Toronto: J.M. Dent & Sons, 1923.

McMullin, Stanley Edward. *Anatomy of a Seance: A History of Spirit Communication in Central Canada*. Montreal: McGill-Queen's Press, 2004.

O'Malley, Sheila. "LM Montgomery on 'The Twentieth Plane,' by Albert Watson." *Sheila Variations*, May 20, 2004. Accessed November 29, 2016. www.sheilaomalley.com/?p=898.

Panayotidis, E. Lisa. "Mavor, James." *Dictionary of Canadian Biography*. Accessed November 29, 2016. www.biographi. ca/en/bio/mavor_james_15E.html.

"Professor Mavor Proposes A Test." *Toronto Daily Star*, January 18, 1919.

"Prof. Mavor on the Watson Book Dates." *Toronto Daily Star*, January 10, 1919.

"Prof. Smith Detects Flaws in 20th Plane." *Toronto Daily Star*, February 1, 1919.

"Stead Not Available, So Coleridge Spoke." *Toronto Daily Star*, March 12, 1919.

"Torontonians Claim They Speak with Spirits of the Twentieth Plane." January 7, 1919.

"20th Plane Probe Drops." *Toronto Daily Star*, March 10, 1919.

"Twentieth Plane Reads the Papers." *Toronto Daily Star*, January 13, 1919.

University of Toronto: Roll of Service, 1914–1918. Toronto: University of Toronto Press, 1921.

Watson, Albert Durrant. *Birth Through Death: The Ethics of the Twentieth Plane.* Toronto: McClelland & Stewart, 1920.

———. *The Twentieth Plane: A Psychic Revelation.* Toronto: McClelland & Stewart, 1919.

"Watson Accepts Mavor's Proposal." *Toronto Daily Star,* January 25, 1919.

23. THE MOST DANGEROUS WOMAN IN THE WORLD

Avrich, Paul. *Anarchist Voices: An Oral History of Anarchism in America.* Oakland: AK Press, 2005.

Bortolotti, Attilio. "Between Canada and the USA: A Tale of Immigrants and Anarchists." *Kate Sharpley Library.* Accessed January 7, 2016. www.katesharpleylibrary.net/ 8pk1h4.

"The Bortolotti Case." *Toronto Daily Star,* February 26, 1940.

"Brilliant Disquisition on Ibsen by Emma Goldman." *Toronto Daily Star,* November 30, 1926.

Bucklin, Mel, dir. *Emma Goldman.* United States: Nebraska ETV Network, 2004.

"The Emma Goldman Papers." *Berkeley Library.* Accessed January 7, 2016. www.lib.berkeley.edu/goldman.

"Emma Much Shocked Assault on Liberty." *Toronto Daily Star,* March 19, 1927.

Ferguson, Kathy E. *Emma Goldman: Political Thinking in the Streets.* Lanham, MD: Rowman & Littlefield, 2011.

Filey, Mike. *Toronto Sketches 6: The Way We Were.* Toronto: Dundurn, 2000.

Goldman, Emma. *Living My Life.* New York: Alfred A. Knopf, 1931.

Gornick, Vivian. *Emma Goldman: Revolution as a Way of Life.* New Haven, CT: Yale University Press, 2011.

Griffin, Frederick. *Variety Show: Twenty Years of Watching the News Parade*. Toronto: Macmillan, 1936.

Nicholson, C. Brid. *Emma Goldman: Still Dangerous*. Montreal: Black Rose, 2009.

Plummer, Kevin. "Historicist: Throwing Intellectual Bombs." *Torontoist*, May 19, 2012. Accessed January 7, 2016. http://torontoist.com/2012/05/historicist-throwing-intellectual-bombs.

Romalis, Coleman, director. *Emma Goldman: The Anarchist Guest*. Toronto: Romalis Productions, 2000.

Tomchuck, Travis. *Transnational Radicals: Italian Anarchists in Canada and the U.S., 1915–1940*. Winnipeg: University of Manitoba Press, 2015.

Wainwright, Kaitlin. "Emma Goldman." *Heritage Toronto*, January 18, 2013. Accessed January 7, 2016. http://heritagetoronto.org/emma-goldman.

"Was Born a Rebel Miss Goldman Says." *Toronto Daily Star*, December 10, 1927.

Whitaker, Reg. "Official Repression of Communism During World War II." *Labour/Le Travail*. Accessed January 7, 2016. www.lltjournal.ca/index.php/llt/article/viewFile/2492/2895.

"World's Woman Anarchist Emma Goldman Dies Here." *Toronto Daily Star*, May 14, 1940.

24. I'LL NEVER SMILE AGAIN

Carter, Sue. "The Unknown Canadian Behind Some of Frank Sinatra's Biggest Hits." *National Post*, December 11, 2015. Accessed May 24, 2016. http://news.nationalpost.com/arts/the-unknown-canadian-behind-some-of-frank-sinatras-biggest-hits.

Harbury, Martin, dir. *I'll Never Smile Again: The Ruth Lowe Story*. Edmonton: Great North Productions, 2001.

"Heritage Toronto Mondays: Shea's Hippodrome," *Urban
    Toronto*, July 19, 2010. Accessed May 24, 2016. http://
    urbantoronto.ca/news/2010/07/heritage-toronto-mondays-
    sheas-hippodrome.

Holden, Alfred. "The Streamlined Man." *Taddle Creek* 4
    (2000).

"I'll Never Smile Again: Sinatra Song of the Century #26."
    Steyn Online. Accessed June 13, 2016. www.steynonline.
    com/6915/ill-never-smile-again.

Jones, John Bush. *The Songs that Fought the War: Popular
    Music and the Home Front, 1939–1945*. Lebanon:
    Brandeis University Press, 2006.

Levinson, Peter. J. *Tommy Dorsey: Livin' in a Great Big Way, a
    Biography*. Cambridge: Da Capo, 2006.

"Put Your Dreams Away (For Another Day)." *Canadian
    Songwriters Hall of Fame*. Accessed May 24, 2016. www.
    cshf.ca/song/put-your-dreams-away-for-another-day.

Rayburn, John. *Cat Whiskers and Talking Furniture: A
    Memoir of Radio and Television Broadcasting*. Jefferson:
    McFarland, 2008.

Schweitzer, Ruth. "How a Jewish Songwriter from Toronto
    Launched Frank Sinatra's Career." *Canadian Jewish News*,
    December 11, 2015. Accessed June 12, 2016. www.cjnews.
    com/culture/arts/how-a-jewish-songwriter-from-toronto-
    launched-frank-sinatras-career.

Sullivan, Steve. *Encyclopedia of Great Popular Song Recordings*.
    Vol. 2. Lanham, MD: Scarecrow Press, 2013.

"What Press Agents Say about Coming Events." *Toronto Daily
    Star*, April 6, 1935.

25. JOURNEY'S END

Adams, James. "Lucy Maud Suffered 'Unbearable Psychological
    Pain.'" *Globe and Mail*, September 24, 2008. www.

theglobeandmail.com/news/national/lucy-maud-suffered-unbearable-psychological-pain/article17971634.

Cavert, Mary Beth. "L.M. Montgomery and World War I: The Dedication in L.M. Montgomery's *Rainbow Valley* 1919." *L.M. Montgomery Literary Society.* Accessed November 4, 2016. http://lmmontgomeryliterarysociety.weebly.com/uploads/2/2/6/5/226525/l.m._montgomery_and_world_war_1.pdf.

Edwards, Owen Dudley, and Jennifer H. Litster. "The End of Canadian Innocence: L.M. Montgomery and the First World War." In *L.M. Montgomery and Canadian Culture,* edited by Irene Gammel and Elizabeth Epperly. Toronto: University of Toronto Press, 1999.

Gammel, Irene. "The Fatal Disappointments of Lucy Maud." *Globe and Mail,* November 15, 2008. www.theglobeandmail.com/arts/books-and-media/the-fatal-disappointments-of-lucy-maud/article1199004.

Gammel, Irene, ed. *The Intimate Life of L.M. Montgomery.* Toronto: University of Toronto Press, 2005.

Lefebvre, Benjamin. "Introduction: A Life in Print." In *The L.M. Montgomery Reader,* vol. 1, *A Life in Print,* edited by Benjamin Lefebvre. Toronto: University of Toronto Press, 2013.

Macdonald Butler, Kate. "The Heartbreaking Truth about Anne's Creator." *Globe and Mail,* September 27, 2008. http://v1.theglobeandmail.com/servlet/story/RTGAM.20080919.wmhmontgomery0920/BNStory/mentalhealth.

Montgomery, Lucy Maud. *The Blythes Are Quoted.* Toronto: Penguin, 2009.

Rubio, Mary Henley. *Lucy Maud Montgomery: The Gift of Wings.* Toronto: Doubleday, 2008.

Stein, Sadie. "I Tried Always to Do My Best." *Paris Review.* Accessed September 25, 2016. www.theparisreview.org/blog/2015/11/30/i-tried-always-to-do-my-best.

26. HOW TOPPY TOPHAM DIED

Bishop, Arthur. "Valour to the End: Part 18 of 18." *Legion Magazine*, November 1, 2006. Accessed November 10, 2011. https://legionmagazine.com/en/2006/11/valour-to-the-end.

"The Canadian Army." *London Gazette*, August 3, 1945. Accessed January 7, 2017. www.thegazette.co.uk/London/issue/37205/supplement/3965/data.htm.

"F.G. Topham, Won the Victoria Cross." *Toronto Daily Star*, June 1, 1974.

"Frederick George Topham." *National Defence and the Canadian Forces.* Accessed January 7, 2017. www.cmp-cpm.forces.gc.ca/dhh-dhp/gal/vcg-gcv/bio/topham-fg-eng.asp.

"Frederick George Topham." *Runnymede Collegiate: Worth Studying.* Accessed November 10, 2011. http://schoolweb.tdsb.on.ca/runnymedeci/schoolinfo/alumni/walloffame/frederickgeorgetopham.aspx.

Jones, Donald. "In Praise of Toronto's Most Valorous Heroes." *Toronto Star*, June 4, 1994.

"Medal Set: Object Number 20050010–001." *Canadian War Museum.* Accessed November 10, 2011. www.warmuseum.ca/collections/artifact/1805563/?q=topham&page_num=1&item_num=0&media_irn=1098873.

"Metro VC Winner Lives After 4000-Volt Shock, Fall." *Toronto Daily Star*, April 20, 1968.

"Unit History." *1st Canadian Parachute Battalion.* Accessed November 10, 2011. http://users.eastlink.ca/%7Ebsmills/UNIT_HISTORY/unit_history.html.

Worthington, Peter. "Salute to 1st Canadian Parachute Battalion." *St. Catharines Standard*, October 4, 2010. Accessed January 7, 2017. www.stcatharinesstandard.ca/2010/10/04/salute-to-1st-canadian-parachute-battalion-2.

27. TORONTO HEARTS STALINGRAD

Anderson, Jennifer. "Propaganda and Persuasion in the Cold War: The Canadian-Soviet Friendship Society, 1949–1960." Ph.D. diss., Carleton University, 2008.

Avery, Donald. *The Science of War: Canadian Scientists and Allied Military Technology During the Second World War.* Toronto: University of Toronto Press, 1998.

Hastings, Chris. "Deathbed Confession of Spy Who Betrayed Atom Bomb Secrets." *Telegraph*, January 26, 2003. Accessed March 20, 2013. www.telegraph.co.uk/news/uknews/1420088/Deathbed-confession-of-spy-who-betrayed-atom-bomb-secrets.html.

"Igor Gouzenko." *Canadian Intelligence Resource Centre Archives.* Accessed March 20, 2013. http://circ.jmellon.com/history/gouzenko.

"Keep Faith with Stalingrad Millions; Send Clothes." *Toronto Daily Star*, January 23, 1945.

McKay, Ian, and Jamie Swift. *Warrior Nation: Rebranding Canada in an Age of Anxiety.* Toronto: Between the Lines, 2012.

"Send Clothes to Firehalls for Orphans of Stalingrad." *Toronto Daily Star*, January 12, 1945.

"Toronto Changed Motion But Did Not Reject It." *Ottawa Citizen*, December 1, 1943.

"Urges 'Adoption' of Soviet Cities as Concrete Token." *Ottawa Citizen*, November 15, 1943.

"Will Ask Every Home to Assist Stalingrad." *Toronto Daily Star*, February 2, 1945.

28. DISASTER!

"1949: 118 Die Aboard Cruise Ship SS *Noronic*." *Morningside.* Toronto: CBC Radio, August 18, 1977.

Bateman, Chris. "A Brief History of the S.S. Noronic Disaster."

blogTO, September 8, 2012. Accessed January 24, 2012.
www.blogto.com/city/2012/09/a_brief_history_of_the_
ss_noronic_disaster.

Bilton, Chris. "Hurricane Hazel and the Evolution of Flood
Control in Toronto." In HTO: Toronto's Water from Lake
Iroquois to Lost Rivers to Low-flow Toilets, edited by
Wayne Reeves and Christina Palassio. Toronto: Coach
House, 2008.

Bradburn, Jamie. "Historicist: Disaster at Hogg's Hollow."
Torontoist, March 20, 2010. Accessed March 2011. http://
torontoist.com/2010/03/historicst_disaster_at_hoggs_
hollow.

"The Burning of the Noronic." Walkerville Times Magazine.
Accessed January 24, 2012. www.walkervilletimes.com/
28/noronic1.html.

Connor, Kevin. "Hogg's Hollow Disaster Remembered."
Toronto Sun, March 16, 2010. Accessed March 5, 2011.
www.torontosun.com/news/torontoandgta/2010/03/16/
13254706.html.

Feeny, Edwin. "Mother Clutching Baby to Breast, Both Dead
Reporter's First Sight." Toronto Daily Star, September 17,
1949.

Gifford, Jim. Hurricane Hazel: Toronto's Storm of the Century.
Toronto: Dundurn, 2004.

"Horror, Heroism Mingle as Fire Sweeps Luxury Cruiser
Noronic: Call for Divers to Seek Dead." Toronto Daily Star,
September 17, 1949.

"Hurricane Hazel: 60 Years Later." Toronto and Region Conser-
vation. Accessed August 12, 2016. www.hurricanehazel.ca.

"Hurricane Hazel — Storm Information." Environment and
Climate Change Canada. Accessed August 13, 2016. www.
ec.gc.ca/ouragans-hurricanes/default.asp?lang=En&n=
5C4829A9-1.

"Hurricane Hazel Impacts — Humber River" Environment
and Climate Change Canada. Accessed August 12,

2016. www.ec.gc.ca/ouragans-hurricanes/default.
asp?lang=en&n=BD91538F-1.

Iacovetta, Franca. "Defending Honour, Demanding Respect:
Manly Discourse and Gendered Practice in Two
Construction Strikes, Toronto, 1960–1961." In *Gendered
Pasts: Historical Essays in Femininity and Masculinity
in Canada*, edited by Kathryn M. McPherson, Cecilia
Morgan, and Nancy M. Forestell. Toronto: University of
Toronto Press, 2003.

———. *Such Hardworking People: Italian Immigrants in Post-
War Toronto*. Montreal: McGill-Queen's University Press,
1992.

Kennedy, Betty. *Hurricane Hazel*. Toronto: Macmillan, 1979.

Plummer, Kevin. "Historicist: Queen of the Great Lakes
Aflame." *Torontoist*, September 10, 2011. Accessed
January 24, 2012. http://torontoist.com/2011/09/
historicist-queen-of-the-great-lakes-aflame.

"Shipwreck Investigations: Investigating the *Noronic*." *Library
and Archives Canada*. Accessed January 24, 2012. www.
collectionscanada.gc.ca/sos/shipwrecks/002031-4200-e.
html.

Varhola, Michael J. and Paul G. Hoffman. *Shipwrecks and
Lost Treasures, Great Lakes: Legends and Lore, Pirate and
More!* Guilford, CT: Globe Pequot, 2008.

Versace, Vince. "Hogg's Hollow Tragedy Changed Ontario's
Construction Industry." *Journal of Commerce*, March 16,
2010. Accessed March 5, 2011.

29. NEIL YOUNG'S HEARSE AND A DEAD MAN'S NAME

Einarson, John. *Neil Young: Don't Be Denied*. Kingston: Quarry,
1992.

Halliwell, Martin. *Neil Young: American Traveller*. London:
Reaktion, 2015.

Henderson, Stuart. *Making the Scene: Yorkville and Hip Toronto in the 1960s*. Toronto: University of Toronto Press, 2011.

James, Rick, and David Ritz. *Glow: The Autobiography of Rick James*. Toronto: Atria, 2014.

Jennings, Nicholas. *Before the Gold Rush: Flashbacks to the Dawn of the Canadian Sound*. Toronto: Viking, 1997.

"John Kay & Steppenwolf: Biography." *John Kay & Steppenwolf*. Accessed September 24, 2016. http://steppenwolf.com/p-4118-biography.html.

Jones, Josh. "When Neil Young & Rick James Created the '60s Motown Band, The Mynah Birds." *Open Culture*, May 1, 2014. Accessed September 24, 2016. www.openculture.com/2014/05/when-neil-young-rick-james-created-the-60s-motown-band-the-mynah-birds.html.

McDonough, James. *Shakey: Neil Young's Biography*. Toronto: Random House, 2002.

"Neil Young on His Famous Hearse." *YouTube*. Accessed September 24, 2016. https://youtu.be/0BCtNw_ljxA.

Warburton, Nick. "Rick James and the Mynah Birds." *Ear Candy Mag*. Accessed September 22, 2016. www.earcandymag.com/rrcase-mynahbirds-part2.htm.

Young, Neil. *Waging Heavy Peace*. Toronto: Penguin, 2012.

———. *Super Deluxe*. New York: Blue Rider, 2014.

30. SHOESHINE BOY

Bateman, Chris. "Historicist: The Murder of Emanuel Jaques and the Cleanup of Yonge Street." *Torontoist*, June 11, 2016. Accessed December 25, 2016. http://torontoist.com/2016/06/historicist-emanuel-jaques.

Beare, Margaret E., and Tonita Murray. *Police and Government: Who's Calling the Shots?* Toronto: University of Toronto Press, 2007.

Brunton, Colin and Kire Paputts, directors. *The Last Pogo Jumps Again*. Toronto: Screamin' Banshee, 2013.

McLaren, Ross, director. *Crash 'n' Burn*. Toronto: Canadian Filmmakers Distribution Centre, 1977.

Smith, Sarah E.K. "General Idea: Life & Work." *Art Canada Institute*. Accessed December 26, 2016. https://www.aci-iac.ca/general-idea/biography.

Sutherland, Sam. *Perfect Youth, The Birth of Canadian Punk*. Toronto: ECW Press, 2012.

The Curse. *Teenage Meat*. Other Peoples Music OPM-2110, 1997.

Worth, Liz. *Treat Me Like Dirt: An Oral History of Punk in Toronto and Beyond, 1977–1981*. Toronto: Bongo Beat, 2010.

31. NO SAD SONGS

"1983–2003: ACT Timeline." *AIDS Committee of Toronto*, June 24, 2003. Accessed November 7, 2016.

Bradburn, Jamie. "Historicist: Raiding the Bathhouses." *Torontoist*, June 26, 2011. Accessed November 4, 2016. http://torontoist.com/2011/06/historicist_raiding_the_bathhouses.

Hannon, Gerald. "Dying to Live." *Body Politic*, August 1985.

Hays, Matthew. "Doc Classics: No Sad Songs." *Point of View Magazine*. November 1, 2010. Accessed November 4, 2016. http://povmagazine.com/articles/view/no-sad-songs.

"HIV and AIDS Statistics — Toronto." *AIDS Committee of Toronto*. Accessed November 7, 2016.

Morford, Mark. "The Sad, Quotable Jerry Falwell / It's Bad Form to Speak Ill of the Dead. Good Thing This Man's Own Vile Words Speak for Themselves." *SF Gate*, May 18, 2007. Accessed November 4, 2016. www.sfgate.com/entertainment/morford/article/The-Sad-Quotable-Jerry-Falwell-It-s-bad-form-3302297.php.

Robertson, Mark L. "An Annotated Chronology of the History of AIDS in Toronto: The First Five Years, 1981–1986." *Canadian Bulletin of Medical History* 22, no. 2 (2005). Accessed November 4, 2016. http://yorkspace.library.yorku.ca/xmlui/bitstream/handle/10315/2482/Chronology%20of%20the%20History%20of%20AIDS%20in%20Toronto.pdf?sequence=1.

Sheehan, Nik, director. *No Sad Songs*. Toronto: CeLL Productions, 1985. http://hotdocslibrary.ca/en/detail.cfm?filmId=25156.

32. THE FALLING LAWYER

Armstrong, Christopher. "Austin, James." *Dictionary of Canadian Biography*. Accessed January 7, 2017. www.biographi.ca/en/bio/austin_james_12E.html.

Arthur, Eric. *Toronto, No Mean City*. Toronto: University of Toronto Press, 1986.

Boles, Derek. "Toronto's First Railway — The Ontario, Simcoe and Huron Railway." *Toronto Railway Historical Association*. 2011. Accessed January 7, 2017. www.trha.ca/resources/111015.Toronto.1st.Railway.by.Derek.Boles.pdf.

———. "Toronto Locomotive Works — 1853." *Toronto Railway Historical Association*. Accessed January 7, 2017. www.trha.ca/thetoronto.html.

Bonham, Mark S. "Toronto-Dominion Bank." *Canadian Encyclopedia*, June 5, 2006. Last modified August 19, 2016. www.thecanadianencyclopedia.ca/en/article/td-bank-financial-group.

Bozikovic, Alex. "New TD Centre Signage Reflects a Time When Brands Trump Architectural Vision." *Globe and Mail*, July 5, 2015. Accessed January 7, 2017. www.theglobeandmail.com/life/home-and-garden/architecture/td-centre-signage-reflects-a-time-when-brands-trump-architectural-vision/article25253309.

Fiennes-Clinton, Richard. "#45 ~ Old Banks of Toronto,
    Then and Now, Part Two." *Toronto Then and Now*,
    March 27, 2014. Accessed January 7, 2017. http://
    torontothenandnow.blogspot.ca/2014/03/45-old-banks
    -of-toronto-then-and-now.html.

Gee, Marcus. "Five Things that TD Centre Can Teach Us About
    How to Build Toronto." *Globe and Mail*, May 1, 2015.
    January 7, 2017. www.theglobeandmail.com/news/toronto/
    five-things-the-td-centre-can-teach-us-about-how-to-build-
    toronto/article24227818.

Gibb-Clark, Margot. "Toronto Law Firm to Go Out of
    Business." *Globe and Mail*, December 18, 1995.

Granger, Alix. "Banking." *Canadian Encyclopedia*,
    February 1, 2012. Last modified March 4, 2015. www.
    thecanadianencyclopedia.ca/en/article/banking.

"History of the Toronto Dominion Bank." *Marmora
    Historical Foundation*. Accessed January 7, 2017. www.
    marmorahistory.ca/history-of-the-td-bank.

Marsh, James. "Architectural Masterpiece Replaced by
    Another." *Toronto in Time*. Accessed January 7, 2017.
    http://citiesintime.ca/toronto/story/architectura.

———."Railway History." *Canadian Encyclopedia*, March 25,
    2009. Last modified March 4, 2015. www.thecanadian
    encyclopedia.ca/en/article/railway-history.

Metzger, Patrick. "Toronto Urban Legends: The Leaping
    Lawyer of Bay Street." *Torontoist*, January 3, 2010.
    Accessed January 7, 2017. http://torontoist.com/2013/01/
    urban-legends-the-leaping-lawyer-of-bay-street.

"Our Roots: From Grain to Nation-Building." *TD*. Accessed
    January 7, 2017. www.td.com/about-tdbfg/corporate-
    information/tds-history/ourroots.jsp.

Schulze, Franz. *Mies van der Rohe: A Critical Biography*.
    Chicago: University of Chicago Press, 2012.

Tyler, Tracey. "End of Era as Toronto Law Firm Collapses."
    Toronto Star, February 26, 1996.

————. "Skyscraper Windows Met Standards: Engineers."
    Toronto Star, July 13, 1993.
Warkentin, John. *Creating Memory: A Guide to Outdoor Public
    Sculpture in Toronto*. Toronto: Becker Associates, 2010.

CONCLUSION: THE WORK OF REMEMBERING

Archaeological Services. "A Master Plan of Archaeological
    Resources for the City of Toronto." *Interim Report*.
    August 2004. Accessed January 7, 2017. www1.toronto.
    ca/city_of_toronto/city_planning/urban_design/files/
    pdf/masterplan_arc.resources.pdf.
Gerster, Jane. "Thousands of Huron-Wendat Remains Reburied
    After Decades as Archeological Artifacts." *Toronto Star*,
    September 14, 2013. Accessed January 7, 2017. www.thestar.
    com/news/gta/2013/09/14/thousands_of_huronwendat_
    remains_reburied_after_decades_as_archeological_artifacts.
    html.
Kapches, Mima. "Ossossané Ossuary: The Circle Closes."
    Archaeology of Eastern North America 38 (2010).
    Accessed January 7, 2017. www.jstor.org/stable/40914538.
Labelle, Katie Magee. "Review of *Collections and Objections:
    Aboriginal Material Culture in Southern Ontario*, by
    Michelle A. Hamilton," *H-Canada, H-Net Reviews*,
    September 2011. Accessed January 7, 2017. www.h-net.
    org/reviews/showrev.php?id=33330.
Martin, Joel W., and Mark A. Nicholas. *Native Americans,
    Christianity, and the Reshaping of the American Religious
    Landscape*. Chapel Hill, NC: University of North
    Carolina Press, 2010.
Ormsby, Mary. "Sacred and Secret: The GTA's Hidden Burial
    Sites." *Toronto Star*, May 21, 2011. www.thestar.com/news/
    gta/2011/05/21/sacred_and_secret_the_gtas_hidden_
    burial_sites.html.

Seeman, Erik R. *The Huron-Wendat Feast of the Dead: Indian-European Encounters in Early North America*. Baltimore: Johns Hopkins University Press, 2011.

Sioui, Georges E. *Huron-Wendat: The Heritage of the Circle*. Vancouver: UBC Press, 1999.

Truth and Reconciliation Commission of Canada. *Calls to Action*. Winnipeg: TRC Canada, 2015. www.trc.ca/websites/trcinstitution/File/2015/Findings/Calls_to_Action_English2.pdf.

United Nations, General Assembly Resolution 61/295, *United Nations Declaration on the Rights of Indigenous Peoples*. March 2008. www.un.org/esa/socdev/unpfii/documents/DRIPS_en.pdf.